DATE DUE

FAR AS THE CURSE IS FOUND

THE COVENANT STORY OF REDEMPTION

MICHAEL D. WILLIAMS

P&R

PUBLISHING

P.O. BOX 817 • PHILLIPSBURG • NEW JERSEY 08865-0817

Page design and typesetting by Lakeside Design Plus

Printed in the United States of America

Library of Congress Cataloging-in-Publication Data

Williams, Michael D., 1952–
    Far as the curse is found : the covenant story of redemption / Michael
D. Williams.
       p. cm.
    Includes bibliographical references and indexes.
    ISBN-13: 978-0-87552-510-5 (pbk.)
    ISBN-10: 0-87552-510-5 (pbk.)
    1. Redemption—Biblical teaching. 2. Covenants—Biblical teaching.
3. Covenant theology—Biblical teaching. I. Title.

BT775.W695 2005
234'.3—dc22
                                    2005042988

To the faculty and staff of
Covenant Theological Seminary,
a community for whom *covenant*
is more than the name on the door

CONTENTS

PREFACE

Noted author and scholar C. S. Lewis believed that Christianity is a life-and-death issue for all people. To be born into this world means "either an eternal surrender to God or an everlasting divorce from Him."[1] Yet, Lewis noted that few people seem to know what Christianity is all about. Walter Hooper recounts a conversation with Lewis:

> One day he and I were speculating as to what would happen if a group of friendly and inquisitive Martians suddenly appeared in the middle of Oxford and asked (those who did not flee) what Christianity is. We wondered how many people, apart from voicing their prejudices about the Church, could supply them with much in the way of accurate information. On the whole, we doubted whether the Martians would take back to their world much that is worth having.[2]

Lewis and Hooper are right: most people—believers as well as non-Christians—cannot give a credible answer to the question What is Christianity about?

How do we account for this state of affairs? Given the life-and-death urgency of Christianity, we stand desperately in need of a rever-

1. C. S. Lewis, *God in the Dock: Essays on Theology and Ethics* (Grand Rapids: Eerdmans, 1970), 9.
2. Ibid., 9–10.

sal of the damning disparity between the eternal importance of the Christian faith and the apprehension of it by its advocates. Christianity is a revelatory religion. This means that God has revealed himself, his ways, and his will most clearly and fully in the Scriptures of the Old and New Testaments. Christianity is, therefore, a religion of the book. Thus, if believers do not understand the core issues of the Christian religion, it is because they fail to grasp or appreciate the Bible in some fundamental way.

Why might people have failed to understand or appropriate the message of the Bible? It can be a confusing book. To the casual reader it might appear a perplexing mix of historical stories, legal codes, doctrinal discourses, apocalyptic tales, morality plays, and proverbial sayings. Yet we confess that the Bible is the Word of God. This implies that we expect it to comprise a coherent message within a unified whole. If not, we should not call it the Word of God but perhaps the words of God or an anthology of revelation (*The Best of Yahweh* or *God's Greatest Hits*).

When we look a bit more closely at the Bible, we find that the majority of its content is narrative in character. It is a storied revelation. This fact suggests that the unifying, insight-producing feature that gives the Bible its coherence as revelation is the story it tells. Indeed, the Bible as a whole is best understood as a story or drama. To be sure, the Bible does more than tell a story. Scripture includes psalms and proverbs, songs and prayers, moral instruction and doctrinal reflection. But what holds all of it together, what makes it a unified revelation is the storyline, what theologians often call the drama of redemption. The nonnarrative pieces fit into and make sense only within their appropriate contexts in the biblical storyline.

Every good story has at least four fundamental elements. The first element of a story or narrative drama is the prologue, an introduction to the principal characters and their starting relationships. The prologue also sets the stage for the unfolding drama, the context within which the story will transpire. Any good story will also include a conflict that arises and that the characters must face. The conflict forms the dramatic problem of the story. Third, the conflict must be resolved or dealt with in some fashion. And finally, there is a summing up or a conclusion in which the reader or listener is told how the original relationships were modified by the dramatic problem and its resolution.

In its most basic structure, the Bible follows this dramatic pattern. It has an introduction, a dramatic problem that arises, a resolution to the problem, and a summing up or conclusion. We might refer to these four elements within the biblical storyline as creation, fall, redemption, and consummation. The story that the Bible relates has a prologue that sets the context for the entire drama: God's creation of a wonderful universe. It describes a conflict of cosmic proportions: our first parents' fall into sin and God's response to their sin in covenant curse. Yet the biblical story does not end there. In the midst of God's judgment of sin, the Bible presents the resolution to the fall in God's mighty acts that judge sin and bring redemption, deeds which culminate in God's redemptive purpose in Jesus Christ. Finally, the Bible's story ends with a summing up: God brings his creation and humankind to his promised consummation. "The essence of the Christian religion consists in this," said Herman Bavinck, "that the creation of the Father, devastated by sin, is restored in the death of the Son of God, and recreated by the Holy Spirit into the kingdom of God."[3] The triune God acts covenantally in history: the Father creates, the Son redeems, and the Holy Spirit recreates.

The creation-fall-redemption-consummation storyline is the central theme of Scripture, and it forms the Bible's overarching literary structure. This storyline, in its given sequence, is fundamental to the drama Scripture relates. Each successive event in the story assumes the entire preceding sequence. Creation is the environment that the fall and redemptive events modify. Fall and redemption are meaningless outside of the context of God's good creation. From what do we fall? God's good creational intention. To what standard are we redeemed? God's intention that his creatures glorify him, an intention given in creation. Creation is the presupposition of the fall story,

3. Herman Bavinck, *Gereformeerde Dogmatiek*, 4th ed., 2 vols. (Kampen: Kok, 1928), 1:89.

and creation and fall together are the presupposition of the history of redemption centering in Jesus Christ.

As the story that Christians believe is the one true story that tells us the truth about God, ourselves, and our world, the Bible is a progressive revelation. God's revelation of his response to sin and its effects upon humankind and the world takes place not in an instant but rather over centuries, through a series of redemptive historical acts. These special events in the biblical story are often characterized by covenant making or are otherwise typified as covenantal in character.

But what does history have to do with the covenant? And what is a covenant? While no single definition of covenant can do it justice, a covenant is nothing less than a historical relationship between persons. To say that a personal relationship is historical is to state the obvious, but it is this very reality that is so often overlooked when we talk about God's ways and relationships. God works in history, which is to say that he works covenantally. God enters into relationship with his people, which is to say that he calls them into covenant.

God's promises to Adam, Noah, Abraham, Moses, and David find their culmination and definitive fulfillment in Jesus Christ (1 Cor. 1:20). He is both the goal and the key to "the covenants of promise" (Eph. 2:12), for the entire biblical story pivots upon Jesus of Nazareth. Thus we will begin our discussion with Christ. Indeed we begin with the resurrection. While it might seem odd at first that our telling of the story begins at Easter morning, the empty tomb is the most fitting time and place to embark upon the drama of redemption and the covenantal purpose of God that undergirds it. All that comes before Christ's victory in rising from the dead looks forward to it, and all that comes after the resurrection in the biblical story is an explication of it.

The theme that undergirds the first two chapters is that the Christian religion and its gospel are about God's acts in our world on our behalf. Dorothy Sayers had it right when she wrote:

That man should play the tyrant over God and find Him a better man than himself is an astonishing drama indeed. Any journalist, hearing of it for the first time, would recognize it as News; those who did hear of it for the first time actually called it News, and good news at that, though we are apt to forget that the word *Gospel* ever meant anything so sensational.

Perhaps the drama is played out now, and Jesus is safely dead and buried. Perhaps. It is ironical and entertaining to consider that once at least in the world's history those words might have been spoken with complete conviction, and that was upon the eve of the Resurrection.[4]

Biblical religion holds that the central event in all human history was the execution of a wandering first-century Palestinian preacher and his rising from the dead two days later in fulfillment of God's covenant promises. This is the gospel. To return to Lewis's and Hooper's question: What is the real issue of Christianity? We must answer that the biblical story is the message of the God who "so loved the world" as to enter into it, and ultimately to die for it. What was promised to Adam and Eve in the midst of their guilt and shame, what was prefigured over and over again throughout the Old Testament story of Israel (another story often characterized by guilt and shame) came to pass in a Judean backwater town when God "became flesh and made his dwelling with us." As Sayers so powerfully puts it: "When He was a man, He played the man. He was born in poverty and died in disgrace and thought it well worthwhile."[5]

All of this suggests that the Christian religion is not an ethereal or eternal doctrine about the nature of deity or a polite philosophical discussion about the relation of spirit to matter but the historical unfolding of God's covenantal involvement in the world, the acme of which is God's coming into the world in the person of Jesus Christ. It is unfortunate that when many believers think of revelation or doctrine, what comes to mind all too often is a somewhat sterile collec-

4. Dorothy L. Sayers, *Creed or Chaos?* (Manchester, N.H.: Sophia Institute Press, 1949), 9.
5. Ibid., 4.

tion of eternal ideas and notions about a transcendent and unchanging realm of pure thought, a realm that is safely removed from this world and its vicissitudes, alterations, and complexities.

The saving events to which Scripture testifies, however, take place within our world. It is the history of this world—not some metaphysically timeless heaven—that is the sphere of God's redemptive plan. It is in history that he triumphs over humanity's sin through Christ and reconciles the world to himself (2 Cor. 5:19). It is in history that God acts to bring man to himself. To be sure, God is transcendent; he stands supremely above our world in immutable majesty. But the biblical story is that God is neither locked up in heaven nor remains there. He is ever the coming one, condescending to his creatures in order to forge relationship, judge sin, redeem his people, shower them with the benefits of Christ, and ultimately to bring them and his creation to the consummation of recreation. And God's way in all this, his way in the historical drama, is the way of covenant.

What shall we say to Lewis's and Hooper's religious seekers from another planet? Bavinck's answer that Christianity is a trinitarian story is an excellent start. Handing the Martians a copy of the Apostles' Creed, also a trinitarian drama, would do as well, for the creed has served that very purpose for the better part of two millennia. This book is not written for inquisitive Martians but for those who would tell the story. To tell it we must first hear it ourselves. And to tell it as it is—a dynamic historical drama of God's creative and redemptive actions within our world—we must hear the unfolding story of the covenant.

Our goal is to tell the biblical story through the episodic unfolding of God's covenant way in history. The first two chapters will concentrate on the two premier redemptive events in Scripture: the resurrection of Jesus Christ in the New Testament and God's deliverance of Israel out of Egypt in the Old. These two chapters of the redemptive drama were—and are—fundamental moments in God's revelation of his true character, his historical purpose, and the destiny of his covenant people. We will then follow the covenant storyline of Scripture from creation to new creation by examining each of the biblical episodes in the developing drama. This will constitute the greater part of our study. Finally, we will examine the question of Christ's relationship to each of the covenant episodes, and briefly reflect upon the postbiblical epoch in covenantal perspective by asking what significance the covenant has for those who live the contest of faith in what Lewis called "the cosmic spring" of the resurrection.

I

THE RESURRECTION
The Single Best Page of the Story

This book is a retelling of the biblical story of God's unfolding covenant relationship with his people. The case has been made that it is important to see that the Bible tells a story. Like all stories, the biblical drama has a sequence that must be honored in the retelling. For it to be the story that it is, we must tell about the way things were at the beginning, what went wrong, how it was resolved, and how it ended. Each episode sets the context for the next. It is critical to the story to set human rebellion and God's redemption in the context of the beginning of the story, God's creation. If you don't, you end up with a different story.

Nevertheless, this first chapter begins with Jesus—God come in the flesh and raised from the dead. Is this to deface the storied character of the Bible's witness? No. Rather, it underscores that the story is the unfolding drama of God's coming to and redeeming his treasured people. It is to say that the story is all about Jesus. Jesus is, as C. S. Lewis noted, "the chapter on which the whole plot turns." Beginning as we are with Jesus, we are taking a peek ahead to see what the story is about.

IT'S ALL ABOUT JESUS

The Story's Early Chapters Point to Jesus

Beginning with Jesus highlights the fact that the early chapters of the story point to a future resolution. Moving through them we ought to see that they draw us into patterns that intimate an as-yet unrevealed final word. The Old Testament is an uncompleted story, a promise waiting for its fulfillment. Jesus is that fulfillment. He is the one who was to come, that one to whom all the law and prophets witness. There is a sense in which we cannot understand the beginning chapters apart from what they point to. Nor, once Jesus has come, can we read the Old Testament Scriptures without reference to him. Jesus changes everything. Isaiah, writing of the man of sorrows, could never have predicted Jesus of Nazareth. But we, having known Jesus of Nazareth, can no longer read Isaiah 53 without him in mind.

In Jesus We Glimpse the Final Chapter

Jesus is the one to which the early chapters point. Jesus is also a sneak preview of the last chapter. Once we see Jesus, God's final Word, we can tell how the story is going to turn out. Jesus is the beginning of the end of the ages. In Jesus we get a good idea of what God is up to. We see it best in Jesus' bodily resurrection from the dead. God's unstoppable goal is nothing less than the restoration of his good creation, the eradication, not of it but of the sin that has damaged it, even the triumph of the body over death itself. We cannot write the story of future intervening years. But we don't have to. We have a view of the end that we need to give us hope for each day: Jesus risen from the dead.

Jesus Sheds Light on the Character and Intentions of God

So Jesus is the key to the story. Jesus is the key, as well, because he expresses undeniably the character and intentions of the story's protagonist, God. If we think that the biblical story is about how we can ascend to God, we have it completely wrong. God is the one who comes to his people to enter into intimate covenant relationship with them and to be with them forever. Jesus, Emmanuel, God with us, comes in the flesh. The Old Testament draws us to recognize and respond in love to the coming God. The final chapters of Revelation confirm that God's dwelling with his people, ever his concern from the beginning, is his ultimate goal in which he will ultimately be satisfied. But his best expression of himself, the one that had we been there we could have touched, is Jesus.

Jesus Makes the Story Our Story

Jesus is the key to the story, finally, because he is the Christian's Redeemer. He is the one who by his death purchases us for God. He is our way into the story, the one who makes the story ours. He is the one who opens our eyes to see it and embrace it. We do not come to God, first of all, by looking at his creation. In fact, without Jesus, we cannot rightly grasp the significance of his creation. For us then, the story begins with Jesus.

In this we identify with Thomas, Jesus' disciple. We, like him, behold Jesus. In John's Gospel, Thomas delivers the punch line of the story, the crowning confession of the gospel. Thomas confesses the reality of Jesus' bodily, public resurrection, and he expresses its ultimate significance. For us to grasp the drama of redemption in its fullness, for our lives to be changed by it as his was, we must understand what Thomas understood.

THOMAS AND THE EVIDENCE OF TOUCH

We tend to recall about the apostle Thomas simply that he doubted. What's more, the church has often condemned him for this doubt. The hymn "These Things Did Thomas Count as Real" criticizes Thomas as being unspiritual because he wanted physical evidence of the resurrection:

> The vision of his skeptic mind
> was keen enough to make him blind
> to any unexpected act
> too large for his small world of fact.

After a lecture I once gave on the importance of Christ's resurrection for our understanding of redemption, a woman, looking increasingly disturbed, stabbed her hand into the air: "You're making way too much of this bodily resurrection stuff," she complained. "According to 1 Corinthians 15, the resurrection was a spiritual event, not a physical one. You're just like Thomas. You want a Jesus you can touch."

Yes, Thomas wanted physical evidence. But Christians have often gotten the story wrong: Thomas was right, not wrong, to want it.

A Jesus You Can Touch—among the Disciples

On that first Easter evening, Jesus' disciples huddled together behind securely locked doors, hiding from the Jewish rulers who had engineered Jesus' arrest and death, and who might, for all the disciples knew, be targeting them. Into this fear-tinged atmosphere suddenly came Jesus. Is this a ghost, they wondered? Apparently, belief in ghosts was easier to accept than resurrection from the dead, for the resurrection stories were discarded as idle talk.[1] Yet here he was, right before their eyes, fully as physical as he had been three days before, when they had witnessed him beaten and then dying.

The disciples recognized the risen Jesus. He spoke and they heard him with their ears. John the writer goes out of his way to mention that Jesus showed the disciples his hands, which had been nailed to the cross, and his side, which had been punctured by the soldier's spear. The marks on his body not only declared the cost of the *shalom* he had won for them but also established that Jesus, the one who died, was now present bodily among them. According to Luke, he even ate some boiled fish in their presence, showing that he was

---

1. Those who had not actually seen the risen Christ for themselves refused to accept the stories. The responses of the disciples to the resurrected Christ (Luke 24:37), Thomas's reaction (John 20), and the responses of the Stoic and Epicurean philosophers to Paul's proclamation of the resurrection (Acts 17:16–34) suggest that the idea of a dead man living again was no less intellectually scandalous for people of the first century than it is for us. They had no more natural reason to accept the idea of resurrection than we do, and their suspicion of the resurrection story shows that they were not naturally bent toward a superstitious and gullible frame of reference.

physically there (Luke 24:42–43). I do not mean to be sacrilegious, but Luke's account almost suggests that Jesus said, "I haven't eaten a thing in three days. Anybody have a fish sandwich?" When the disciples were faced with the body of evidence (if you will excuse the pun), confronted with the Word become flesh, and shown the wounds of his struggle, wounds that demonstrated his triumph over death, they had to believe.

The subsequent multiple appearances of Christ tell the same story. Even though the Jewish officials and the Roman military took every possible precaution to secure the body in the tomb, the grave and the supposed finality of death could not hold the Lord of life. Except for a few grave clothes, everything that went into the grave came out. Both the empty tomb and the resurrection appearances argue for a bodily resurrection, a physical continuity between Jesus' preburial and resurrection life. "Death could not hold its prey." By the power of God, Christ is risen.

And when God resurrects, he goes big time. This is no merely spiritual resurrection in the hearts of those who desperately wanted Jesus to live again. If the resurrection were anything other than a physical, historical event, the empty tomb story is unnecessary and irrelevant. In fact, it is misleading. The body is not and cannot be in the tomb, because it is risen.

The disciples cowering in the upper room came face to face with a physical, fish-eating Jesus. His tangibility was just the point: God had raised Jesus bodily from the dead.

A Jesus You Can Touch—with Thomas

One of the disciples was not present at Jesus' first appearance. When the others told Thomas that they had seen Jesus, their statement was met with blank incredulity. Thomas must have surmised that the others had fallen prey to wishful thinking. But he was not going to be taken in. Even when they told him how they had identified the Lord by the nail prints and the spear wound, Thomas was not persuaded. Even seeing would not be enough for him. Only if he put his finger into the nail prints and his hand into the spear wound would he believe. Only the evidence of touch would convince him of solid flesh. Quite literally the text reads: "If I do not see . . . and put my finger . . . I will never believe" (John 20:25).

With that statement Thomas has come down to us as doubting Thomas, Thomas the skeptic, Thomas the crass materialist. But Thomas doubted no more than the others. The other disciples had thought the resurrection story an idle tale until Jesus appeared to them and proved the tale true. His bodily appearance among them had moved them to belief.

A week later they were all in the house again, with doors shut and bolted, as before. This time, Thomas was present. Jesus came and greeted them. The Lord had a special word for Thomas. He extended his hands and invited Thomas to use his sense of touch as well as sight. "Put your finger here: see my hands. Reach out your hand and put it into my side." And Jesus extended the further invitation: "Stop your disbelieving, and become a believer."

Without any further demonstration Thomas burst forth with the greatest confession of the gospel story: "My Lord and my God" (John 20:28). He may have been slower than his fellow disciples to believe in the risen Christ, but when he did so, he expressed his faith in language that went beyond that of the other ten disciples.

Like all the others mentioned in John 20, Thomas believed because he had seen. Peter and John had seen the empty tomb and grave clothes. Mary had seen, heard, and touched the Lord. The disciples had examined the wounds left upon his body by the crucifixion. For all of them, physical evidence, Jesus Christ bodily risen from the grave, was the crucial item that moved them to belief.

Jesus also said to Thomas: "Because you have seen me, you have believed. Blessed are those who have not seen and yet have believed" (John 20:29). This was a special message for the Gospel's first readers as well as for those who read it today. Those first readers had not physically seen the Lord. Neither have we. We belong to that group of people who asked John to write it down, to get it on paper, to tell us about Jesus. Since the passing of the apostolic generation, all believers in the crucified and risen Lord have believed without see-

6

ing. To them is assured the special blessing pronounced here by Jesus. Today we do not have living witnesses, but we have the inspired record of those who were witnesses, of those who heard, and saw, and touched the Word of life (1 John 1:1–4). But they were witnesses because they touched him.

Thomas didn't miss the point. Perhaps more emphatically than anyone else, he got it. Your faith and mine rests on a resurrected Jesus who can be touched. And when you put your own fingers in the wounds, the realization can't help but rock your world: This is Jesus embodied—"My Lord and my God!"

THE BEGINNING OF THE STORY: THE WORD BECAME FLESH

Thomas understood that for Jesus to have been resurrected, Jesus would have to be bodily the same physical Jesus after as before. Thomas also understood that for Jesus to be the fulfillment of God's ultimate promise, Jesus would have to be bodily the same physical Jesus as before. Touching Jesus in that moment, Thomas knew that Jesus was God, and God's Messiah.

The promise of the Old Testament, the subject of later chapters in this book, was that God would come to his people, that he would come to dwell with his people, that he would come and stay. God's Messiah would make God visible, approachable, present—God in the flesh, embodied, particular, with us because he is one of us. Thomas was right to settle for nothing less than what he could touch. And having touched Jesus after the resurrection, he grasped—literally—that God had come in the flesh, fulfilling his central promise.

Thomas's confession constitutes the climax of John's Gospel, for it confirms the proclamation of the book's prologue: The Word was in the beginning; it was with God; it was God (John 1:1). And Jesus of Galilee is that Word made flesh (John 1:14). Thomas, looking at embodied Jesus, confessed, "My Lord and my God!" John's case is made.

Jesus—the Logos

John asserts that the Word is God. The Greek word that John used for "word" is *logos*. The philosophers of ancient Greece held that true reality is both unchanging and rational, distinct from and underlying the ever-changing world that we sense. They used *logos* to refer to the underlying rational principle that gives order and stability to our world. But where the Greeks thought of "word" as "thought," the Hebrews used their word *dabar*, which translates into Greek as *logos*, as "deed." For the Greek, *logos* was the unchanging essence of reality, but for the Hebrew the *logos* was dynamic, having the power to effect and affect reality. For the Hebrew, the word is historical; for the Greek, intellectual or mental.[2]

John, like the Old Testament authors, thought in concrete historical terms. The *logos* is not just a word, as vocal speech, but also deed. What after all is a word but a vocal event? How does God create? By his word: "And God said, 'Let there be light, and there was light' " (Gen. 1:3). By his word, his explosive action, the heavens were made. The *logos* did not refer to an idea in the mind or some abstract principle of order. For John it referred to the creative power of God. Notice the intentional allusions to Genesis 1 in John's prologue. The Hebrew God acts, and he acts in history.

Thus, the Word became flesh, the fullest conceivable expression of a dynamic God who acts in history and who promises his people that he will come to them. Unlike the *logos* of the Greeks, this Word is a historical event by nature. The *logos*, the Greek principle of all order, does not enter and cannot enter physically into the world. The Greeks often dismissed history as unworthy of philosophical interest. History was no more than the sphere of endless and repetitive

2. James Barr's *The Semantics of Biblical Language* (London: SCM, 1961) took the biblical theology movement of the 1950s to task for what Barr judged to be its overly easy distinctions between the Greek and Hebrew "mind." While accepting the warning that the idea of a national mind is abstract and that the distinctions between the Greek and Hebrew mind can be overstressed, it is nevertheless the case that there existed a decidedly different worldview among the Greek philosophers than that which we see in the Old Testament. Further, I would also argue that the worldview commitments a person or nation hold will influence the linguistic choices and usages possible for them.

change. Meaning could be found only in transcendence, the explicit rejection of history. The Greeks tended to think spatially and statically rather than historically. Man's historical, creaturely life seemed an obstacle to his true being. The highest good could be attained only through liberation from the appetites and drives of historical existence. As endless and meaningless change, history was without purpose, without a goal. The essence of perfection was the changeless realm of eternal ideas, and such changeless perfection could not arise from the contingencies of human history. The *logos* may be the principle of the world, but for the Greeks it was foolishness to suggest that it could become historical, that it could become part of the world.

John 1:14 declares: "The Word became flesh and made his dwelling among us. We have seen his glory, the glory of the One and Only, who came from the Father, full of grace and truth." In three simple words, John turns the religious thought of the first century on its ear. "Word became flesh." The connection with the first sentence of John's Gospel cannot be overlooked. The one who was in the beginning with God, and who was in fact God himself, became flesh. That is history, an observable and datable event. In space and time God took on humanity. Just as each one of us was born into the world, the Word, Jesus Christ, who was in the beginning with God and who was God, was born into the world and became flesh. John the Evangelist sought to contextualize the gospel story for a Hellenistic culture, even as he signaled to the Hebrews that Jesus was just what they expected God to be: the God who comes to be with his people.

John brought the *logos* into the stuff of creation and of history. The one who was God became flesh and blood, with all the limitations of space and time, all its physical handicaps of fatigue, hunger, and susceptibility to the vicissitudes of earthly existence. The power that called the world into being takes on the weakness of createdness. The one who is truly God is now so truly man that the word *flesh* can be used to describe him. Contrary to the universality and changelessness sought by the philosophies of the Greeks, John declares that meaning and truth are to be found in historical particularity, a specific, particular, historical person. The *logos* is the man Jesus Christ, born in Bethlehem, executed as a heretic and political criminal thirty years later in Jerusalem. There is nothing abstract or universal here. John drives home his point: In Jesus the incarnate Word of God made his home with us. He ate our food and drank our water. As a boy, he was taught carpentry by Joseph. He swung hammers, pushed planes, sawed lumber. The second person of the Trinity made chairs. He entered completely into the affairs of this world.

Jesus—Yahweh Dwelling with His People, Made Flesh

In Christ's becoming flesh, and dwelling among us, the glorious presence of the Lord of the universe is manifested to all creation. In Jesus' body, his physical, this-worldly body, his flesh, God is seen and his glory is manifested to man. To see the glory of God, his making himself present in this world, to see God's restoration of humanity and creation, one must look upon the flesh of Jesus Christ. "No one has ever seen God, but God the One and Only, who is at the Father's side, has made him known" (John 1:18). Making God known is the particular business of Jesus: making the coming God of Old Testament promise the present God, showing us up close and personal (in the flesh!) the character and ways of the Creator. In Jesus of Nazareth, God is brought near, made close, personal, available to his people. In the incarnation God enters a young girl's womb and comes into our world to begin the long and blood-covered path to restore and regenerate, to reclaim again all creation, and to fulfill the covenant promise: I will be your God, and you will be my people.

Why must God come to his people? John knows the witness of the Old Testament: God's people need a Savior, one who will redeem them. God must go so far as to provide himself a lamb. The God of all creation, the God who measures out the heavens in the span of his hand and sifts out the galaxies as you might sprinkle salt on your evening meal, had long ago determined that there was but one way that his sin-scarred world could be cleansed of the corruption of sin. God must become man in order to suffer the penalty of sin and guilt. God must come, embodied in history, and as the one who saves.

Throughout John's Gospel runs the refrain: Come and see, the Messiah is here! Behold the Lord. He performs signs, solidly mate-

10

rial deeds demonstrating who he is, so that we might believe in him. John's telling of the gospel story is thoroughly this-worldly. His one all-consuming point is that God has acted visibly and definitively in Christ in order to take away the sin of the world. Thus, upon seeing Jesus, John the Baptist exclaims: "Look, the lamb of God who takes away the sin of the world." He's the one, the one I told you about, the promised Messiah of God. And there he is. *Look!*

John the Baptist's confession expresses the gospel's one fundamental proclamation: Jesus is the Lamb of God—God present with his people, with them in flesh and history, poised to save. Thomas confesses, "My Lord and my God!" If it's Jesus, and his is a pierced, resurrected, body, here with us, then Jesus has to be our God. Thomas's confession does not merely acknowledge the reality of the resurrection but also expresses its ultimate significance: Jesus is the conqueror of death because he is none other than the creator of life. Now the story is told. The wound of the Garden is healed. On resurrection morning God was able again to say what he had exclaimed over his creation so long ago: "It is good. It is very good."

It matters that Jesus was restored bodily, because it signaled that Jesus was the Creator and promised Redeemer who covenants with his people, who promises to come to them, and who keeps his promises. Jesus the one and only has made Yahweh known. With Thomas we confess that he is God, and we are his.

THE RESURRECTION PREVIEWS THE FINAL CHAPTER: THE RESTORATION OF CREATION

The flesh Jesus takes on in the incarnation is a flesh he never lays down. It is there in his ministry: Immanuel, God with us, come in the flesh to cure his broken world. And that same flesh, repaired, renewed, and glorified in resurrection, is there in the risen and ascended Christ. In Jesus' bodily resurrection we view with Thomas the very meaning of the resurrection: the restoration of creation.

G. C. Berkouwer once observed that if we conceive of the Christian faith—and what it proclaims about human destiny and the goal of all things—apart from reference to the resurrection of Christ, without appreciating its nature as the restoration of all things, then we have not truly grasped the nature of redemption. Since we have been born again to "a living hope through the resurrection of Jesus Christ from the dead" (1 Peter 1:3), the hope of the believer "rests on a promise inseparable from the salvation already granted" in Christ's resurrection from the dead.[3] In God's mighty act of raising Jesus bodily from the grave we are right to glimpse the final chapter of the drama of redemption. Indeed, an understanding of redemption that fails to take its moorings from Christ's victory over sin and death via bodily resurrection, and the promise of ultimate restoration of all things declared by the empty tomb, is not a biblical understanding of redemption at all.

Jesus Invaded History

There is an altogether marvelous quality to the concreteness, the this-worldliness, even the earthiness, of the drama of redemption. This history does not transpire within some ethereal and bloodless realm of perfection. Quite the contrary, the events spoken of in Scripture take place within the same world in which you and I live. The redemption of Jesus Christ was not worked out in heaven. It all took place right here, in this world, the same world in which you and I rear our children, pay our bills, and shovel our snow-covered walks. Matthew began his Gospel with a place and date: "After Jesus was born in Bethlehem in Judea, during the time of King Herod" (Matt. 2:1). Luke does the same. God was made man in the year that Caesar Augustus was taking a census in connection with a scheme of taxation (Luke 2:1). They tell us that about thirty-three years later Jesus was executed "under Pontius Pilate," much as we might say, "when the Russian Republic replaced the Soviet Union," or "when George W. Bush was the president of the United States." It is as definite and concrete as that. The biblical authors were committed to the historicity of the events they related. They knew that faith without real world, historical fact, is not faith but mere superstition.

3. G. C. Berkouwer, *The Return of Christ* (Grand Rapids: Eerdmans, 1972), 171.

God's Complete Restoration Will Invade History Also

The distinctive thing about the biblical emphasis upon the historicity of these events is the belief that history has a redemptive goal. Biblical religion is oriented toward the future. Israel's hope of the kingdom of God was always an eschatological hope, a hope for the future.[4] From the Garden forward, Scripture addresses the question of how the Lord will answer human rebellion. The promise that comes to fulfillment in Christ's resurrection is first sounded in the Garden of Eden. The expectation of the coming Redeemer is proclaimed in the mother promise of Genesis 3:15. Anthony Hoekema writes, "From this point on, all the Old Testament revelation looks forward, points forward, and eagerly awaits the promised Redeemer."[5] The rest of redemptive history is a historical unfolding of that promise.

Because Israel experiences the LORD as a promise-making and promise-keeping God, it can place its hope in his promised kingdom. From an Old Testament perspective, the *eschaton*, the promised future, was seen as beginning with the coming of Messiah and ending with the judgment and the restoration of all things to God. From the foreshortened perspective of the Old Testament the *eschaton* was often understood as a single, comprehensive event or a matrix of events that would transpire in serial and quick succession.

Jesus—A Down Payment on the Coming Restoration

The resurrection is the first event of God's promised resolution to the rebellion of the Garden. Jesus Christ's resurrection is the payment on a promise made when the world was both very young and suddenly made very old by the foolishness and selfishness of sin.

The resurrection is something of a foretaste, a movie trailer or commercial for God's ultimate future, for in Christ's resurrection we

---

4. The word *eschatological* means "pertaining to the future." It comes from the Greek word *eschatos* ("last"). Eschatology is the study of the biblical witness to the future, either the approximate future as in the warnings of covenant judgment in the Old Testament prophets, or the ultimate future: the return of Christ and the events surrounding his return.

5. Anthony Hoekema, *The Bible and the Future* (Grand Rapids: Eerdmans, 1991), 11.

have a picture of the future given before its arrival. The end is seen ahead of time. As the beginning and foretaste of the future, the resurrection is the firstfruits or the first stage of the coming redemption. The bodily resurrection of Christ not only signifies God's victory over sin and death but also declares the nature of that victory. It is total, comprehensive; so comprehensive that it claims that history is moving toward nothing less than a fully restored and glorified universe. Those who are in Christ, along with the entirety of creation, will receive his resurrection life upon his appearing (Rom. 8:21–25).

This means that Christ is the center of the biblical story. Throughout its length, Scripture has a Christ-centered thrust: he will come! The Bible tells the redemptive story of the promised Messiah who came to redeem. That thrust must define our understanding of the nature of Scripture and the way we read it. As we look back to earlier chapters in the story, we must see that the coming of the Messiah fulfills the covenant promise to Adam that God will crush the power of the evil one (Gen. 3:15). The coming of the Messiah forms the foundation for God's covenant promise to Noah that creation will be sustained for all time (Gen. 8:22). The coming of the Messiah energizes God's covenant promise to Abraham that he and his posterity will be a blessing to all nations (Gen. 12:3). And the coming of the Messiah burns in the covenant promise to the prophets that God will write his law on the hearts of his people and will give them the gift of the Holy Spirit (Jer. 31:31–34). In the resurrection of Christ God has begun to make good on his promise. The primary difference between the Testaments is that the Old looks toward Christ and the New moves out from him and toward the consummation, a new heavens and new earth, heaven on earth, God dwelling with his people. Thus Scripture is not a series of isolated divine acts but an integrally unified narrative. Because God's plan of salvation is fulfilled in Christ, Jesus is the leading player, the protagonist of the biblical drama of redemption.

All of this strongly suggests that if we want to understand that redemption, we must pay heed to the resurrection. As Christ's saving work is the central theme of the Bible, and his resurrection is the sign of the fulfillment of that work, so his resurrection is the anticipation of the goal of redemptive history, a peek ahead, if you will, at the last page of the story. Biblically, the best single term to catch the nature of redemption and the character of the Christian hope is resurrection.

The restoration of all things signified and promised in the resurrection is at one and the same time the hope of the believer and the horizon in which he must understand all reality, for it is the direction in which the believer is traveling. Faith means having something to which we can confidently look forward. It means having a goal. The basis for informed Christian action is its vision of the future, and that future can be stated in one word: resurrection.

The usual or popular notion of faith is that it is a trust in something transcendent, anti-creational, otherworldly, anti-scientific, and heavenly. Faith is believing in spite of the facts; and it has nothing to do with anything historical. Faith is believing in what we cannot see. Faith is geared toward spiritual rather than physical things, right?

Well, no. "Now faith is being sure of what we hope for and certain of what we do not see" (Heb. 11:1). The text is not talking about the heavenly, the otherworldly, or something that contradicts this-worldly reality. The author of the Epistle to the Hebrews is talking about a faith that places its trust in that which comes to us in history. What the church hopes for is the bodily return of the Lord to consummate the kingdom. That is an event in history, albeit a future event. What we do not see is that which we as yet have not experienced. As the chronicle of redeemed sinners (Heb. 11:4–40) makes plain, faith is being sure of God's promise of the future. That promise is anchored in God's absolute faithfulness to the covenant history of his people.

Believing in something spiritual is easy. Very few people actually refuse to believe in a deity of some sort. But believing that God acted in Jesus Christ, raising him from the dead, and that his resurrection is God's absolute promise that he will be victorious over sin and death and will reclaim his fallen creation in the glory of Christ's return, now that's faith.

15

You and I, by faith, know how the story ends: complete, physical, earthly restoration of all that our sin has broken in God's world. Having glimpsed the future in the resurrection of Jesus, we live our days now in joyful hope.

THE RESURRECTION AS PUBLIC EVENT AND CONFESSION

Thomas's grand confession helps us comprehend the scope of divine redemption, from the first chapter to the last. It also leads us to consider how we come to recognize it and embrace it.

Thomas believed and confessed Jesus as Lord because of the tangible evidence of touch. Yet not all who affirm Jesus' resurrection respond with repentance and faith. We need to see that the resurrection is at once a public event and also one whose significance is grasped only through the work of the Holy Spirit. Thomas believed because he touched, and that is as it should be. But he also believed because the Spirit removed his blindness.

For All to See

Christianity is a religion grounded in history. Unlike religions that seek to transcend history, as if it were a thing to be scorned or ignored, the good news of Jesus Christ is news, the telling of things that have happened. The gospel is the recital of a great event: the mighty act of God in raising Jesus from the dead in fulfillment of his covenant promise.

The fact that the resurrection is a historical, public event anchors the entire gospel. The apostle Paul insists that if Christ is not risen on Easter morning, the entire Christian faith is fallacious and futile. If Christ is dead, the proclamation of the faith is valueless, and all testimony to Christ is false. If God did not raise Jesus, those who place their trust in him perish without hope and no sins are forgiven. Take away his resurrection, and Christians are the most miserable of all people (1 Cor. 15:14–19).

Paul and the other writers of the New Testament do not offer the resurrection as a spiritual truth, a heavenly reality, a secret insight

16

unavailable to the mass of humanity, or something that requires some special illumination. Paul addresses this directly: The good news of Jesus Christ is not secret, spiritual knowledge, but the declaration of a historical event that is open to all: "By setting forth the truth plainly we commend ourselves to every man's conscience in the sight of God" (2 Cor. 4:2). The gospel is nothing less than a telling of the truth, an exposition of the world-transforming, historical fact of the birth, career, death, and resurrection of the Messiah of God. That birth, life, death, and resurrection are fact. They are open and public, as open, public, and factual as gravity or the Korean War. The disciples believed because they saw the risen Christ.

So Why Don't All See?

The question naturally and rightly arises, Why do not all believe? If the gospel is as historically sure as Hannibal crossing the Alps, why do so few people accept it? Not all who saw Jesus in the flesh accepted him as the Messiah. Not all who hear John's testimony of the risen Lord are moved to faith.

In this we recognize the blinding effects of sin (2 Cor. 4:4) and the mystery of God's sovereign election. The gospel is not a secret truth given to some. Rather, the Holy Spirit removes the blindness of the fall. Thus faith is not a *super additum* but the removal of sin's misperception. By the witness of the Holy Spirit, seeing produces knowing. John links these two verbs with the act of faith throughout John 20 and John 21. Vision, the experience of the risen Christ, must move on to knowledge, commitment to and intimate familiarity with Jesus Christ.

Events are not, of course, self-interpreting. While they are open in the sense that they are moments in history that can be experienced by witness and testimony, their significance is not equally open. Sifting through the historical evidence for the resurrection of Jesus Christ will not make believers of all. I heard of an atheist who, upon examining the evidence for the resurrection of Jesus from the dead, accepted the factuality of the event. When asked how he could affirm

17

the reality of the resurrection without becoming a Christian, he replied, "Strange things happen in history."

Thus, while we affirm the historicity of Christian faith, we must also recognize that there is no such thing as a brute fact, a self-evident truth, or an event that carries its own self-contained significance. The Gospel of John's understanding of witness helps us here. Herman Ridderbos has stated that in the witness of the Spirit "facts and their meanings coincide." The events of biblical history can become redemptive history only through the witness of the Spirit to the believing community as it responds to the biblical story. The recital of the event, then, becomes a proclamation of and a witness to God's redemptive activity in the world. This activity is open to all; it is a public event, able to be seen by all. But the redemptive significance of that activity is known only through the Spirit of God. The resurrection, like all of God's acts in history, beginning from his creation of the world, are public events whose significance believers grasp only as the Holy Spirit removes the scales from our eyes.

A Vision That Changes Everything

The resurrection was no private or internal event. Jesus appeared in the flesh to more than five hundred people at once (1 Cor. 15:4–8). But to accept the risen Christ, one must be converted, changed in mind as well as heart. The New Testament word *metanoete*, usually translated as "to repent," etymologically means "to change one's mind." Every new fact we experience calls us to rearrange our mental furniture, perhaps only a small bit, perhaps a great deal. Making room for the new calls for a conversion, a change of the topography of the mind. The gospel calls for a reordering, a conversion that makes the fact that Jesus Christ is not lying dead in a tomb but is alive, the key to understanding all reality. Lesslie Newbigin says:

> The simple truth is that the resurrection cannot be accommodated in any way of understanding the world except one of which it is the starting point. Some happenings, which come to our notice, may be simply noted without requiring us to undertake any radical revision of our ideas. The story of the resurrection of the crucified is obviously

18

not of this kind. It may, of course, be dismissed as a fable, as the vast majority of people in our society do. This has nothing to do with the rise of the modern scientific worldview. The fact that a man who has been dead and buried for three days does not arise from a tomb was well known before the invention of electric lights. If it is true, it has to be the starting point of a wholly new way of understanding the cosmos and the human situation in the cosmos.[6]

It is possible that people can refuse to believe John's testimony, functioning as if Jesus' tomb has a No Vacancy sign hanging outside it. It is also possible that we verbally affirm the resurrection and still fail to be changed by it. The Spirit's work is essential. But when he works, as Thomas demonstrates, the resurrection radically transforms our lives. The resurrection, the key to understanding the biblical story, becomes the key to our story as well, the key to a new way of understanding and living in the world.

6. Lesslie Newbigin, *Truth to Tell: The Gospel as Public Event* (Grand Rapids: Eerdmans, 1991), 11.

2

THE EXODUS
God Sets the Pattern of Redemption

Reformed theologians have often said that what is latent (concealed) in the Old Testament is patent (fully revealed) in the New. While this statement is something of a cliché, it nevertheless conveys the Reformed commitment to the historically progressive relationship between the Testaments. The Old Testament and the New Testament are intimately connected, and the connection is best expressed as promise and fulfillment: What an all-confident and all-competent God, Yahweh, promises in the Old Testament, in the New Testament he fulfills. More pointedly, the history of redemption recorded in the Bible finds its center in the saving revelation of God in Jesus Christ. S. G. De Graaf captures the centrality of Jesus Christ within the drama of redemption: "The Old Testament is the book of the Christ who is to come, while the New Testament tells us of the Christ who has come."[1]

---

1. S. G. De Graaf, *Promise and Deliverance*, 4 vols. (St. Catherine's, Ont.: Paideia, 1977), 1:21.

Thus in the last chapter we began with Jesus' bodily resurrection, the linchpin of the biblical drama. But now we turn back to explore the patterns in the Old Testament that pointed beyond themselves to their fulfillment in Jesus. A thoughtful look at the Old Testament reveals one pattern that centers all the others in pointing to Jesus: it is the story of Israel's exodus, God's redemption of the Hebrew people from slavery in Egypt.

WHY BEGIN WITH THE EXODUS?

In this chapter we begin again, this time with the exodus. Again we must ask, Why are we not beginning with creation? Why is the exodus our point of entry into the story? One important reason is what we might call the revelational priority of redemption over creation. God first saves his people, and then he gives them his word. As John Calvin expressed it in his *Institutes of the Christian Religion*, while God is first the Creator and then the Redeemer, we must first know him as Redeemer, and then we know him as Creator. Outside of God's gracious redemption, we will not read aright his revelation in his creation.

While the sequence of the biblical storyline is nonnegotiable, we see that the order of revelation does not always follow the order of the storyline. In fact, the revelation of the book of beginnings is given to the exodus community. The first audience of Genesis was the newly redeemed Hebrew slaves, now camped on the far side of the Red Sea, wondering about the God powerful enough to triumph over the forces of Egypt. A reliable principle for the interpretation of biblical texts is to inquire about the text's first hearers. And thus we begin where they began, learning to know the God who has just so undeniably and powerfully made them his people.

Another important reason to begin with the exodus is that it is the deliverance that draws together Old Testament events the way the resurrection draws together the whole story. It is kind of a prefatory linchpin.

21

HOW THE EXODUS IS CENTRAL FOR ISRAEL

A thoughtful perusal of the Old Testament reveals that for Israel, throughout its history and repeatedly in its writings, their formative exodus from Egypt is ever central to their identity and to their confession. Every subsequent event in the Old Testament story takes its cue from the exodus. It is the one event that is assumed by every other writer and piece of literature in the Old Testament. Psalmists, prophets, and chroniclers continually look back to this event as the central act of redemption and the model for future events of redemption. They speak of it as the high water mark of the faith, the most spectacular example of God's redemption (Judg. 19:30; Hos. 13:4; Jer. 7:25; 23:7–8). The nation dates their existence as a nation from the exodus (1 Kings 6:1). Throughout the Old Testament, the exodus is repeatedly celebrated as the ground for Israel's hope and basis for God's future deliverances.

Old Testament Pattern

There are a number of reasons why the exodus is so central to the Old Testament faith. First, the exodus set the model of redemption as deliverance from oppression and reception into divine blessing. Redemption, the exodus shows, is a coming out and a going in, a coming out of the bondage of sin and a going into the family and presence of God. God does not seek merely the political liberation of Israel from Egypt. Leaving Egypt was only the first step toward the goal of Israel coming into God's presence. God's mighty act of delivering his people from Egypt and bringing them into a place of sonship and blessing in his presence sets the model of biblical redemption.

Thus the exodus affords God's people a type, as such models can be called.[2] Former redemptive events begin a pattern to which later

2. This modeling is often spoken of in Scripture under the notion of typology. One thing, person, or event is a type of or analogous to some other thing, person, or event. Typology is the recognition of a historical correspondence, a likeness, between the past and the present. Certain constant elements characteristic of the pattern and the new event

events conform in some way. This patterning of God's faithful ways in history is crucial for his people to be able to interpret his ways in the future. They recognize and grasp the significance of a new redemptive event by analogy with the pattern. The type creates a pattern for the antitype, the historical precedent against which the antitype can be understood. If they are familiar with the pattern, the new event occasions an "aha!" moment, a "we've seen this before, and thus we know how to understand its significance" recognition.

The exodus was not the first act of divine redemption in Scripture, but it was the event that set the pattern. There must, of course, be more than one event in order to speak of a pattern. When God delivers Israel through the heaped-up waters of the Red Sea, there begins to emerge an important interpretative marker for God's redemptive act: deliverance through water. Water events become typical in the story. Already previous to the Red Sea God had delivered baby Moses through water, in the mini-ark. That story reminds us of a water event in the yet deeper past of the prepatriarchal history, the Noahic flood. In Noah's flood and the story of Moses in the bulrushes, God uses water as a medium for the revelation of his deliverance and grace. We see the same pattern in the Red Sea event.

Israel's prophets looked back upon the exodus as the quintessential redemptive event, the event to which all later redemptive events must conform. Isaiah would later speak of the exodus as the golden age of Israel, and thus would speak of the return from exile as a new exodus, a new deliverance from oppression (e.g., Isa. 11:15).

In the New Testament, the typological centrality of the exodus in redemption comes to fruition in the events of Jesus' life and ministry.

- The baby Jesus' flight into Egypt and return recapitulates the Moses typology, establishing Jesus as the new Moses, the new

---

would act as the interpretative clues for recognizing later events or persons. While the type anticipates or prefigures the antitype, we should not think of the type as being merely a kind of the antitype. It would be better to think of the type as setting a pattern for the antitype. Such an understanding preserves the integrity and content of the type and allows the antitype to be the fulfillment of what was promised in the typological pattern.

23

lawgiver, before he ever preached the Sermon on the Mount (the new covenant law) (Matt. 2:13–23).

- John the Baptist's confession of Jesus as "the lamb of God" reminds us of the Passover lamb who preserved Israel from the final plague immediately prior to Israel's departure from Egypt (John 1:29).
- The celebration of the Lord's Supper as a new covenant replacement of the Passover meal, celebrates the resurrection as Israel was instructed to celebrate the Passover.
- The new covenant rite of baptism fulfills the water theme, symbolizing immersion into God's presence (union and communion with God) and into the community of faith as well as cleansing from sin.

Thus, God's delivering Israel through the Red Sea sets the pattern of redemption and blessing by which his people would forever recognize God's mighty action, most centrally in Jesus Christ.

Old Testament Creed

Second, the exodus was also central for Israel's faith because it formed the center of the Old Testament confession of faith. If you were to ask a New Testament believer what single event is crucial for biblical faith, he or she would name the resurrection of Jesus Christ from the dead. Ask an Old Testament believer the same question and the answer would be the fact that God delivered Israel from the Egyptian brick pits. Indeed, Deuteronomy 26:5–9 is often called the little credo.

> My father was a wandering Aramean, and he went down into Egypt with a few people and lived there and became a great nation, powerful and numerous. But the Egyptians mistreated us and made us suffer, putting us to hard labor. Then we cried out to the LORD, the God of our fathers, and the LORD heard our voice and saw our misery, toil and oppression. So the LORD brought us out of Egypt with a mighty hand and an outstretched arm, with great terror and with miraculous

signs and wonders. He brought us to this place and gave us this land, a land flowing with milk and honey.

Every Israelite recited this confession of faith publicly when presenting the tithe of firstfruits to the priest. Thus, it functioned similarly to the early Christian confession that "Jesus is Lord" and to the historic church's Apostles' Creed. In addition, Israel was to recite the story from generation to generation in the Passover feast (Ex. 12:21, 28).

Understanding God

Third, the exodus formed the foundation for Israel's understanding of God. The next section explores this claim. Here we note that God revealed his identity to his people in his mighty acts surrounding the exodus experience. Again, if you were to ask an Old Testament believer about his or her God, the answer would be that God is the one who delivered Israel from Egyptian bondage. God's mighty deeds, striking Egypt with plagues and delivering Israel through the Red Sea, demonstrated that he alone is God. God's purpose was not simply to force Pharaoh to let Israel go, to bring political or economic liberty to Israel. Rather, it was to demonstrate and vindicate his rights over Israel, rights that would be remembered by Israel, "that you may tell your children and grandchildren how I dealt harshly with the Egyptians and how I performed my signs among them, and that you may know that I am Yahweh" (Ex. 10:2).

Thus, for the people of God in the Old Testament, their beginnings in God's deliverance from Egypt centered their faith and their hope. And even as it identified them as a nation, in it God identified himself to them.

GOD REVEALS HIMSELF TO HIS PEOPLE: A CRUCIAL CONVERSATION

God had commissioned Moses to seek the release of Israel from Egyptian thralldom. But things got off to a rather rocky start. For when Moses relayed to Pharaoh God's command to release the

Israelites, Pharaoh told Moses that the instruction of some unknown deity was meaningless to him. There was no reason why the mighty Pharaoh of Egypt should obey the command of some desert deity, the god of a debased slave people.

You see, Pharaoh knew some things about gods. They talk a lot, that is, their priests talk a lot, always trying to get Pharaoh to do something: build this, outlaw that, subsidize something else. But the deities themselves never did anything. They stood there on the wall, forever lifeless. (As per Howard Carter's 1928 discovery of the tomb of Tutankamen, the boy king, Egypt's lifeless gods still have not moved.)

Declaring ignorance of Moses' God, Pharaoh refused to let Israel go. Furthermore, because of Moses' effrontery, apparently having the time on his Israelite hands to dream up such hooey, Pharaoh commanded that Israel now make bricks without straw.

At this turn of events occurs a crucial conversation in which God reveals himself and his plans to Moses and through him to his people. Looking at it carefully helps us also to know our God, the one who enters into covenant relationship with his people, binds himself to his own promises and calls us to loving response.

Moses openly charges God with breach of promise. God had sent him to seek the release of Israel from bondage. But instead, Israel has been subjected to even harsher oppression than it knew before. God has not rescued Israel. "Is this why you sent me?" asks Moses belligerently (Ex. 5:22–23). God, what are you doing?

In an immediate reply, God promises that Israel's freedom is future but sure. Pharaoh will indeed let Israel go (Ex. 6:1). In fact, God will make things so uncomfortable for Egypt that Pharaoh will not only emancipate Israel but virtually expel it from the land of Egypt.

And then God says to Moses:

I am Yahweh. I appeared to Abraham, to Isaac and to Jacob as God Almighty, but by my name Yahweh I did not make myself known to them. I also established my covenant with them in the land of Canaan, where they lived as aliens. Moreover, I have heard the groaning of the

26

Israelites, whom the Egyptians are enslaving, and I have remembered my covenant.

Therefore say to the Israelites: "I am Yahweh, and I will bring you out from under the yoke of the Egyptians. I will free you from being slaves to them, and I will redeem you with an outstretched arm and with mighty acts of judgment. I will take you as my own people, and I will be your God. Then you will know that I am Yahweh your God, who brought you out from under the yoke of the Egyptians. And I will bring you to the land I swore with uplifted hand to give to Abraham, to Isaac and to Jacob. I will give it to you as a possession. I am Yahweh." (Ex. 6:2–8)[3]

In response to Moses' urgent question, God discloses himself as Yahweh, and he reveals his plans for his people in a series of promises.

GOD REVEALS HIS NAME, YAHWEH

Not once but four times in this conversation, God identifies himself by the name Yahweh. Besides introducing and concluding God's reply to Moses (Ex. 6:2, 8), the divine name also confirms God's promise of redemption (Ex. 6:6) and underscores God's promise to adopt Israel as his son (Ex. 6:7). The final declaration of the divine name also confirms God's promise of the land that he swore to give to the patriarchs.

What's in a name? Nowadays not much. My wife and I named our son, Peter, after a close pastor friend, and we gave our younger son the name Sawyer simply because we liked the name. But in ancient Israel people attached great importance to names. A name said something about the person who bore it. It captured something of that person's status, reputation, and character. For Israel the name by which God identifies himself is quite important. While God throughout the Old Testament reveals his character to Israel in a number of ways, this divine disclosure of the name *Yahweh*, in order that Moses can call upon him, is one of his most significant.

---

3. The NIV text has been changed from "I am the LORD" to "I am Yahweh" for reasons that will become apparent immediately.

27

Unfortunate Church Traditions

We often miss the profound significance of this revelation, due in part to ways the church has over the centuries handled the term *Yahweh*. Most English versions render the divine name as "the LORD." Why has the church, instead of using "Yahweh," opted to change it to "the LORD"?

The Hebrew text reads *YHWH*, the name that God revealed to Moses. During the intertestamental period, however, around the fourth century B.C., the Jews began thinking that the name of God was too holy to be spoken aloud. Influenced by Assyrian and Babylonian magical incantations and rites during their exile, they apparently accepted the notion that to know the name of a deity was to possess a certain kind of power over it. By calling up the name, one controls or manipulates the deity. Consequently, whenever they read *YHWH* in the Hebrew Bible, they spoke *adonai*, the Hebrew word for "master" or "lord," instead. The Septuagint, the late-third-century Greek translation of the Hebrew Bible, followed the intertestamental tradition, rendering *YHWH* as *kurios*, the Greek word for "master" or "lord." Today our English versions that render *YHWH* as "the LORD" follow in that tradition.

The irony of this tradition is that it chooses to use a circumlocution instead of the name that God gives to Israel to call upon him. It obscures the fact that God is revealing his name here, not a title or an office. In this it can keep from us the radical import of this disclosure.

Second, church tradition has inadvertently obscured the powerful impact of God's name with respect to the derivation and meaning of the Tetragrammaton ("the four letters") *YHWH*. The name appears to be a play on the Hebrew verb *to be*. The church typically throughout its history has taken *YHWH* as meaning something like "I am, I exist, or I am the one who exists."

For example, the medieval tradition understood *YHWH* not as a name but as a statement of self-existence, a statement of the certainty of God's existence. God is disclosing the meaning of his person as existence. He is the one who most completely exists and thus is the source or derivation of all being. In his *Summa Theologica*

28

(1.2.3), the thirteenth-century theologian Thomas Aquinas understood *YHWH* not as a name but as a philosophical assertion of being or existence. By calling himself Yahweh, God is saying that he is the deity who truly exists over against the idols who do not exist.

Further confirmation of this traditional understanding was drawn from God's earlier expression of his name as "I am who I am."

> Moses said to God, "Suppose I go to the Israelites and say to them, 'The God of your fathers has sent me to you,' and they ask me 'What is his name?' Then what shall I tell them?"
>
> God said to Moses, "I AM WHO I AM. This is what you are to say to the Israelites: 'I AM sent me to you.' "
>
> God also said to Moses, "Say to the Israelites, 'the LORD, the God of your fathers—the God of Abraham, the God of Isaac and the God of Jacob—has sent me to you.' This is my name forever, the name by which I am to be remembered from generation to generation." (Ex. 3:13–15)

Tomes have been written on the translation and meaning of the words "I am that I am" and the divine name in this text.[4] Etymological and philological studies on the Tetragrammaton have proved less than fully helpful and certainly less than convincing, for the term itself remains puzzling. Most scholars today would agree that thinking of *YHWH* merely as a statement of being, as "I am" or "I exist," is highly dubious.

I Will Be There for You

A closer look, however, at the context of Exodus 3:15 and Exodus 5:22–6:8 leads us away from a bare philosophical approach to God's self-disclosure and toward a historical and covenantal understanding. Contextually, "I am that I am" (Ex. 3:15, which probably carries the same force as Yahweh) may well be taken as "I will be to you as I was to them" (the fathers of Ex. 3:13), or "I will be there—with you in Egypt—as I am here." It might be best to combine the two together,

4. See Paul R. House, *Old Testament Theology* (Downers Grove, Ill.: InterVarsity Press, 1998), 92–94, for a recent discussion of the argument about the divine name in Ex. 3:13–15.

as Exodus 6:2–5 ties to God's past action on behalf of the patriarchs and Exodus 6:6–8 is directed toward the future.

In its other occurrences, the name Yahweh appears in covenantal contexts, in the midst of God entering into personal relationship with his people. Thus, Yahweh is the divine name associated with the ark of the covenant, the tabernacle, and the temple—primary emblems of God's presence with Israel. Yahweh also tends to be the central name of God when the issue is God's historical action, whether past, present, or future. While there may be some claim of existence in the name Yahweh—though it is unlikely that Moses would doubt the reality of the Sinai epiphany—it is the covenantal and historical reality of God that is fundamentally at issue in the name *Yahweh*.

Yahweh is thus the covenant name for God: I am the one who keeps promise. I am the one who is always faithful. I am the one who is there for my people. I am the one who is here for you. I am the one who acts in your behalf. In giving his name, God promises his covenant presence to his people. He might be saying, "Call me Dad. I'm the one you can count on."

Thus, by announcing his name, God reveals his essential character to Moses. It is not so much about being as about presence. He is active, dynamic, working in history, entering into relationships, giving and fulfilling promises.[5] This was the great Word to Moses and to that first generation that came through the waters of the Red Sea.

The Living, Acting God

To Moses and Israel, this disclosure of God's name would have held radical significance. In it God is revealing himself as powerful and active. For 430 years the Israelites had seen Pharaoh's gods. As the Egyptians' slaves, the Israelites had built the monuments, the tombs, the shrines. They had seen the statues and paintings on the walls. And they knew, like Pharaoh, that the gods do not act; they

---

5. For a further discussion on the divine name here see Geerhardus Vos, *Biblical Theology: Old and New Testaments* (Grand Rapids: Eerdmans, 1948), 115–19; R. Alan Cole, *Exodus* (London: InterVarsity, 1973), 69–70; John I. Durham, *Exodus* (Waco, Tex.: Word, 1987), 38–39.

do not speak. The gods are impotent, mute, and probably deaf. In the exodus, however, they see and hear something different. Yahweh is different, for Yahweh acts. The issue is not existence but life and action.

Later in Israel's history, Isaiah argues with powerful sarcasm that the issue between the biblical God and the idols of the ancient Near East is not some philosophical discussion concerning existence but rather one of action and character (Isa. 44). The carpenter cuts down a cedar or oak. He measures and draws a character on the wood. He roughs out his work with hammer and chisel. Should he get tired, he will stop and rest. Should he hunger, he cuts off a portion of the log and uses it for cooking fuel to bake his bread. Late in the day the weather turns foul and cool. He cuts off another piece of the log to build a fire for warmth. From what is left of the log he carves his own likeness, man in all his awesome glory. He bows down to his own likeness and worships. He prays to it and says, "Save me; you are my god."

Existence is not the issue. Of course the gods exist. Man makes them. He can hold his idol in his hand. The issue is action, person, character. The false god of the idol maker is blind; it sees nothing. It does nothing, for it is made of wood. It can speak no word that man does not first give it. It is an impotent dead thing. Yahweh is no such manmade, lifeless god. He is not the thing made. Yahweh is the maker of all. What sets Yahweh off from the idols is the fact that he is the sovereign one, the one who comes to us, not the one who comes from us.

The issue between Yahweh and the idols is central to the exodus story as well. Yahweh's deliverance of Israel from Egypt featured his resounding defeat of Egypt's lifeless gods. The plagues were not simply designed to break down Egyptian resistance to Moses' demands to "let my people go." The plagues primarily demonstrated Yahweh's superiority over the deified forces of nature that the Egyptians worshiped. Albert Baylis appropriately comments:

> These plagues vindicate Yahweh as the true God in a land of gods, a land ruled by a Pharaoh regarded as the incarnate son of the god Re.

Pharaoh is to learn that the earth is Yahweh's (Ex. 9:29). So Yahweh announces, "I will bring judgment on all the gods of Egypt; I am Yahweh" (Ex. 12:12).

In fact, many of the individual plagues directly demonstrate Yahweh's power over the gods. The Nile River was considered sacred, yet it was turned to blood. Associated with the river were the gods Khnum, Hapi, and Osiris (for whom the Nile served as his bloodstream). The goddess Heqt, the wife of Khnum, was represented by a frog . . . And there was the sky goddess Nut, from whose domain came the hail. Isis and Seth, responsible in part for agricultural crops, seem to have been overwhelmed. A number of gods were identified with the sun, including the sun god Re. Certainly these gods failed in allowing a heavy darkness to blanket Egypt for three days.[6]

The name Yahweh means that God can be grasped and understood only by his actions and his words. Only his action reveals his presence and character. Humanity cannot discover it or forge it. Israel can know God and learn of his true nature only through his acts on its behalf. By giving his name to Israel, Yahweh is saying: If you want to know me, you will have to watch my actions and listen to my words. My faithfulness to my covenant is the key to my character.

The God Who Personally Relates

The revelation of God as Yahweh is also significant in the exodus story because it presents God as personal. The giving of his name is the promise of his personal presence. By and large, the deities of the ancient Near East were impersonal deities, little more than personifications of natural forces. And religion consisted in mere acts of appeasement. There is no relationship, no communication, no reciprocal action, no moral obligation. There is only formal service, a service conducted by man for the gods.

In the exodus, however, Israel and Egypt see and hear the revelation of a God who enters into covenant relationship with people, who makes promises to them and keeps them, a God who is a person, a

6. Albert H. Baylis, *From Creation to the Cross: Understanding the First Half of the Bible* (Grand Rapids: Zondervan, 1996), 107.

person who proves his existence by his moral character and his faithful action. By giving his name to Israel, Yahweh says to them, "You can count on me. And my deeds on your behalf will be my proof."

That a people would enter into a personal relationship with their god would have been a startlingly new concept in the ancient Near East. It is as if this God gives his people his business card, but in doing so, he turns it over and writes on the back of it an additional number: "Here's my private line."

This God cannot be known coldly, speculatively, or abstractly. Knowing God, for Israel in the exodus, and for God's people in every age, is not a question of philosophical definitions of essence or being. He can be known only as all persons are known: in the existentially relevant warp and woof of historical existence, and only as he gives himself to be known.

GOD MAKES PROMISES TO HIS PEOPLE

To establish his intent to be Moses' God, Yahweh makes a series of promises to Moses (Ex. 6:6–8). "I will bring you out," Yahweh says first; then, "I will free you from being slaves, I will redeem you, I will take you as my people, I will be your God, I will bring you to the land I swore to give to Abraham, and I will give it to you as a possession."

The litany of promises is tied up with the bow of his name: "I am Yahweh," God says, as if to make it absolutely sure that Moses knows with whom he is dealing. "I, Yahweh, promise these things to you." God's name and promise are so intimately tied together that the promises are a test of his name.

The seven "I will" statements express four promises. God promises Israel

> . . . deliverance from oppression:
> * I will bring you out;
> * I will free you;
> * I will redeem you.
> . . . creation of a community:
> * I will take you as my people.

... personal relationship:
- I will be your God;
- Then you will know that I am Yahweh.
  ... abundance and blessing:
- I will bring you to the land I promised;
- I will give you the land.

About the Promises

We may note three things about the promises in general. First, the guarantee for the fulfillment of God's promises rests on him alone: "I will." His name, Yahweh, guarantees his promise. God's name, one commentator says, is his personal signature on the check, his personal declaration of power and faithfulness to work out his promises for his people.

Second, the promises together express the nature of redemption. The promise of the exodus is far more than mere release from oppression. The initial act of physical deliverance is just that, initial. More is to come. For all believers, salvation is more than deliverance from the oppression of sin, guilt, and death. God wants not only to save but also to enter relationship with his covenant community and to bless that community. Relationship and blessing lie alongside deliverance at the heart of redemption.

Third, the promise is not new. God says to Moses, "I appeared to Abraham, to Isaac, to Jacob, as God Almighty" (Ex. 6:3). God had already committed himself to the patriarchs by way of the covenant. The promise of community, divine presence, and blessing through the land had been sounded many times in the patriarchal history of Genesis—to Abraham (Gen. 12:1–3; 15:18), to Isaac (Gen. 26:3), and to Jacob (Gen. 28:19; 35:9–12). God is telling Moses that he remembers and honors the promise that he made to Abraham: As I was there with them and for them, so I am here with you.

Yet there is something new. According to our text, God is revealing a new name, Yahweh. The patriarchs knew God as Elohim, or, as in this text, El Shaddai (God the powerful provider). Elohim is a somewhat generic word for God. In Genesis, Elohim refers to God's power and transcendence. Elohim is the majestic Creator. The name rarely designates the personal God who enters into covenant with Israel.

But the name Yahweh, while extremely rare, was not unknown before God's promise to Moses. While it appears some sixty-eight hundred times after Exodus in the Old Testament canon, it is used only a handful of times in the Genesis narrative. The Genesis occurrences include use by the patriarchs and by God. Vos mentions that Moses' mother's name, Jokhebed, is a compound name built from Yahweh (Ya). From this Vos concludes that Exodus 6:3 does not require the absolute previous unknowability of the word. The patriarchs did not as yet possess practical knowledge and experience of the side of God's character that finds expression in Yahweh.[7]

What is new here is not a new name but a new understanding of God's presence, a presence that is proclaimed and promised by the name. Now Israel will experience the reality of this name in a way their fathers could not have dreamed.[8]

Redemption from and to

Now to the promises. The first and the last promises go together: I will bring you out; I will bring you to. God saves his people from something and to something. Salvation is a negation of something and the positive possession of something.

Far too often we limit redemption to negation, to deliverance from sin. When we do, we also tend to regard sanctification as merely a matter of denial. But negation is not enough. Fleeing evil, as important as that is, does not secure righteousness or redemption. Turning and running 180 degrees from what is wrong may put you into a direction that leads to similar folly. The good and true must be sought for its own sake. The Christian life is never merely a matter

---

7. Vos, *Biblical Theology*, 115.

8. William Dyrness, *Themes in Old Testament Theology* (Downers Grove, Ill.: Inter-Varsity Press, 1979), 33, suggests that Exodus 6:3 could be rendered: "In the character of my name Jahweh I did not make myself known to them." God is filling up the meaning of his name in the events surrounding the exodus. That is the new thing here.

of negation. It has positive content, as we will see as we encounter these two sides of redemption over and over again.

I Will Be Your God, and You Will Be My People

The middle two promises, community and relationship, go together as well. Connected in God's declaration, "I will be your God and you will be my people," they occur twenty-five times in Scripture. This declaration is so common in the biblical text that scholars often call it the covenant formula. It expresses God's intent in all his dealings with his people. God's plan for community and relationship form the context for his promises of deliverance and blessing.

The covenant formula includes a demand as well as a promise. The promise, God's initiative, is "I will be your God," that is, "I will be here for you." Our response is, "We will be his people."

We are elected to the covenant, chosen by God's grace for that relationship. It comes from God just as sovereignly as the promises of his presence and divine kingship. We saw that God and his name guarantee the covenant promise.

While the covenant rests on God's sovereign monergistic act, it is also two-sided or bilateral. The covenant involves mutuality, for by its nature a covenant is a relationship. There is always an appropriate response to God's initiative. We hear and obey his command. The covenant brings or calls its parties into a committed relationship in which both have obligations and responsibilities. This interplay between divine initiation and human response is consistent throughout the covenantal story of Scripture.[9]

Community

It is crucial to note that the covenant formula envisions a community, not an individual. God's redemptive relationship is always

---

9. Thus I tend to think that the common distinction between so-called conditional and unconditional covenants is not very helpful. God's promise is always the guarantee of the covenant, and covenant always comes sovereignly from him, but we are called to live in its light. While some covenant episodes will emphasize human response more than others, the necessity of belief and obedience are always present in the biblical covenant.

with a people. This was true, for example, in God's covenant with Noah: "I now establish my covenant with you and with your descendants after you" (Gen. 9:9). Similarly, in his covenant with Abraham, God has Abraham's descendants in view (Gen. 12:1–3).

In fact, God often does deal with one person in Scripture. But that one functions as covenant representative for the group. He stands for or represents the people. He mediates the covenant between God and the covenant people.

But it is the group, rather than the isolated individual, that is center stage in the covenant. The fundamental unity of Hebrew society was the group, not the individual as in the modern West. Modern man starts with the rights of the individual. The Bible does not. God always addresses his word to a people. That word applies to individual persons insofar as they are part of the group.[10] Biblical religion always involves a covenantal relationship between God and the covenant community.

Relationship: Intimate, Natural, Moral

What God promises to his people is his presence. His dwelling with them will characterize the life of Israel. Thus what God seeks, in his redemption of a covenant people, is the kind of relationship that he had with Adam before the fall, when God walked in the Garden in the cool of the day and talked with man. This goal never leaves the biblical story.

"You will know that I am Yahweh your God, who brought you out from under the yoke of the Egyptians" (Ex. 6:7). God calls Israel to be his people so that it will know him. God's promise means, "among other things, that he offers himself to be known. He invites his people into the adventure of knowing him."[11]

Knowledge of God includes knowing about God. But the emphasis, in God's revelation of himself, always falls upon relationship rather than mere information. To be sure, there is a great deal to be

10. See my "Individualism and Biblical Personhood," *Pro Rege* 21.3 (March 1993), 6–22.
11. Elmer A. Martens, *God's Design: A Focus on Old Testament Theology* (Grand Rapids: Baker, 1981), 18–19.

known about God and his purposes, but this knowledge is always and only relevant in covenantal relationship. God wants our knowing of him to push beyond the merely historical and discursive. God is calling a people to himself.

The knowledge of God in Scripture is primarily a matter of personal intimacy: knowing the ways of the other, spending time with the other, experiencing personal intimacy. To know God as Yahweh is to experience his promise, his promise of deliverance from sin, his promise of blessing, his promise of coming into his family, and his promise of personal intimacy with his people.

This is the goal of the biblical story. Yahweh makes himself, his ways, intentions, and demands known to Israel so that it will believe and live in his grace.

The remarkable fact that Yahweh is a God who relates is central to biblical faith. It means that he is personal. It means that, though he is the transcendent one, utterly distinct from his creation, for us to enjoy his presence, he must and does choose to enter our world. He is also utterly free to enter into the world he has made and work within it. Immanence (God's relating to creation, his personal and moral proximity) is as central to the biblical story as is transcendence.

Relating to creation is not a problem for the God of Scripture. It is natural. We never have the feeling that God does not fit in the world, that his appearances are out of place, that he is fundamentally a hermit who dislikes contact with human beings or creation. The thoroughly concrete character of his appearances underscores this. More than sixty times the Book of Exodus uses the verb *see* in connection with God's presence: "And God appeared . . . and Moses saw . . ." God declares his glory (his visible presence) at Mount Sinai before Moses. He engages other senses besides vision. Exodus also speaks of hearing and even smelling.

There is no vague spiritual awareness here, but a tangible experience, an overwhelming one. We tend to reduce religious experience to the scope of our private feelings. We would do well to remember this biblical truth: God is absolutely free to enter into his creation, and when he does so, we are suddenly aware that it is our existence, not his, that is tentative and fragile. It is our existence, not God's that is questionable.

From the start, the relationship between God and his people has a moral dimension. God had commanded Abraham: "Walk before me and be blameless" (Gen. 17:1). The response God expects from his people toward him is a moral one. Indeed, without moral expectation and obligation, there would be no relationship.

We moderns seem to have developed the strange habit of thinking of relationships in amoral categories. Thus we argue about whether our public officials should be held to moral standards or whether business should be conducted in an ethical manner. It is as if morality were optional, something we do on top of or added to other endeavors or enterprises. We think of morality as a dimension of life and social relationship that is separable from the rest of life, a voluntary and often intrusive one.

Such thinking is impossible within the covenant. God's relationship with his people is never merely formal or legal. This is so not only because of the nature of the covenant but also because, within the biblical reality, a nonmoral relationship is like a square circle. It not only does not exist; it cannot exist.

Human beings live in an inherently and inescapably moral universe, because its Creator is a person. Every relationship between persons is moral. Every act and intention of persons is moral. When God calls his people into relationship, he calls them to morally upright action in the world, for he is morally upright. You do not get to call upon the name of God without him also being able to call upon you and make you accountable to him.

And so it is that Israel meets Yahweh. Delivered miraculously from Egypt through the water of the Red Sea, with a display of power and life that thumbs a nose at Egyptian idols, Israel finds itself drawn into the presence of, and intimate relationship with, this God who binds himself to faithfulness even as he summons the nation to obedience. The exodus constitutes Israel's identity as God's people, even as it reveals his identity, and his redemptive ways, to them. Israel, beloved covenant people, behold your God.

3

CREATION
Covenant-Historical Introduction

In his jubilant Song by the Sea, Moses praises Yahweh for delivering Israel from Egypt and defeating Pharaoh's army:

> I will sing to the LORD,
>   for he is highly exalted.
> The horse and its rider
>   he has hurled into the sea.
> The LORD is my strength and my song;
>   he has become my salvation.
> He is my God, and I will praise him,
>   my father's God, and I will exalt him.
> The LORD is a warrior;
>   Yahweh is his name.
> Pharaoh's chariots and his army
>   he has hurled into the sea.
> The best of Pharaoh's officers
>   are drowned in the Red Sea. (Ex. 15:1–4)

Moses' song asks, rhetorically:

Who among the gods is like you, O Yahweh?
  Who is like you—
  majestic in holiness,
  awesome in glory,
  working wonders? (Ex. 15:11)

Israel has just witnessed an awesome display of divine power that has pointedly triumphed over the entire pantheon of Egyptian deities. Now, suddenly, in a tide of dramatic events, Israel is delivered out of Egypt.

The revelation of Yahweh comes upon Israel, and Egypt, in a rush. Egypt, of course, had not known Yahweh. But Israel, we may surmise, at the point of the exodus, had not known much about him, either. Even though God had blessed Joseph's family in Egypt by greatly multiplying their numbers, Israel had experienced more than four centuries of slavery and oppression. The sands of Egypt contained the graves of countless Hebrews. Undoubtedly, they retained some stories about God's dealings with the patriarchs, but they had no written revelation. It's quite possible, even probable, that all Israel possessed before the events of the exodus were some dimly remembered tales and traditions about Abraham, Isaac, Jacob, and Joseph.

WHO IS THIS DELIVERER?

The plagues upon Egypt, the exodus of Israel out of the land, the deliverance and debacle at the sea thus bring momentous questions to the fore. Who is this God of the Israelites? How could he defeat mighty Pharaoh? How could the god of a no-account slave people so embarrass the gods of Egypt? And what claim does he have on Israel? Why us?

Genesis in Historical Context

It is important to realize that the revelation of the Book of Genesis had not been given before the time of the exodus. The Israel God rescued from Egypt through the Red Sea and led to the wilderness of Sinai was the first audience of the Book of Genesis, the first people to hear

41

or read the Book of Genesis as a written revelation. While the creation of the world, the fall into sin of our first parents, the stories of the Noahic flood, Babel, and the patriarchs predate the exodus, the written revelation of these events does not take place until the wilderness.

People have reasons for writing, and they write to someone. This is no less true of the books of Scripture than it is for the last letter (or e-mail) you wrote to your mother. Thus, interpreting texts involves not merely discerning what is being said but also discerning the author's purpose or intention, the context of the writing, and how the original hearers, the first audience, would have heard the message of the writer. That is the emphasis of the word *historical* in the Reformation principle of grammatical-historical interpretation. In order to interpret with integrity the book of beginnings, then, we must consider it in light of what Israel, recently redeemed from Egypt and camped in the wilderness, would have been asking and what they would have heard.[1]

Genesis a Covenant-Historical Introduction

What is more, it was not simply that the awesome display of power and the grand rescue called for explanation. Presumably the redeemed are now in some way obliged to the Redeemer. So grand a rescue hinted of covenant relationship, in the past and in the future. Israel would be asking for the story that led to this event, asking to understand how it was that Yahweh came to rescue them—who he was, not only with respect to the Egyptian deities, but also who he was to Israel.

The Book of Genesis is a covenant history, a covenantal-historical introduction to the exodus events. God is telling his people who he is. He is introducing himself to Israel in the creation story, and in so doing he tells them how he—in spite of the might of Egypt and its

---

1. In *Let the Reader Understand*, Dan McCartney and Charles Clayton talk about what they call "sane imagination," by which they mean the act of placing oneself in the situation of the original audience of a biblical text (*Let the Reader Understand: A Guide to Interpreting and Applying the Bible*, 2d ed. [Phillipsburg, N.J.: P&R, 2002], 145–46). This chapter employs that approach.

gods—was able to deliver Israel to himself at Sinai. He also reveals much of Israel's prehistory to the wilderness community. God's declaration of himself, the story of his early dealings with humanity from the Garden of Eden up to the call of Abraham, and the patriarchal stories tell Israel how and why Yahweh has redeemed her from slavery and into covenant relationship.

Structurally, ten occurrences of the introductory phrase *toledot* unite the Book of Genesis. *Toledot*, the Hebrew word for "generations," carries the prevailing idea of "this is the story of" or even "this is the history of." The *toledots* of Genesis give us a narrative that is presented in eleven panels (the first *toledot* appears in Genesis 2:4).[2] Each occurrence of the phrase forms an episode in the history of God's dealings with creation and humankind up through the death of Joseph in Egypt.

Genesis does not provide an exhaustive history of the world before the exodus. There are many things Moses does not address. He tells us nothing of the many cultures that rose and fell before God's exodus revelation. There is no word here about dinosaurs or ice ages. The episodic linkages created by the *toledot* structure of the text indicate that Genesis is not a mere telling of primeval history. Rather, it draws attention to the fact that the book is best understood as a "redemptive-historical way of looking at the past as a series of interrelated events."[3] Moses' intent is to give a situational prehistory of the exodus.

2. Following the creation story of Genesis 1, there are ten *toledots*, which along with Gen. 1 form eleven panels or narratives in all.
   1. The *toledot* of the heavens and the earth (Gen. 2:4–4:26)
   2. The *toledot* of Adam (Gen. 5:1–6:8)
   3. The *toledot* of Noah (Gen. 6:9–9:28)
   4. The *toledot* of the sons of Noah (Gen. 10:1–11:9)
   5. The *toledot* of Shem (Gen. 11:10–26)
   6. The *toledot* of Terah (Gen. 11:27–25:11)
   7. The *toledot* of Ishmael (Gen. 25:12–18)
   8. The *toledot* of Isaac (Gen. 25:19–35:29)
   9. The *toledot* of Esau (Gen. 36:1–43)
   10. The *toledot* of Jacob (Gen. 37:1–50:26)
3. Willem Van Gemeren, *The Progress of Redemption* (Grand Rapids: Zondervan, 1988), 70.

In some ways, that prehistory begins with God's call of Abraham, the father of Israel (Gen. 12). The story of Abraham and the patriarchs is immediately prior to the exodus. If Moses had begun there, he would have explained why God is acting in history on behalf of Israel but would indicate no larger picture.

But more introductions farther back in Genesis answer more fundamental questions. The stories of Noah and his sons (Gen. 6–11) preface God's call of Abraham. They explain God's election of this one Semitic tribesman and his descendants, for they tell us of God's covenantal concern for all humankind and that he calls the tribe of Abraham to mediate his claims to all.

But by inspiration Moses takes the covenantal history yet farther back. The narrative of Genesis 3 tells Israel how it is that humanity lives in a sin-scarred world, how we got from the perfection of God's original creation to the fallen world in which we live. The creation story (Gen. 1–2) provides the ultimate introduction to the whole story. Israel learns from it why Yahweh is so powerful, why he could trample upon the gods of Egypt as if they are but blades of grass. And here Israel learns the true nature of the world in which we live, and the nature and purpose of human existence in it.[4]

WHAT IS A COVENANT?

Thus, especially when we take into consideration that the recently redeemed Hebrew people are the first hearers of the contents of Genesis, it makes sense that the accounts in its early chapters function primarily as a covenant-historical introduction, and how, in light of that, we are to interpret them. What do we mean by "covenant"?

4. The sheer volume of attention given to the patriarchs in Genesis shows that the principal interest of the book is covenantal history. Gen. 1–11 is often spoken of as a prehistory, an introduction to the call of Abraham. And so it is. Many scholars have suggested that the prehistory found in Gen. 1–11 is somehow less historical, less factual than Gen. 12–50. The *toledots*, however, argue strongly against any idea of Gen. 1–11 being mere legend, saga, fable, myth (whatever word one might employ to suggest a nonhistorical story). Again, the very idea of the word *toledot* is "this is the history of." Gen. 1–11 claims to be every bit as historical, event-centered, and factual as any other part of Scripture. To interpret it otherwise is to make the Bible argue against itself.

Reformed theologians have proposed for centuries that the idea of covenant may be a fundamental engine that drives forward the biblical story.[5] But not until the mid-twentieth century did scholars of the vast field of oriental law and culture attend to the cultural context of the Old Testament understanding of the covenant. Indeed, G. E. Mendenhall has shown that the *berith* was a staple of ancient Near Eastern political and commercial relationships.[6] A covenant (Hebrew: *berith*) was a typical way of describing a relationship typified by promises and obligations.

Since the word *covenant* appears 286 times in the Old Testament, we may surmise that its authors were using an idea already familiar to their readers. We find several types of covenants in the ancient world as well as in Scripture. No single type or covenant paradigm captures God's covenant with his creation in all its historical diversity. Nevertheless, we may justifiably recognize the presence of covenantal features throughout divine action.

For this reason also, to insist on a single definition of covenant, attempting to fit all the covenantal occasions within Scripture to it, would be wrongheaded. "Asking for a definition of 'covenant' is something like asking for a definition of 'mother'," comments O. Palmer Robertson.[7] Definitions tend to be rather static things. One does not define persons or relationships, and a covenant is first and foremost a way of talking about persons in relationship.

Rather than a definition, we might perhaps begin with a rough description. Broadly described, a covenant is a relationship between persons, begun by the sovereign determination of the greater party, in which the greater commits himself to the lesser in the context of

---

5. Reflection upon the covenant as a central theme of the progressively unfolding drama of redemption can be found in such sixteenth-century Reformed thinkers as Ulrich Zwingli, Johann Heinrich Bullinger, John Calvin, Zacharias Ursinus, and Caspar Olevianus and was codified in the Westminster standards of 1647–1648 (e.g., The Confession of Faith, chap. 7).

6. G. E. Mendenhall, "Ancient Oriental and Biblical Law," *Biblical Archaeologist* 17.2 (1954); "Covenant Forms in Israelite Traditions," *Biblical Archaeologist* 17.3 (1954).

7. O. Palmer Robertson, *The Christ of the Covenants* (Grand Rapids: Baker, 1980), 3.

mutual loyalty, and in which mutual obligations serve as illustrations of that loyalty.

This beginning description of covenant as relationship highlights important features we may expect to find. As an organic, historical relationship, the covenant deepens and even undergoes change in the biblical story. Any relationship between persons changes over time. If a couple on their wedding day noted the significance of their marriage and then compared their perception thirty years later, they would see differences. The birth of children and grandchildren, vocational changes, medical problems—each issue of life changes us irremediably. The wife is still the girl who walked down the aisle, and her husband still the young man with whom she fell in love. But neither is the exact same person after thirty years. The relationship displays discontinuity, maturity, and change, even as it maintains continuity. Relationships retain the past even as they undergo change.

Similarly, the biblical story displays discontinuity, maturity, and change within its continuous covenantal relationship between God and his people. The analogy is not perfect, for the groom in the biblical story is not given to change. But the human story from creation to new creation does change, and that affects how God administers his creation covenant. Thus, the idea of covenant as relationship offers a helpful way to understand the unfolding drama of Scripture.

THE COVENANT OF CREATION

As we will see, God's dealings with Israel on the farther shore of the Red Sea, in particular his giving of the Ten Commandments, lends itself readily to interpretation as a covenant agreement. The early stories of Genesis, we have seen, introduce the "greater party" to Israel, recounting in covenant fashion the history of his power, his previous actions in behalf of his people, his sovereign right to their allegiance. But Exodus 20 is not the first covenant arrangement between God and his creation. His dealings with Abraham and before that with Noah take covenantal form also. I believe that we may also justifiably and valuably interpret the creation story in covenantal terms.

Is Genesis 1–2 a Covenant Text?

On what grounds may we treat Genesis 1–2 as a covenant text? Since the text does not use the word *covenant* (it first appears in Gen. 9:9), many scholars have argued against the notion of a creational covenant. Further, Anthony Hoekema claims that "the word *covenant* in Scripture is always used in a context of redemption."[8] Because covenant is a redemptive administration or relationship, there could have been no covenantal relationship before the fall, before the need for redemption entered the story.

Nevertheless, there are biblical warrants for a covenant of creation. Castigating Israel for their sin, Hosea says, "Like Adam, they have broken the covenant—they were unfaithful to me" (Hos. 6:7).[9] Here Hosea refers to an original, creationally given relationship.

Jeremiah refers to a creationally given covenant in these words:

> This is what the LORD says: "If you can break my covenant with the day and my covenant with the night, so that day and night no longer come at their appointed time, then my covenant with David my servant . . . can be broken . . .
> "If I have not established my covenant with day and night and the fixed laws of heaven and earth, then I will reject the descendants of Jacob and David my servant . . ." (Jer. 33:20–21, 25–26)

In the midst of exile, the prophet reassures Israel that God's faithfulness to his people is as sure as his faithfulness to his creation. As God has covenantally bound himself to creation, he has no less bound himself to Israel. Thus Jeremiah and Hosea understand God's creation action to involve covenantal action.

---

8. Anthony A. Hoekema, *Created in God's Image* (Grand Rapids: Eerdmans, 1986), 121.

9. It is possible to render the verse, "They like men have transgressed the covenant" since *adam* is not only the name of our first parent but also the Hebrew word for "man." But taking Hosea's statement this way is difficult, for it would then seem to say that Israel is simply following the natural course of all men in his covenant breaking. While that is certainly true, the statement loses most of its force as a criticism of sin. Israel is only doing what is to be expected from fallen human beings.

Old Testament writers often compare God's covenant bond with Israel with a marital bond.[10] While this is not an argument for a covenant of creation, it does, along with Hosea's and Jeremiah's words, undercut restricting the covenant to redemptive contexts. For marriage is a creational ordinance rather than an instrument of redemption.

William Dumbrell offers another justification for viewing the creation account as a covenant. He argues compellingly that the covenant with Noah (Gen. 9) constitutes a promise to continue and protect the creational order and relationships begun at creation. The text presents its covenant as a renewal rather than an innovation, thus implying the previous existence of that which is being renewed. In addition, a large number of sustained parallels link Genesis 1–3 and Genesis 6–9. Noah appears as something of a second Adam.[11] The evidence of Genesis 9 strongly supports a creational covenant.

Individually or cumulatively these arguments may not compel us. The real issue is whether Genesis 1–2 evidences elements essential to the existence of a covenant. Is the creation story the seed plot for the covenantal story of Scripture?

Covenantal Elements in Genesis 1–2

In fact, we may detect in the creation story several elements typical to covenant documents. The first such element, we know from extrabiblical covenant documents, was usually a preamble introducing the sovereign and the parties of the covenant relationship. This undoubtedly occurs in Genesis 1. God is introduced as the all-sovereign Creator, the King over creation—a kingdom he calls into existence by the sheer power and authority of his Word. And the universe created is depicted as the willing and eager vassal to his rule.

In this formative, sovereign act God calls all of creation into covenant relationship. "All things," writes John Frame, "plants, animals, and persons are appointed to be covenant servants, to obey

---

10. See Geerhardus Vos's discussion, *Biblical Theology: Old and New Testaments* (Grand Rapids: Eerdmans, 1948), 256–63.

11. William J. Dumbrell, *Covenant and Creation* (Nashville: Nelson, 1984), 15–26.

God's law, and to be instruments of his gracious purpose."[12] All of creation, the Israel of the exodus learns from Moses, is bound covenantally to Yahweh, and he to it. The lordship of God, by which all of creation is called into being and before which all things are subject, is powerfully put before Israel in the creation story.

A second typical element of ancient covenants was a statement of obligations. This included the promises made by the sovereign (the senior partner) in the relationship and the responsibilities of the vassal (the junior partner) in light of the sovereign's promise. In Genesis 1, by his sovereign, free decision, God covenantally binds himself to his creation. He orders the separate elements of creation not merely with respect to one another but with respect to himself as well. It is by the Word of God that the creation is made, and it is by the Word that creation subsists. He binds himself to be faithful to his Word. The patterns of day and night, seedtime and harvest, mating and giving birth, do not follow impersonal laws but rather the direct command of a God who is ever close.

God appoints a place, an area of responsibility, to each of his creatures. He appoints the sun to govern the day and the moon to rule over the night. Each creature has a covenantal response to the Word of God. As the psalmist put it, "All things serve you" (Ps. 119:91). God commands the waters to bring forth fish and, reciprocally, the fish to multiply and fill the waters. Likewise the sky and the birds, the land and the land animals. All parts of God's creation have their covenantal task.

What we see in Genesis 1 is a totalizing relationship in which all things are vassals to the King of creation. And for this reason the psalmist can declare:

> Let the sea resound, and everything in it,
>> the world, and all who live in it.
> Let the rivers clap their hands,
>> let the mountains sing together for joy. (Ps. 98:7–8)

12. John M. Frame, *The Doctrine of the Knowledge of God* (Phillipsburg, N.J.: P&R, 1987), 12.

Mediator

Genesis 1–2 evidences a third covenantal element: the role of the mediator. Not all extrabiblical covenants possess this element, but in the biblical covenant it is a necessary and constant ingredient.[13] God administers his covenant to the entirety of creation through a covenant mediator. As the one creature called and empowered to bear the image of God within creation, Adam, the human being, is to mediate God's rule to creation. Adam must respond obediently, on behalf of creation, to the rule of God.

In this arrangement, the creation covenant assumes personal and moral aspects. God, as a person, invariably relates personally and morally to all his creatures. The planets, physical laws, and animals, nonpersonal creatures, do not respond in kind. No personal intentionality or moral accountability is ascribed to the raindrop, the solar system, or the oak tree. Their obedience is involuntary, instinctive, even automatic. By contrast, the response of humankind is personal and always moral. At the very heart of biblical covenant stand the divine promise and the response of the mediator to the divine provision.

Humankind is free—free to obey. Man is not free to obey or disobey the Word of God as he pleases. Disobedience is never free, for it always brings slavery. The creational freedom of the mediator is not the alleged freedom of modern autonomous choice. Gordon Spykman says, "By divine design we are never free to disobey. Obedience to God's Word is the only open door to a liberated and liberating life."[14]

The responsive freedom of the human is also a responsible freedom. As the representative of creation, human response to God affects all other creatures. "We are responsible *to* God and responsible *for* his other creatures, accountable *to* our Maker *for* his cos-

---

13. While the covenant mediator is absent from the Hittite suzerainty covenant, it is a fundamental aspect of some other forms of covenant making in the Late Bronze Age (1500–1000 B.C.).

14. Gordon J. Spykman, *Reformational Theology: A New Paradigm for Doing Dogmatics* (Grand Rapids: Eerdmans, 1992), 251.

mos."[15] Mankind's choices, his obedient and faithful or disobedient and faithless responses toward God, will affect the entire created order.

This suggests a fourth covenantal element of Genesis 1–2: a declaration of blessing and curse, the blessing promised upon covenant fidelity and the warning of curse that covenant faithlessness brings. The Tree of Life (Gen. 2:9) symbolizes the blessing that will come upon man and all of creation so long as humankind obeys the Word and will of God. The Tree of the Knowledge of Good and Evil, however, simultaneously declares that the human is not ultimate, that he is a creature under the Word of God, and warns of a most serious penalty for covenant unfaithfulness (Gen. 2:16–17).

The presence of covenant elements within the creation text, therefore, supports our interpreting it as itself a covenant. Far-reaching implications flow from this claim. Covenant indeed shapes the biblical story from cover to cover.[16] The biblical drama displays the fundamental, unfolding continuity of a personal relationship. We may view covenant history not as a series of disconnected installments but as a single line. Each new covenant presupposes and renews what went before. Specifically, God's redemptive acts do not oppose or deny his creative intent, but come as restorative promises in relation to creation.

God covenants with all things, not simply with his people. All created things, not just people, and not just his people, are bound covenantally to God. All things stand before him either as covenant breakers or as covenant keepers. In appointing yet another covenant mediator, Israel, God never reduces the scope of his redemptive concern: Israel will be his agent of redemption, not as an end in themselves but for the redemption of the world. This humbling sense of his (and thus their) larger purpose God revealed to the newly freed

---

15. Ibid.

16. Not all biblical truth, however, may be reduced to covenantal theology. See John H. Stek, " 'Covenant' Overload in Reformed Theology," *Calvin Theological Journal* 29.1 (April 1994), 12–41. John Murray rightly argues that it would be inappropriate, for example, to apply a covenantal construal to the relation between the persons of the Godhead ("Covenant Theology," in *Collected Writings of John Murray*, 4 vols. [Edinburgh: The Banner of Truth, 1982], 4:234–38). Covenant is a historical relationship.

Hebrew slaves in the Sinai wilderness. The creation story reveals that their constitution as God's people implicates them in a larger design that predates the exodus.

WHAT ISRAEL LEARNED ABOUT GOD

In addition to the fact that they had entered into a larger story, what would the wilderness community have learned when God first inspired the writing of the creation story of Genesis? The creation story would have provided them, its first hearers, a full explanation of their identity and calling, in relationship to their God, their world, and humankind.

God Is the Sovereign King over All Things

First, Israel would have heard a powerful declaration that God is the almighty, transcendent Creator and the sovereign King over all things. Genesis 1 does not begin with an extravagant introduction to God, contrary to the way many extrabiblical covenant preambles introduced a monarch by grandiose claims of might, authority, intellect, or beauty. His actions are the revelation and the proof of who he is. Willem Van Gemeren says, "God brought forth the cosmos, and in so doing he made himself known."[17]

The text uses the Hebrew verb *bara* ("to create"). Scripture in general uses the verb quite sparingly elsewhere. Only God creates. Human beings might make or fashion things, but we are not creators. Further, the creative act appears supremely effortless. The casual verb *to do* is often used as a parallel to God's creating. Creation is God's doing by his Word. He speaks and it is done. God's creation by the sheer might of his Word moves the psalmists to awe and adoration. For example:

By the word of the LORD were the heavens made,
their starry host by the breath of his mouth.

17. Van Gemeren, *The Progress of Redemption*, 7.

> He gathers the waters of the sea into jars,
>> he puts the deep into storehouses.
> Let all the earth fear the LORD;
>> let all the people of the world revere him.
> For he spoke, and it came to be;
>> he commanded, and it stood firm. (Ps. 33:6–9)

The creative word of God is effective; nothing frustrates it. There is nothing against which God must struggle.

Since the verb *bara* ("create") is never used with any statement of raw material (as in God created the heavens and the earth out of ABC), the classical tradition has held that God created the universe *ex nihilo* (out of nothing). God, and only God, is the source of creation. He creates purely by his Word, without using any antecedent material. While the verb *bara* (Gen. 1:1) does not require this doctrine, *bara* does connote God's effortless, totally free, and unnecessary act of creation.

Dissenters from the doctrine of *creatio ex nihilo* have postulated a primordial chaos out of which God fashions his creation, some hostile force against which God must battle, an unruly chaotic order upon which God must impose his creative intent. They have alleged that the words *shapeless and void*, the *darkness*, and the *deep* (Gen. 1:2) support this view. But this dualistic interpretation is profoundly foreign to the creation story of Genesis. The text does not depict an imagined battle of the gods. Instead, it depicts the act of creation as free and effortless. By an executive command, the sovereign Creator speaks, and the thing is done. The execution sequence is extremely terse: "Let there be light. There was light." It is even starker in the Hebrew text: "be light, was light." We may more naturally interpret the "formless and void" of Genesis 1:2 as the fruit of the implied command of Genesis 1:1, the raw, unformed matter that will be fashioned into the creatures of God. Further, no deep evil symbolism need be read into the darkness or the deep. The "deep" may refer simply to the unformed stuff God calls into existence, and "darkness" merely to the absence of light.

God Has the Right to Rule over All

The great teaching of Genesis 1 is that God is the majestic King over his world. The creation story proclaims his authority as well as his power. All things do his bidding, answer his command, and bend to his decree. God not only creates but also names the creatures he speaks into being: the day, night, sky, land, sun, moon, sea, man. To have the right to assign a name is to exercise the right of lordship, authority, and possession. By naming his creatures God declares his kingly rights over them. The proclamation of kingship, the right to rule over his creation-kingdom, makes Genesis 1 a most fitting prologue to the entire Pentateuch, which is itself dominated by the covenant, the administration of the kingdom of God.

Yahweh Alone Is God

At the time it was formulated, the proposition that one God created all things and authoritatively reigns over all was anything but commonplace. The creation story's declaration of a single God (monotheism) was absolutely startling in the world of Moses and ancient Israel. It would have stood in marked contrast to the creation stories of Israel's pagan neighbors.

The pagan creation myths were full of tales of how the gods themselves were born and of the birth of the universe as the result of their contests or their love affairs and reproductive activities. Genesis is the great exception. The first verse dismisses all the mythologies of the ancient world.

For ancient people, the mysterious powers that seemed to reside in all things appeared as deities: the god of water, the god of fire, of sky, of sun, moon, animals, and so on. Genesis refutes and rejects all the pretended gods of human imagination. Only this God, this one God—Elohim Yahweh (the God whose name is Yahweh)—is supremely distinct from the world and sovereign ruler over it.

We moderns often come to Genesis 1 assuming that this text is presenting an argument against (a polemic) the naturalistic, evolutionary story of origins. There is indeed a polemic here, but the polemical intent of Genesis 1 is not aimed at modern naturalistic science but rather ancient pagan mythologies. Moses' intent is to break the back of the pagan gods and mythologies that held ancient people in thrall. Moses is not grappling with issues that arose out of the modern scientific attempts to understand the structure, forces, and processes of the physical universe. The revelation of Genesis 1 may be inconsistent with the naturalistic story of modern science (and I believe it is), but the text is aiming its polemical guns elsewhere.

Genesis 1–2 answers Israel's question, How could Yahweh, this one God, defeat the many gods of Pharaoh? The answer is both positive and negative, declaratory and polemical. The gods of Egypt are no gods at all. What the pagans worship are merely the creatures of God. The sun is not a deity; it is a creature. The moon is not a god; it is the product of God. The pagan gods are no gods at all but merely part of the same order of creation as man. The gods of Egypt cannot raise a hand in defiance to the God who delivered Israel because the only hands they have are those carved for them by human hands; the only powers they possess are those imagined for them by human powers. Only the God who delivered Israel out of Egypt, the God whom Moses identifies as Yahweh in Genesis 2, is God. He is the maker of worlds, and he alone stands supremely above all created things.

The strongly implied exhortation for a people who long had been exposed to the polytheistic and idolatrous practices of Egypt was that Israel must put away its idols. Israel is to have no other gods, for there are no other gods. There is but the one God, and the world he has made. The exhortation is the same as that which is found in the opening words of the Decalogue:

> I am the LORD your God, who brought you out of Egypt, out of
> the land of slavery.
> You shall have no other gods before me. (Ex. 20:2–3)

Only Yahweh acts. Only he is the Creator. Only he is the deliverer of his people. He alone is worthy of worship.

WHAT ISRAEL LEARNED ABOUT CREATION

The grand teaching of the Genesis creation story is its revelation of God. It is in effect the formal introduction of the Creator God to Israel. But Genesis also reveals something about the world God has made.

Creation Is God's Kingdom

As we have seen, Genesis proclaims that the material universe is God's creation, the kingdom over which he reigns as the great King. To say that God is the great King is to say that he alone has the right to rule over our world. Like the word *covenant*, however, the terms *king* and *kingdom* do not appear in Genesis 1–2. But in demonstrating covenantal elements, the text also implicitly but very clearly declares God's sovereign kingship over creation.[18]

While many approaches toward biblical theology use the covenant as an organizing principle (as we are doing in this work), others center on the kingdom of God theme in Scripture. We can already see that these two grand biblical themes relate. One way of describing their relationship is to speak of the covenant as a kingdom instrument. God maintains and administers the kingdom—his sovereign rule over all things—through covenant means. Or, we might say, covenant looks backward, kingdom looks forward. Covenant suggests the abiding character of God's work by continually looking back to the moment of the constitution of relationship. Think of a wedding ring, the symbol of the marriage covenant bond. It continually reminds the wearer that he or she is a party to an oath-bound relationship. It says in effect, the one who put that ring upon your finger has promised to love and honor you, as you have promised to love and honor the one who wears the matching ring. Whereas covenant is foundation-oriented, kingdom is often goal-oriented in Scripture, looking forward to final fulfillment.[19]

18. While the kingdom of God is an important New Testament theme, the phrase does not appear in the Old Testament. Yet God's kingship over his creation is a recurrent Old Testament theme (e.g., Ps. 93; 103:19).

19. Spykman, *Reformational Theology*, 258.

Creation Is Distinct and Dependent

As the Creator-King, God alone holds the forces of creation together. All things depend upon God and his Word, not on forces of nature, fate, or random happenstance. Nothing and no one within creation is ultimate or eternal. Only God is. Indeed, the biblical story opens on this very point. John Timmer has appropriately said: "When Genesis 1 says 'In the beginning God created the heavens and the earth,' it declares that there are only two kinds of being. There is the Creator and there is the creation. God alone is the Creator; all else is creation. The two are totally and eternally distinct."[20]

Monotheism is the clear implication of the creation story.[21] The text explicitly states the dependence and nondivine status of the created order. Contrary to pagan myths' depiction of the world or humankind as the product of either divine ejaculation or expectoration, creation is not an extension of God's being. Rather, the cosmos is the result of God's spoken will, his Word.

Creation Is the Recipient of God's Providential Care

The relative, dependent nature of creation suggests a continuing relationship between Creator and creation. The Apostles' Creed affirms that God is "the Father Almighty, maker of heaven and earth." God is not just the almighty Creator; he is a fatherly Creator; and a good father never abandons his children. This is the witness of Scripture as well. God's providential care over his creation is a continual and present activity (Neh. 9:5–7; Isa. 40:22–31; Ps. 148). As a good Father and King, he sustains and cares for everything he has made, even the least sparrow. Thus John Calvin proclaimed, "If God should

20. John Timmer, *They Shall Be My People* (Grand Rapids: Bible Way, 1983), 11.

21. The coupling of monotheism with the affirmation of God as the Creator of all things is a common element of Old Testament religion. Ezra's appeal for God's aid in deliverance from slavery is typical. "You are the LORD. You made the heavens, even the highest heavens, and all their starry host, the earth and all that is on it, the seas, and all that is in them. You gave life to everything, and the multitudes of heaven worship you" (Neh. 9:6).

but withdraw his hand a little, all things would immediately perish and dissolve into nothing."[22]

God's work does not end with the original act of creation, for the universe is never self-sufficient. There is no cruise control setting, no autonomous innate principle of self-maintenance and government. This is not to allege anything lacking within creation but merely to recognize that it is a vassal, ever subject to its Creator, ever dependent upon his will and love. The continuation of the universe is just as much the product of the divine will as is the original creative act.

Creation Is Good

The creation story resounds with the sevenfold declaration that the work of God's hands is *good*, even very good. There is not the slightest hint that creation is bad or lacking simply because it is something other than God and dependent upon him. The creation is not to be feared or demeaned, for it is the work of the almighty Father, the King of the cosmos. Thus as the creation story refutes pantheism (the idea that some aspect of the world is divine), it also denies dualism (the idea that the universe or humanity is caught between eternally antagonistic principles).

As the good creation of God, the cosmos displays order, symmetry, and harmony, rather than chaos, accident, or trial-and-error arrangement. Each element and creature receives a divinely designed place and function. Yet for all its harmony and order, creation exhibits divinely intended diversity. A frequent New Testament term for "world" is the word *kosmos*, a word that denotes harmony and beauty. "The term *universe* is related but emphasizes that the (di)versity (the many) is a uni (one). Many parts constitute one product from the Creator's hand."[23]

22. John Calvin, *Commentaries on the First Book of Moses Called Genesis*, trans. John King, 2 vols. in one (reprint, Grand Rapids, Baker, 2003), 1:103.
23. Gerard Van Groningen, *From Creation to Consummation* (Sioux Center, Ia.: Dordt, 1996), 38.

Creation Is the Object of God's Redemptive Concern

The creation story warns Israel against narrowing the scope of God's concern to itself alone. Yahweh will not be reduced to a mere tribal deity (even the tribe of the elect). The creation narrative conveys the cosmic proportions within which the story of Israel is to be placed. The biblical world is not just a world of persons, nor is its story limited to divine-human encounters. The dimensions of the biblical story are as wide as the universe, for the biblical God is the maker of all things.

What Israel Learned about Man

Genesis 1–2 situates man in the universe by relating him to God, the world around, and to other human beings. These three relationships are constitutional in that they define the purpose for human existence. We may say that God creates man to fulfill a threefold covenantal calling or office, for all three relationships are bounded by covenantal responsibilities and blessings.[24]

Man Relates to God

The last creature made, according to the creation narrative, is the human (Hebrew: *adam*). But God's final creative work is no afterthought, for the text appears to move from the creation of lower forms to higher creatures. Man is the acme of God's creative work.

The unique circumstances of man's creation and the charge God places upon him demonstrate this:

Then God said, "Let us make man in our image, in our likeness, and let them rule over the fish of the sea and the birds of the air, over the livestock, over all the earth, and over all the creatures that move along the ground."

24. For more on humans being created in threefold relationship, see Anthony A. Hoekema, *Created in God's Image*, 78–82.

So God created man in his own image,
    in the image of God he created him;
male and female he created them.

God blessed them and said to them, "Be fruitful and increase in number; fill the earth and subdue it. Rule over the fish of the sea and the birds of the air and over every living creature that moves on the ground." (Gen. 1:26–28)

While each of the other creatures is made "according to its kind," this phrase is missing from the narrative of man's creation. Rather, humankind is made after the image of God. Within the created order, the human corresponds uniquely to God. Only the human responds to God reciprocally, as person to person. Because God's own character is relational, he has created man for companionship and covenantal relationship with him. Genesis 3:8 says that God walked in the Garden, implying that God created Adam and Eve for the purpose of personal companionship.

Man Relates to Creation

Genesis 1:26–28 indicates that there is more to bearing the divine image than personal relationship with God. It also involves relationship with creation. The image of God does not make man unique from the created order, but rather unique within the created order. Man is called to be God's agent, the mediator of God's covenant with creation. Man bears God's image for the sake of his calling to rule over and steward creation. Should we miss man's calling, we will miss the purpose of his being the image of God.

The human is uniquely a creature of the earth in special relationship with God for the sake of the whole earth. Polar bears are creatures of God, but they are not persons. Angelic beings are persons, but they are not called to rule over creation. Only humankind is given this dual relatedness, the calling to mediate the covenant of creation.

Genesis 1 suggests that the world without man is incomplete. But we can turn the proposition around: man without the world is incomprehensible. That God has placed us here in this world and called us in service both to himself and to his creation means that we can be comfortable with our creaturely status, with our physicality, our undeniable links with the creaturely. Man is made for the earth. This world is our home.

Humans Relate to One Another

Human beings are not only related to God and related to the created order but also to one another. After God started Adam in his duties as steward over creation, working the Garden and naming the animals, God determined that "it is not good for the man to be alone" (Gen. 2:18). God creates male and female (Gen. 1:27), and marriage as a creation ordinance (Gen. 2), thereby envisioning a larger social relationship for man.

God intends that we be social creatures. Our sexual differentiation and our union in the marriage ordinance should be understood, at least in part, to indicate that humans image God not in individualistic isolation but in relationship to other human beings. As the man is incomplete without the woman, and the woman incomplete without the man, so the human is incomplete without other human beings. Togetherness, not aloneness, is good for human beings. Our calling as image bearers includes relating to others in loving and responsible ways.

The gift of human personhood with its accompanying endowments is not for personal aggrandizement but that we may enrich the lives of others, serving our fellow human beings within God's world. There are no biblical warrants for the idea that the individual person stands alone before God. Personal relationship with God should not be confused with private relationship. While the covenant begins with relationship with God, it is also a relationship with God's good earth and with other human beings. Repeatedly Scripture expresses the covenant formula, "I will be your God, and you will be my people," the continuing theme that God is calling a people. He covenants with a people, not with an individual here and an individual there.

In sum, we may describe man's imaging God as his representative in creation by saying that he is a reflector or mirror. Humans are called to reflect the divine presence, will, and love of the transcendent covenant Lord into the world. We are to reflect, manifest, reproduce, represent, mediate, and act on behalf of God. This is exactly what the verb *to glorify* often denotes in Scripture. Man glorifies God by transcribing, writing out his character in the world in the multiplicity of our divinely designed and intended relationships.

COVENANT AND CREATION

The revelation of Yahweh to the miraculously freed Hebrew slaves came on them in a rush. They found themselves on the other side of the sea from Egypt and embedded centrally in a divine story dating from the dawn of time. They began to hear and observe the ways of their God that would be borne out in every encounter thereafter.

Yahweh enters a covenantal relationship with his creation and with his people. He sovereignly initiates that relationship, choosing and binding himself to the recipients of his steadfast love. The relationship in no way depends on the prior performance of the chosen; it is, from the outset, wholly gracious.

Such a covenant relationship nevertheless involves mutuality. While sovereignly initiated by God, covenant grace calls for covenant response, even as any relationship is sustained only through moral response. Human obligation never precedes or conditions covenant relationship with God; human obligation proceeds from, in response to, divine initiative. Man is responsible to God for right worship, loving his neighbor, and caring for creation. The covenant of creation thus provides for newly constituted Israel what it affords God's people in every age: a full-bodied way of life that we are called to live before God and in the midst of the world.

4

THE FALL
Humanity in Revolt

God created a perfect world, the opening chapters of Genesis proclaim. He appointed every structure, force, and creature a place and task within the perfectly balanced order of the universe. He created Adam and Eve to bear his image within creation, and he established a pattern of life in which human obedience and loving relationship would issue in blessed human existence, the tilling and keeping of the earth, and the glorification of God. But as we are so painfully aware, the history of humankind has not been characterized by the faithful worship of God, the loving service of man to his fellow man, or the obedient protection and development of creation. Adam and Eve rebelled against God's fatherly love and rule.

WHAT SIN IS, AND WHAT IT ISN'T

For us to gauge aright the role of sin in the grand story of redemption, we must pay attention to what the Bible says about sin, and what it doesn't say. Let us begin with the obvious: the fall is not the

63

first event in the Bible. Creation is the first event—God's creation of a beautiful and perfectly ordered universe. The account repeatedly affirms that it was good. When he finishes, God looks at his work and declares it very good. There was a time when there was no sin in God's creation, when sin was not an element of human experience.

An Intruder

By beginning with the story of creation rather than the fall, Scripture proclaims categorically that sin is an intruder. It is not the product of God's creativity. It does not belong.

The Bible does not describe an eternal struggle between good and evil. Sin is not an eternal principle, a necessary or structural element of either the universe or human beings, or the product of God's creative intent. Nor does Genesis seek to make sense of sin, to make rational room for it in our cognitive universe. Sin remains ever a riddle, ever absurd, ever irrational. Augustine quite rightly said that seeking a rational explanation for the origin of sin is like trying to see darkness or hear silence.

What Genesis does tell us is a story of an event, something that happened after the beginning. It narrates an event in which Adam and Eve knowingly and willfully violated the Word of God. Sin is not a defect inherent in creation. Sin has to do with human response to God.

Far too often, those who argue for the historicity of the creation account in Genesis and the historicity of our first parents and the fall do so merely as a reaction to evolutionary science[1] or for the sake of a biblicist point: the Bible says the fall happened, therefore it did happen.[2] The important theological point is often missed: that sin is

---

1. I believe that the biblical witness to creation is incompatible with the evolutionary story of biological origins, but as I argued in the last chapter, the purpose of Gen. 1–2 lies elsewhere than in offering a polemic against Darwinian science.

2. Biblicism can be either a virtue or a vice. Virtuous biblicism is full submission to the inscripturated Word of God. Biblicism becomes a vice, however, when we fail to appreciate the fact that the Bible refers to, is about, and explains a complex of realities external to its pages. The Bible is a referential Word. That is to say, it is about man's life as

a nonoriginal, historical disruption deep in the history of humankind's experience in God's world.

If we miss the biblical emphasis upon the goodness of God's original creation, we will also fail to see the blasphemy of sin for what it truly is: a rebellion against God and his good gifts, a rebellion from the loving word of God, a rebellion that brings discord and fracture into God's creation. Sin is never normal or natural. It never fits.

The fact that the fall story follows the creation narrative in the Book of Genesis strongly suggests that sin is an intruder, that God's creation did and can exist without evil or sin.[3] To recognize that something is wrong with us presupposes an order of right, a way things ought to be. For biblical religion that is what it was before the disobedience of the Garden brought alienation, discord, and the covenant curse of guilt and death.[4]

Human Flight from a Personal God

In essence, sin is man's flight from God. Created to be God's servants, stewards, and companions, Adam and Eve rejected God's call upon them and declared their independence from his rule by defying the divine command. "Our first parents being left to the freedom of their own will, through the temptation of Satan, transgressed the

---

God's creature in God's world. It is a lamp to the feet, a light upon the path of life (Ps. 119:105). It refers to and is for man's life in the world.

3. "The story of the Bible is the story of God's creation of a perfect world, of man's subsequent rebellion and fall from spiritual perfection, the Lord's plan—centering in Jesus Christ—of the restoration and restitution of his lost creation and people, and God's completion of all things in the end and fulfillment of them in eternal life. This is the storyline powerfully and unmistakably suggested by the placement first in the Bible of the story of Adam and Eve and the placement of the Gospels later. This placement suggests strongly that the story of Jesus must be interpreted and seen on the backdrop of the story of Adam and Eve's creation and fall. Moreover, this sequenced order is reinforced by the placement of the Old Testament first in the canon, an interpretive decision made in the canonization process that has more significance than modern theology is incline to grant." Henry Vander Goot, *Interpreting the Bible in Theology and the Church* (New York: Edwin Mellen, 1984), 71.

4. See Cornelius Plantinga Jr., *Not the Way It's Supposed to Be: A Breviary of Sin* (Grand Rapids: Eerdmans, 1995).

commandments of God in eating the forbidden fruit; and thereby fell from the estate of innocence wherein they were created."[5]

The Westminster Shorter Catechism defines sin as "any want of conformity unto, or transgression of, the law of God." We might be tempted to think of such law breaking impersonally, the way we might view circumventing the law of gravity by using aerodynamic lift. Certainly, sin is the transgression of God's law. Paul calls Adam's disobedience in the Garden a transgression of God's law (Rom. 5:14). Yet as we will see, the law is never an end in itself. The law is never merely formal, and most certainly never impersonal. The law is the personal God's declared will for his creatures. To violate it is to rebel against God himself. Consequently, Scripture often describes sin in relational terms. Sin is man's betrayal, desertion, faithlessness, breach of covenant relationship, and treachery, directed against a personal God.

Idolatry

Adam and Eve's disobedience was not only a flight from the good word and fatherly love of God. It was also their attempt to make themselves the master of their own lives. Fleeing God is running toward that which is not God. The Bible also describes sin as *falling short* or as missing the mark. But this is no accidental miss, as one might miss a target because one lacks sufficient skill or power with a bow and arrow. Missing the mark is the product of aiming at the wrong target, of setting one's sights on the wrong goal. Thus sin is a willful and culpable failure.

Scripture expresses the closely related idea that sin is idolatry. In describing sin as idolatry, Paul had something much larger and in its way far more perverse in mind than stone figurines representing pagan gods (Rom. 1:23–25). An idol is anything in creation that man turns to in worship rather than God. Idolatry is not merely one sin among many, but the epitome of all sin, the disobedience that denies God his rightful place over his creation and our lives.

How we cringe to name the awfulness of sin, especially as we know it so intimately as the expression of our hearts! But the fall story,

5. Westminster Larger Catechism, Q. 21.

placed as it is in Genesis 3, also offers the clear and indirectly comforting message: sin is not the way it is supposed to be.

WHAT SIN DOES

When God put the man and the woman in the Garden and appointed them to their calling as his vice regents to preserve and nurture the Garden, he also warned them not to eat the fruit of the Tree of the Knowledge of Good and Evil. In effect this was a command to preserve and nurture (till and keep) the word of God. It was not the nature of the tree that made it dangerous, the bearer of covenant curse and death, but what it stood for: obedience to the word of God.

God had charged man to keep the word of God. God had bound himself to his word also. Now, when man disobeys, God keeps his promise: "When you eat of it you will surely die" (Gen. 2:17). God imposes a series of curses on the participants of the first sin: the serpent whose temptation occasioned the sin, Eve, and then Adam. He expels the man and the woman from the Garden. Henceforth they and their posterity will experience the world as an inhospitable place, a place of toilsome labor and great danger.

Relationships Perverted

An entire demonic panoply of consequences stems from Adam and Eve's disobedience. It perverts humans' relationship to God. The creature meant to be God's image bearer, his covenant mediator within creation, has declared war against God. Alienation takes the place of covenant intimacy. Hostility, rather than obedient servanthood, now characterizes man's relationship to God. The Bible speaks of the corruption that blinds man to righteousness and disposes him toward selfishness, making him a slave to sin.[6]

Yet no sin is ever an isolated event, an issue that is relevant only to the sinner and God. Sin fractures and corrupts man's relationship not only to God but also to other human beings, to the world, and

---

6. E.g., Jer. 13:23; 17:9; John 8:34; Rom. 7:18–19; 8:7–8; Eph. 4:17–19; Titus 1:15–16.

to himself. This is especially so regarding the sin in the Garden. Because Adam acted as the covenant representative of all humankind, his sin alienated the entire human race from God. Every human being comes into the world as a slave to the reign of sin and death (Rom. 5:17).

The scope of Adam's act includes not just the human population but all of planet earth. God cursed the ground because of Adam's disobedience (Gen. 3:17–19). His sin proves catastrophic for creation as a whole, shattering creation's harmony. Paul tells us that the creation groans under the weight of sin even though the effects sin visits upon the world come about through no fault of the material universe (Rom. 8:20).

Hosea observes this covenantal connection between man's moral response to God and the health of creation:

> There is only cursing, lying and murder,
>   stealing and adultery;
> They break all bounds,
>   and bloodshed follows bloodshed.
> Because of this the land mourns,
>   and all who live in it waste away;
> the beasts of the field and the birds of the air
>   and the fish of the sea are dying. (Hos. 4:2–3)

Because Adam was the mediator of God's covenant with all creation, his moral response to God affects all of creation. Man's obedience brings blessing; his disobedience brings curse.

Kingdoms in Conflict

God could have left it at that: a depraved race inhabiting a dying world. He would have been within his rights to let the curse be his last word. But within the curse of Genesis 3 is another word, a very different kind of promise. In cursing the serpent, the Lord says, "I will put enmity between you and the woman, and between your offspring and hers; he will crush your head, and you will strike his heel" (Gen. 3:15).

68

At first glance, this statement does not appear to be a word of hope but a declaration of war. And so it is. As Adam has committed the human race to enmity toward God, God too declares war. But there is a crucial difference. Coming as it does to Satan (in the form of the serpent), God's word declares his hostility, not toward man or the creation but toward Satan and the reign of sin and death.

From this point forward, two opposing forces war in the world: the kingdom of God and the kingdom of Satan, the kingdom of light and the kingdom of darkness, the seed of the woman and the seed of the serpent. Abraham Kuyper spoke of this enmity as the antithesis.[7] Due to the sin in the Garden, two kingdoms stand antithetically to one another, a contention that will pit God against all that is in opposition to his rule. But note that this antithesis is not between earth and heaven, the body and the soul, or the visible and the invisible, but between God and Satan, between God and the kingdom of sin and death. It is between obedience and disobedience. Human beings, the seed spoken of in Genesis 3:15, are either the friends of God or the enemies of God.

The biblical story testifies repeatedly to the antithesis, the spiritual warfare between faith and idolatry, obedience and disobedience. Moses, Joshua, and Elijah all challenge God's people to choose between God and idols, life and death (Deut. 30:15,19; Josh. 24:14–15; 1 Kings 18:20). The psalmist distinguishes between the broad way and the narrow, the wicked and the righteous (Ps. 1). The New Testament witnesses to it in its distinction between God and mammon, the new man and the old, the Spirit of God and the flesh, wheat and tares, sheep and goats.

The warfare between obedience and disobedience is pervasive, running through every aspect of creation and every human endeavor. There is no neutral territory, no area of life that is free from the struggle. Both God and Satan lay claim to all things. What we experience is warring sovereignties, two regimes that stand over against one

7. The word *antithesis* is related to a participle in Gal. 5:17: "For the sinful nature desires *what is contrary* to the Spirit, and the Spirit *what is contrary* to the sinful nature."

another in their contention for everything. And nothing—no aspect of life—is neutral or uncontested.

This means that Scripture brooks no distinction between the sacred and the secular, the religious and the nonreligious, spiritual and unspiritual, moral and amoral. Sin touches every human endeavor from sexuality to automobile design, from showing a three-year-old how to tie a shoe to banking and economic systems, from prayer to politics. And in all these areas of life—and all the rest— God declares his enmity to sin.

GOD PROMISES RESTORATION

But there is a deeply running word of hope in Genesis 3:15 as well. God promises to destroy the power of the serpent, ending Satan's ways. The promise that the seed of the woman will crush the serpent's head, often called the mother promise or the protoevangelium (the first good news), marks a transition in God's response to his fallen creation, from wrath to grace. God here first declares his redemptive intention in the midst of covenant curse. It is a watershed statement in Scripture, for it speaks to a crucial moment in history.

How Radical Is God's New Provision?

Douglas Jones has rightly written that "the most prominent distinction that appears in God's covenant work is that between God's covenant before the Fall and His covenant thereafter."[8] In affirming this distinction, however, it is important that we describe it carefully, noting accurately what changed in the covenantal relationship between God and man and what remained the same. Is it appropriate, for example, to say that God's redemptive promise replaces an old covenant with a new one? What would be the consequences of this description for our understanding of God?

8. Douglas M. Jones III, "Back to the Covenant," in *Back to Basics: Rediscovering the Richness of the Reformed Faith*, ed. David G. Hagopian (Phillipsburg, N.J.: P&R, 1996), 76.

The Westminster standards sought to place due emphasis on the importance of the promise of redemption in Genesis 3:15 by putting forth a two-covenant view of history, a covenant of works and a covenant of grace.

> The first covenant made with man was a *covenant of works*, wherein life was promised to Adam; and in him to his posterity, upon the condition of perfect and personal obedience.
>
> Man, by his fall, having made himself incapable of life by that covenant, the Lord was pleased to make a second, commonly called the *covenant of grace*. (Confession, 7.2–3, emphasis added)

This two-covenant view has been debated hotly within Reformed and Presbyterian circles. Opponents deem it a systematic distinction that lacks clear biblical foundation. It may also give the unfortunate impression that God's covenant relationship with man before the fall was a strictly legal relationship devoid of grace[9] and that his covenant relationship with man after the fall was a strictly gracious arrangement without reference to law or obligation.[10]

While these concerns are valid, there is also much to commend the Westminster distinction. First, it appropriately recognizes that Adam and Eve lived within a covenant with God before the fall. Second, it rightly acknowledges the mediatorial role of Adam in the covenant, something which Paul makes much of in Romans 5:12–19. Finally, the distinction affirms that the fall so affects man's relationship to God that, in order for it to be restored, God must redeem man from sin. Thus, the Westminster language of the two covenants "highlights the sinfulness of sin and the amazing character of God's free grace."[11]

Nevertheless, the Westminster construction, throughout the history of the Reformed tradition, has suggested to many theologians

9. Grace here meaning God's favor rather than his redemptive response to sin.

10. E.g., John Murray, "The Adamic Administration," in *Collected Writings of John Murray*, 4 vols. (Edinburgh: Banner of Truth, 1977), 2:47–49.

11. David B. McWilliams, "The Covenant Theology of the *Westminster Confession of Faith* and Recent Criticism," *Westminster Theological Journal* 53 (1991), 123.

that Adam's relationship to God before the fall was a strictly meritorious arrangement. The Confession says that "life was promised to Adam; and in him to his posterity, upon condition of perfect and personal obedience." Given what we have already seen of God's gracious initiative in creation, as well as what we will see that the Bible says about the relationship of law and grace, it is dangerously misleading to describe Adam's relationship as merit-based.

Adam's obedience was a necessary condition but not the sufficient condition for life in God's favor.[12] Adam was required to obey the covenant instruction not to eat from the Tree of the Knowledge of Good and Evil, and Adam's failure to obey would bring sin and death. But the sufficient condition for the covenant and Adam's life within it was the fatherly and kingly favor of God. What I am suggesting here is that life in covenant relationship with God was something that Adam enjoyed by God's grace. He possessed it as a gift. He could lose that gift by the misapplication of his responsible freedom, his disobedience, but he could not earn or merit it.[13]

David McWilliams argues that this interpretation accords with the Confession of Faith. It states:

12. There is a difference between what philosophers call *sufficient condition* and necessary condition. If X is the sufficient condition for Y, if X happens, then Y happens. Thus if Adam's obedience was the sufficient condition for his life in God's favor, Adam's life was merited by his obedience, for life in God's favor was caused by or was the product of his obedience. However, if X is a necessary condition for Y, the causal relationship is inverted: If Y happens, X happens; or we can say that Y happens *only if* X happens. Thus, throwing a brick through a window is a sufficient condition for the window to break, while putting gasoline in a car is a necessary condition for the car's running. A necessary condition is not therefore necessarily the sole determinative cause of an event, even though the event requires it. It might be just one of a series of conditions for the event.

13. Although addressing the covenant obligation of circumcision in the redemptive context of the Abrahamic covenant, John Murray's words are relevant here, for they address the in principle relationship between divine favor and the covenant conditions God imposes upon his covenant partner: "The grace dispensed and the relation established do not wait for the fulfillment of certain conditions on the part of those to whom the grace is dispensed. Grace is bestowed and the relation established by sovereign divine administration. How then are we to construe the condition of which we have spoken? The continued enjoyment of this grace and of the relation established is contingent upon the fulfillment of certain conditions. For apart from the fulfillment of these conditions the

The distance between God and the creature is so great, that although reasonable creatures do owe obedience unto Him as their Creator, yet they could never have any fruition of Him as their blessedness and reward, but by some voluntary condescension on God's part, which He hath been pleased to express by way of covenant. (7.1)

In this McWilliams notes a strong element of grace:

From the outset the confession makes clear that man qua man needs God's grace. Man's finitude is such that he cannot fulfill his end to glorify and to enjoy God apart from God's enabling grace. Moreover, God's transcendence means that man can never hope to commune with him, glorify and enjoy him, apart from a "voluntary condescension on God's part," which is accomplished in God's covenant. The pervasive personal element of the confession's covenant theology is at this point noteworthy. The confession never maintains that man was created originally in a statically legal relationship to God. The legal element is prominent and essential, but never impersonal . . . The confession clearly represents the prelapsarian covenant as gracious. Anytime that God condescends to fellowship with man, whether considered upright or fallen, it is an act of sheer, unadulterated, sovereign, free grace![14]

It is thus appropriate to see that both before and after the fall, man was related to God in virtue of God's grace. Nor does this, McWilliams also argues, lessen the seriousness of the Adamic fall. As sin introduces death and alienation into creation, the character of God's grace radically changes. Prior to the fall Adam lived within the creational grace of God, the divine condescension to create and sustain man

---

grace bestowed and the relation established are meaningless. Grace bestowed implies a subject and reception on the part of that subject. The relation established implies mutuality. But the conditions in view are not really conditions of bestowal. They are simply the reciprocal responses of faith, love, and obedience, apart from which the enjoyment of the covenant blessing and of the covenant relation is inconceivable. In a word, keeping the covenant presupposes the covenant relation as established rather than the condition upon which its establishment is contingent." John Murray, *The Covenant of Grace* (Phillipsburg, N.J.: P&R, 1953), 19.

14. McWilliams, "The Covenant Theology of the *Westminster Confession of Faith* and Recent Criticism," 110, 114.

and the world, and to call man into intimate personal relationship. While much of this unmerited favor continues as God's common grace after the fall, as a sinner man stands in need of the "grace of mercy and reconciliation." Thus before the Adamic fall the terms of the covenant were addressed to man as creature. After the fall the covenant addresses man not only as creature but also as sinner in need of redemption.

But McWilliams cautions that we not conclude from the gracious nature of Adam's relationship that it was devoid of the obligation of law. Relationship is always bounded by obligation. Indeed, "the grace of God is unintelligible apart from his righteous demands."[15] As both grace and law (love and holiness) are essential to God's character, so the two are inexorably bound together and interdependent within the covenant.

As we will see, the function of law within Scripture is the maintenance of relationship, not the creation of relationship. Legal obligation is not the precondition for life and relationship. Rather, life and relationship form the necessary environment for obligation. I tell my son that he must pick up his room and neatly put his things away. I require him to do it. It is necessary for a healthy and happy relationship between us. But the ground of our relationship is not his picking up of his toys and books. If it were, a visiting playmate could straighten up Sawyer's room and then earn the right to become my son. But relationship precedes obligation.

The biblical model is the fatherly favor of God, with law as his gracious revelation of how to keep the relationship a healthy and happy one. God created Adam and Eve in and for personal covenant communion with himself, and he gave them his righteous requirements as an essential aspect of his gracious provision. Indeed, it is just God's original fatherly and kingly provision for his creation that gives Adam's fall its very character as apostasy.

May we not, therefore, misdescribe the profound change in God's relationship to humans in Genesis 3. Adam never at any time merited God's grace, nor at any time did grace come to him apart from

15. Ibid., 115.

law. For all that, the promise of redemption is radically new, and our sole hope in this life.

Three Gardens Picture the Full Weight of Sin

The fall story explains the brokenness of our experience and our world. In broader redemptive-historical terms, the fall of Adam and Eve in the Garden explains how the world got from God's perfect creation (seven times good) in Genesis 1 and Genesis 2 to the world described in later chapters, the world that leads God to grief and ultimately to send his own Son as a redeeming sacrifice.

Two realities situate and define sin in Scripture: first, the goodness of God's original creation, and second, the lengths to which God is willing to go in order to address the problem of sin, to return man to a spiritual condition in which he will again obediently and eagerly glorify God, and indeed, enjoy him forever. As sin can only be known for what it is in the context of a sense of the creational order (however dimly perceived by the fallen mind) and our sense of loss and fracture, likewise the true nature of sin as the enemy of man's relationship to God is most clearly displayed in God's redemptive work in Jesus Christ.

It is of more than passing interest that the Old Testament fails to illuminate the ultimate nature of sin. To be sure, it recognizes and names it. Sin is covenant faithlessness, disobedience to God's word, autonomy, and rebellion. God hates sin and in his holiness cannot approach it with approval. The Old Testament repeatedly records the debilitating effects of sin, how it corrupts human relationship, breaks the covenant harmony of creation, and makes every person its willing slave and an enemy of God. But for all that, the Old Testament ends without articulating a complete doctrine of sin. As seriously as the Old Testament treats sin, it is finally incapable of taking sin's full measure.

There is one event to which the Old Testament does not again refer explicitly after its first telling—one crucial character it does not bring to the fore in later texts. The Old Testament alludes time and again to Abraham and Moses. But Adam and the fall are left without comment in the Old Testament Scriptures.

The fact is, the fall of Adam and Eve introduces a problem whose full scope and gravity cannot be put into perspective—and certainly not resolved—until "the Son of God takes our flesh, assumes our burden, and bears it away on the cross as the one, true Lamb of God (cf. John 1:29)."[16]

When Jesus comes, prays the prayer of the garden, suffers the pains of crucifixion, cries out in dereliction, dies and is buried, then and only then can we really appreciate the full character of sin. Only then do we see the seriousness and blasphemy of sin in all its stark reality. Adam's sin, and ours, has meant nothing less than the death of the Son of God. Thus Anselm of Canterbury asked, "Who has truly pondered the weight of sin?" and rightly answered, "the one who has truly pondered the weight of the cross."

It is a story of gardens. The solution to Eden's problem is requested in Gethsemane's prayer and answered in an empty garden tomb.

Knowing the cure tells you a lot about the gravity of the disease. In the cross we see what was needed to cure the wound of sin, and we see to what lengths God was willing to go to cure it. Thus we see its true character as something so reprehensible to God, as something so unfit for inclusion in God's covenant kingdom, that his own Son must suffer. And finally, it is then that we see God's character as the one who goes all the way, who bears the full burden of the covenant upon himself. We see a love beyond all love.

While we may not trace sin to the work of God, it is God's work that puts sin into historical and personally relevant context. The fundamentally inexplicable reality of sin is to be understood against the backdrop of God's creation (God's revelation of how the world and man were meant to be) and his promised re-creation (God's revelation of what the world and man will be).

16. Bernard Ramm, *Offense to Reason: A Theology of Sin* (New York: Harper & Row, 1985), 39.

FINDING JESUS IN THE OLD TESTAMENT?

Here in our discussion of Genesis 3:15 we have moved naturally to speak of Jesus. We identify the seed of the woman that crushes the serpent's head with Jesus. Is the interpreter of Scripture within his rights to do so? This text offers an occasion to scrutinize the principles we apply when we interpret Scripture. We all would agree that it is imperative that we treat all scriptural texts with integrity. But we may not be so clear about what is involved and how to do it well.

Three Principles of Interpretation

1. One fundamental principle of interpretation, relevant to Scripture or any other form of communication, is that persons speak with intention. If my wife tells our son that it's bath time, he is not free to interpret her words as meaning that he may eat as much ice cream as he likes. A successful act of communication requires that the hearer or reader rightly interprets the meaning that the speaker or writer intended.

Applying this principle of authorial intention to Scripture, we should take the text to mean what the author intended to say. But authorial intention should not be thought of as some meaning behind, before, or separate from the text of Scripture. The primary key to the author's intended meaning is the text itself: what the author means to communicate is in fact communicated by the text.

The evangelical and Reformed tradition has long held that the author's intended meaning is best pursued through a grammatical-historical interpretation of the biblical text. This involves letting the Bible speak for itself by paying attention to the normal rules of grammar, syntax, genre, and context and situating the text within the historical context of the author and his first audience. In fact, a good way to integrate authorial intention and historical context is to ask: How would the original audience have heard the text? How would those who shared the author's historical circumstances, language, and ways of seeing the world have understood the author's message? This is precisely what we were doing in the last chapter when we asked how the exodus community would have understood the creation story of Genesis 1–2.

2. To this we must add a second fundamental principle of hermeneutics, the analogy of Scripture (sometimes referred to as the analogy of faith). The analogy of Scripture is based upon the presupposition that the Bible consists of an organic, consistent, and coherent revelation. Since the Bible is a unified revelation rather than a collection of disconnected and contradictory writings, a passage that is eminently clear on a particular issue or doctrine can shed light on a passage that is more difficult to understand. Thus, all interpretation is to respect the entirety of the biblical canon.

Obviously, the analogy of Scripture is an important tool for the systematic theologian, whose task it is to draw together the entirety of the biblical teaching into a synthetic statement. Nevertheless, because the analogy is topically oriented rather than oriented to the historical sequence of Scripture, it can be abused. The inherent danger is that the theologian might flatten the text into an ahistorical collection of doctrinal propositions. While the analogy proceeds under the correct assumption that the Bible holds together as God's authoritative redemptive revelation, and thus one part illuminates another, we must give care not to forget the historical and progressive nature of Scripture.

3. Our third principle, *sensus plenior* (the fuller sense) may at first glance appear to override authorial intent, but actually it is a legitimate extension and historical application of the analogy of Scripture. The biblical text, unlike Philip Schaff's *The Creeds of Christendom* or an auto repair manual or a note left on the refrigerator reminding me to take the dog to the vet, is inspired. That is to say, it has a level of authorship that transcends the human author and the original audience—even as God transcends the historical particularity of the human author. God is the ultimate author of his Word, and it is possible that God's intention for his Word transcends the intention of the human author. Thus a text may have a fuller meaning—a fuller sense—than the author or his community of faith could have been aware of. In particular, later redemptive history may call

attention to a sense of the text unseen by the author or the original audience.

As Christ is the center of Scripture, the Old Testament is as much a revelation of Jesus Christ as is the New, for Jesus completes the Old Testament story and fulfills the Old Testament promises. Thus Paul can say that all of God's promises are " 'Yes' in Christ" (2 Cor. 1:20). The principle of *sensus plenior* suggests that some events in the history of redemption bear multiple references. While not losing their original meaning for the author or his first audience, they can take on expanded meanings as new revelatory events and occasions transpire. The principle of *sensus plenior* derives from the fact that Christ is the center of the progressively unfolding biblical drama, Old Testament as well as New.

A careful interpreter thus must read the Old Testament with two horizons in mind: the horizon of the original author and the text's first audience, and the horizon of the fulfillment of promise in Christ. Thus when reading the Book of Genesis we ask: What was God's word for the exodus community? and What additional levels of significance does the story take on in light of Christ? Similarly, for the first hearers of the narrative about the binding of Isaac (Gen. 22), the story did not have an explicit messianic reference. It was about the seed promised to Abraham and the testing of Abraham's faith in God's promise. But for us, the story points to Christ and does so in such a way that we will miss its message if we leave Jesus out. Christ is both the obedient son who is willing to be sacrificed for the salvation of the world and the ram that takes the place of another and becomes the sacrifice. Paul probably had the binding story in mind when in Romans 8:32 he wrote, "He who did not spare his own son, but gave him up for us all—how will he not also, along with him, graciously give us all things?"

We appropriately employ the interpretive principle of *sensus plenior* when we find a reference to Jesus in Genesis 3:15. Yes, it does go beyond authorial intent. For Moses and the exodus community, the seed promise of Genesis 3:15 referred to the godly line coming from Eve, a posterity who would be graced by God and be a faithful mediator of the covenant. This interpretation would be deepened and particularized in the seed promised to Abraham and Sarah (Gen. 12–22) and in the Davidic covenant of 2 Samuel 7, in which David was promised that his seed would sit on the throne of Israel forever.

But in the New Testament Paul claims that the seed finds its fullness of meaning in Jesus Christ. In Galatians 3:16–29 he explicitly says that Christ is the seed who was promised to Abraham. It is highly unlikely that the exodus community who first received the revelation of the Book of Genesis or the first readers of 2 Samuel understood the seed as referring to Christ, but in the fulfillment of God's promises in Christ, Paul can declare that Jesus is the promised seed. And indeed, when we go back and read Genesis 3:15, Genesis 12:1–3, and 2 Samuel 7, it is clear that neither Seth nor Isaac nor Solomon could fulfill the entirety of the promises declared in those texts. They are fulfilled only in Christ.

The Wrong Way to Find Jesus in the Old Testament

Scripture is bound together by its organic unity in Jesus Christ. That unity is expressed frequently in the Bible by its use of typology, in which what was done in the past provides an indication of God's acts in the future. Recognizing the divine *modus operandi* in history, typology interprets the present in light of the past. Thus typology functions in the normal linear history of cause and effect, past to present.

There is an obvious similarity between typology and the idea of *sensus plenior*, for both seek to discern the connections between former and later occasions within redemptive history. The two are different sides of the same promise-and-fulfillment coin. Typology looks at the fulfillment in Christ through the patterns of expectation established earlier in the history of redemption. *Sensus plenior*, however, uses the fulfillment in Christ to shed light on earlier events in redemptive history.

Previously we noted that typology is wrongly employed when it is used backwards, when it reads Christ into the Old Testament rather than seeing God's work in Christ as the fulfillment of the Old

Testament patterns and expectation. When this happens, the reality of the Old Testament revelation is lost and an allegorical kind of interpretation replaces the redemptive-historical story of Scripture. Old Testament persons, events, or places evaporate away, replaced by a spiritualized interpretation. Allegorical interpretation keys on merely verbal or accidental correspondences and creates ahistorical and unnecessary connections between texts and ideas.

Some theologians reject the use of *sensus plenior* because it may easily be confused with bad typology, disrupting the historical flow of cause and effect, or the movement from past to present to future. Some dismiss it because they suspect that it is little more than a sneaky way of introducing allegorical interpretation, in other words, of finding things in the text that are simply not there.

For example, it was common in medieval theology to hold that the coverings that God fashioned for Adam and Eve after the fall typified Christ because the word *atone* means "to provide a covering." Many held that the scarlet thread that Rahab hung out the window typified the blood of Christ because blood is red. But neither of these interpretations is warranted by their original Old Testament situations or hinted at in the New Testament. They proceed merely by accidental correspondence and a desire to read Christ into the Old Testament texts.

Interpreting Scripture with Integrity

What controls might guide a legitimate use of *sensus plenior*? How can we be sure that a second referent, an additional christological meaning, is intended by God? Sidney Greidanus has rightly pointed out that when interpreters go beyond original intentionality, the possibility of reading fanciful interpretations and subjective opinions into the text becomes very real. But we safeguard against such abuse of the Old Testament, not by denying the reality of the fuller sense but by insisting that that fuller sense be established only as an extension of the original sense and solely on the basis of subsequent bib-

81

lical revelation.[17] "It is not a substitute for a grammatical-historical exegesis, but a development from such exegesis."[18]

Thus authorial intention and the principle of the analogy of Scripture are primary. *Sensus plenior* interpretation must be a development of what is said via authorial intention. The fuller sense should be just that, a fuller sense of what is already present, not an entirely other sense, as one finds in allegorical interpretation. While it is fair to see an oak within an acorn, it is not fair to see a cow within an acorn. But we must not lose sight of the author and his intention. Do not ignore or empty the acorn of its reality, but know that ultimately the oak is the point.

Sensus plenior is thus appropriately applied when the original text points toward and expects further development. That is to say, the text calls for something more. Something has been left undone. Many of the faulty christological interpretations of Old Testament texts fail here. Rahab's thread (Josh. 2) does not call out for further development. It stands on its own. The story is complete. The same is true with the Lord covering the man and the woman with animal skins (Gen. 3:21). There is no reason within the text to see anything more here than God's merciful provision for Adam and Eve. The mother promise of Genesis 3:15, however, clearly looks to the future and is fulfilled only in Christ's victory over Satan. The passage requires the victory of Christ over Satan in order to be fully cogent. Jesus is the seed of the woman whom God promises will crush the serpent's head.

17. Sidney Greidanus, *The Modern Preacher and the Ancient Text* (Grand Rapids: Eerdmans, 1988), 71–72, 111–12.
18. Ibid., 72.

5

THE FLOOD
God Refuses to Give Up

Some episodes within the biblical drama get no respect. The Genesis story of Noah and the flood certainly falls into this category. It's a Bible story, something we tell our children. Its color, detail and action keep the kids quiet in children's church, but poor old Noah never quite makes it into the sanctuary.

Believers of a more liberal bent consider the story of Noah a myth, not completely to be believed, full of too many questionable elements. Evangelicals, by contrast, if they concern themselves with the story at all, attempt to prove that the flood actually happened, that it is not a myth but a historical fact. Thus we conservatives approach Noah in much the same way that we approach Eden, namely, with the primary interest of refuting the liberal denial of historicity.

As important as defending the Bible's historicity is—and it is crucially important—if historicity is our fundamental concern, we will miss the point of the narrative. Not only the event but also the meaning of the event is important. There is a message in the story.

Moses could have included in the Genesis story any number of things from the ancient past. But Genesis does not tell us everything

83

that happened in human history before Israel went into Egypt. We find not a word about where Cain and Abel got their wives, no references to dinosaurs or continental drift, nothing about many peoples and cultures that existed before the election of Israel. If Moses had meant merely to chronicle the distant past, the great gaps in his story would become difficult to explain. Obviously, Moses selected events from the early history of humankind that were important to the larger story he wished to tell: the story of God's redemption.

The question to ask when we read a biblical narrative is not merely What happened? but What was God doing? Why is this episode part of the grand biblical narrative? How does this small story contribute to the larger story of God's redemptive intention in the world? The story of the Noahic flood speaks volumes if we will but listen.

Sandwiched as it is between the creation and fall narratives and the calling of Abraham, the Noah story develops and graphically underscores for the believer the fatherly character and redemptive concern of the God with whom we find ourselves in covenant, and the implications and impact of our involvement with him and in the world. Set in the larger context of the historical unfolding of God's redemptive mission, the story acquaints us more profoundly with God, creation and man, and human sin, judgment, and grace. It confirms what God cares about, what he is up to, and how he goes about it, and what he has for humans to be and do. There is much more to the story than its historicity. And the story is much more than an isolated event.

HUMAN SIN AND DIVINE JUDGMENT

Genesis tells the story, many commentators have noted, of the pervasive spread of sin in the world. When Adam and Eve were expelled from the Garden, they took the fruit of their disobedience with them. After sin broke into the Garden (Gen. 3), it broke out into the whole world (Gen. 4–11). Adam's sin leads to a sorry picture. God warns that "sin is crouching at the door" (Gen. 4:7). Only one generation away from the Garden, man engages in fratricide. Cain murders his brother Abel and reaps divine punishment for not being his brother's

84

keeper (Gen. 4:8–16). By the seventh generation, Lamech can boast of his many murders (Gen. 4:23–24). The flood (Gen. 6–7) is occasioned by the intermarriage of the "sons of God" with "the daughters of man." This may refer to the confusion of the two seeds first introduced in Genesis 3:15: the faithful seed (the Sethites) is threatened through accommodation and assimilation by the godless seed (the seed of Cain).[1] After the flood, sin again increases upon the earth until finally at Babel man says, "Come, let us build ourselves a city, with a tower that reaches to the heavens, so that we may make a name for ourselves and not be scattered over the face of the whole earth" (Gen. 11:4).

Thus the trajectory from the Garden to Babel moves from the illicit promise of moral autonomy in the serpent's lie to a full-blown culture of godlessness in which every human energy is employed in "the ultimate act of rebellion—the total denial of God in the absolute assumption of self-sufficiency. This is sin in totality, with finality."[2] Lamenting both the extensiveness of sin (it had corrupted all things) and its intensiveness (it had inclined every human thought toward evil), God determines to wipe out the human race, to wash away the stain of sin and cleanse his creation.

> The LORD saw how great man's wickedness on the earth had become, and that every inclination of the thoughts of his heart was only evil all the time. The LORD was grieved that he had made man on the earth, and his heart was filled with pain. So the LORD said, "I will wipe mankind, whom I have created, from the face of the earth—men and animals, and creatures that move along the ground, and the birds of the air—for I am grieved that I have made them . . ."
>
> Now the earth was corrupt in God's sight and was full of violence. God saw how corrupt the earth had become, for all the people on earth had corrupted their ways. (Gen. 6:5–7, 11–12)

---

1. See John Murray, *Principles of Conduct* (Grand Rapids: Eerdmans, 1957), 243–49, for a reasoned presentation of this interpretation.

2. B. Davie Napier, *From Faith to Faith* (New York: Harper & Row, 1955), 56.

While the flood was by no means merely an opportunity for God to teach man a lesson, it does tell us something about the character and effects of sin. O. Palmer Robertson states that the flood provides us with "an appropriate historical demonstration of the ultimate destiny of a world under sin."[3]

Sin Affects All Creation

First, the flood graphically demonstrates the scope of sin's spread and power. Man's sin so touches creation that God must address not only us but the world as well when he deals with sin. Sin and judgment, and thus also redemption, can never be limited to some alleged private or personal sector of life. Sin is a matter of the heart, but from the heart all of life is affected.

When the covenant mediator fails, no relationship works right. Man's failure to function as divinely intended brings debacle upon the entire created order. Called to be a blessing, he has instead become a curse. The threat to life that man introduces extends to every creature and every relationship. The animal world lives in fear of man, and the creation that was meant to be man's ally is now his enemy. The conditions of the Edenic peace have been broken, and the whole of creation groans in travail. Because man, the covenant mediator, has fallen, he has rendered himself incapable of fulfilling his calling of walking with God, serving his fellow human beings, and stewarding God's creation.

Sin Requires God's Judgment

Second, the historical reality of the flood warns sinful man of the surety of judgment (2 Peter 3:3–6). Later biblical writers employ the flood as the model for God's future judgment (see Zeph. 1:2; Matt. 24:36–41).[4] Victor Hamilton emphasizes that there is a "clear-cut

---

3. O. Palmer Robertson, *The Christ of the Covenants* (Grand Rapids: Baker, 1980), 114.

4. Thus, none of this is to suggest the impossibility of hell. Hell is the absolute and final denial of grace beyond historical life for fallen man. Yet as judgment serves God's gracious ends, the threat of this ultimate covenant curse preserves the grace of God in its own particular way in that it presents a sobering and realistic warning to a sinful world.

moral motivation behind sending the flood."[5] It is not an arbitrary act of divine wrath but rather the righteous judgment of God upon a sinful race. The orderliness and beauty of God's original creation and intention for man in the world have been undone by the disobedience of man. The creation order established by God is everywhere flaunted, for "all the people on earth had corrupted their ways" (Gen. 6:12). The just order and divinely instituted constitution of creation is breached, and violence is upon the face of the earth (Gen. 6:13).

Sin Breeds Corruption

Third, the consequences of sin are not accidental. Sin invariably breeds corruption. In the judgment of the flood God to some extent blots out the human stain of sin and begins anew, giving man a second chance in the world. But this second chance only confirms the effect that sin has upon man and the world. While the ark delivers Noah and his family from the judgment of the flood, the root disease that brought on the flood was also a passenger on the ark. When the boat docks, Noah beholds a world very much different from the one produced by the sin in the Garden. But it is not an utterly different world, for there remains a point of continuity: the fallen human heart. The sin problem has not been done away with. A sinful world comes from fallen people. A sinful human culture comes from fallen people, even born again fallen people.

GOD REDEEMS IN SPITE OF HUMAN SIN

It is only after the confusion and dispersion effected by God's judgment against Babel that God calls Abram. Some interpreters have drawn the conclusion that the history of God's redemption begins with Abram's call, and not before. But such an approach is possible

---

Beyond this life lies a final judgment, and the man who has not lived in God's grace will forever know the curse of the covenant.

5. Victor P. Hamilton, *The Book of Genesis*, chapters 1–17 (Grand Rapids: Eerdmans, 1990), 273.

only if we interpret Genesis 4–11 as merely a story of sin and judgment.

While we are naming our tendencies to mistreat the Noah story, let us note two more. People tend to think that it is merely about sin and judgment, overlooking its message about redemption and grace. And second, when we do note its redemptive aspects, we tend to see only God's care for humans and not his care for creation.

The Pattern of Divine Faithfulness

Sin and judgment is at best only half the story. While it is certain that the pre-Abrahamic revelation tells "a story of rapid degeneration, so guided by God as to bring out the inherent tendency of sin to lead to ruin, and its power to corrupt and debase whatever of good might still develop,"[6] nevertheless God's kingdom and redemptive promise are recorded here as well. The point is rather to communicate God's resolve to redeem in spite of fallen man, and that sin cannot thwart the promise made in the Garden. It is about grace, that God will protect the seed of the woman and will effect his plan to redeem in spite of sin's power and allure. Like all of Scripture, the story is about the faithfulness of God.

For its every episode concerning the spread of sin, Genesis records a movement of divine grace breaking through the corruption of sin. Cain's murder of Abel threatens the promise of the seed (Gen. 3:15). But God responds in grace by raising up the faithful line of Seth. God's grace is further evidenced in the genealogy (Gen. 5). While it may be too much to claim that Mahalalel (Gen. 5:15) was a believer simply because his name means "praise to God," we learn that Enoch (Gen. 5:22) walked with God and that Lamech (Gen. 5:28–29) believed that his son Noah would be used by God. And as we shall see, the flood story is as much about God's grace to Noah and his family as it is about judgment.

Genesis 4–11 sets out a recurring pattern of sin and grace. We may enumerate four elements in the pattern:

6. Geerhardus Vos, *Biblical Theology: Old and New Testaments* (Grand Rapids: Eerdmans, 1948), 45–46.

1. Divine provision or promise
2. Man's covenant disobedience
3. God's judgment (covenant curse) against sin
4. God's gracious redemption (covenant blessing)

We note this pattern in the Garden story, in the narrative of the line of Seth leading up to Noah, and in Noah's experience immediately after the flood. Indeed, the pattern recurs throughout the Old Testament. In Deuteronomy 4:21–31 Moses applies it to the future history of Israel.

At the heart of the pattern of sin and grace lies the fact that God remains ever faithful to his covenant promises even though man proves himself faithless to the covenant. This is the issue that sets up God's judgment in the flood and his covenant with Noah. In light of the fact that the creature who was created, gifted, and commissioned to be the mediator of God's covenant to all of creation has become a curse upon the land, what steps must God take to preserve his creation and protect the promise of the seed? What must God do to protect the creation from man? What must he do to insure his promise of redemption in spite of the sinfulness of man?

God's Preservation through Judgment Serves His Larger Gracious Intent

God's judgment in history is never an end in itself, but rather a means toward God's promised covenantal *shalom*. God's judgment in the flood, his covenant curse, comes in order to preserve the covenantal relationship between God and his creation, and between God and his appointed covenant mediator. Divine judgment is never arbitrary. Rather it has a purpose. Judgment is never an end in itself.

God knows that ultimately the problem of sin cannot be resolved by judgment and curse. Judgment has serious limitations. By itself, apart from the context of grace and God's covenantal concerns, all judgment does is kill. It does not bring life. And it does not change the human heart. God's judgment upon sin always takes place for the sake of grace, for the sake of creation, for the sake of covenant. God judges the world in the flood in order to preserve the promise, to preserve the seed of the woman, and thus to preserve his gracious intentions toward his creation.

God Preserves the Believing Seed

Though God's stated intention is to wipe humankind from the face of the earth (Gen. 6:7), to put an end to all people (Gen. 6:13), God extends grace to Noah. In the midst of a judgment poured out as a massive flood upon an unbelieving world, God remembers his promise in the Garden and preserves the believing seed. Noah and his family are saved so that they could be God's agents for the fulfillment of his promise.

God Promises to Preserve the Creation

After the floodwaters have subsided and Noah and company disembark, Noah builds an altar and sacrifices a thank offering to God. To this Yahweh responds:

> Never again will I curse the ground because of man, even though every inclination of his heart is evil from childhood. And never again will I destroy all living creatures, as I have done.
>
> As long as the earth endures,
> seedtime and harvest,
> cold and heat,
> summer and winter,
> day and night
> will never cease. (Gen. 8:21–22)

At first glance, God's promise to preserve the earth might seem like a *non sequitur*. Never again will the earth be destroyed on man's account, even though man is sinful. Covenant faithlessness brings covenant curse. And as Adam is the mediator of the covenant, his failure to keep the covenant should bring the effects of that failure to all of creation.

But here God in his mercy is withholding the curse. He will not allow the sin of man to undo the creational order or thwart God's redemptive purpose. Quite simply, God must protect the creation from the creature called to be his image bearer, his moral reflection within the creation. Though the creature, who was called to rule on God's behalf, employs his giftedness for that commission against God and God's cause, God steps in and declares that he will preserve the created order in spite of man. Man's godless way in the world will not thwart the divine intent.

This is an expression of what is often called common grace. The term does not refer to redemptive action toward man on God's part but rather God's continuing providential care over human life in the world even though "man is totally depraved, inclined toward self-destruction, and worthy of judgment."[7] In other words, God does not allow man to become as fully evil as his fallen heart would otherwise lead him to become. Although the consciences of individual men may become so seared to evil that it loses its horror and becomes a friend, and though through the efforts of such people whole societies may become particularly perverse and destructive, man's historical existence as a whole is not allowed to degenerate into absolute depravity. God's merciful preservation of fallen man involves God's restraining the effects of sin upon man, his society, and the creational order.[8] God preserves man and the created order in the Noahic covenant because, even though covenant curse is the deserved outcome of man's enmity toward God and corruption of God's good gifts, God has bound himself to redemption rather than wrath by his Garden promise.

God Reaffirms Man's Covenantal Place within Creation

God not only preserves the creational order in spite of the covenant mediator in the Noahic covenant; he also reaffirms man's covenantal place within creation, in phrases intentionally reminiscent of

---

7. Robertson, *The Christ of the Covenants*, 115.

8. Common grace may be defined as "every favor of whatever kind or degree, falling short of salvation, which this undeserving and sin-cursed world enjoys at the hand of God." See John Murray, "Common Grace," in *Collected Writings of John Murray*, 4 vols. (Edinburgh: Banner of Truth, 1977), 2:96. See Murray's essay for further definitions of common grace within the Reformed tradition.

God's commission of Adam as covenant representative. As man was originally commissioned in God's image (Gen. 1:26), he is recommissioned in God's image (Gen. 9:6). Noah and his descendants are instructed to bring forth new generations, care for the earth, and respect human worth, "for in the image of God has God made man."

God had commanded Adam to fill the earth (Gen. 1:28). In almost identical language he gives the same command to Noah (Gen. 9:7). As God brought the animals to Adam to be named (Gen. 2:19), he brings the animals to Noah to be delivered (Gen. 7:15). As man was originally appointed as the steward of the earth, that appointment still stands, even though now the ground is cursed because of man, and the fear of man falls upon every beast, bird, and fish (Gen. 9:2).

As Noah and his family are the germ of a new humanity bonded to God in covenant relationship, so the creational order is called anew to the same bond. As the various species of animal life enter the ark, they wordlessly declare the sovereignty of God and the reality of man's covenant rule over the nonhuman creation. Man's rule over creation as God's appointed representative continues, though now exercised in the unnatural context of terror and dread.

The essential point here is that nothing of God's original instructions to Adam and Eve are annulled. To be sure, the situation is now radically different. But as God holds himself to his word, so too does he hold man responsible to it. The God who jealously refuses to give up his original purpose for man and the world will not allow man— even sinful man—to give up either.[9]

God does not give up on his original intention of glorifying himself through man's caring for and development of the created order. Gabriel Fackre thus refers to the "irrevocability" of the covenant. "God does not go back on the divine intention. The No of the world cannot turn aside the Yes of the Word. Covenant is for keeps."[10] Even though the world resists God's purposes, he refuses to abandon it to self-destruction.

---

9. In the Adam narrative the image of God appears as the basis for man's identity, and in the Noah story it appears as the basis for man's protection.

10. Gabriel Fackre, *The Doctrine of Revelation: A Narrative Interpretation* (Grand Rapids: Eerdmans, 1997), 63.

God's covenant with Noah is not a replacement of his first covenant. Rather than think in terms of a series of covenants, we might better think of the covenant episodes in Scripture as just that, episodes in a single, organic, ongoing story. The many parallels between the Noahic covenant and the creation story should not surprise us.

God Covenants with All of Creation

God does not make his covenant only with Noah. Noah is the mediator, the representative of a much larger community. Yahweh tells Noah that he establishes his covenant with him and his descendants and the animals that he placed into Noah's care (Gen. 9:9). He declares that he makes an "everlasting covenant" between God and "all life on the earth" (Gen. 9:15–17), a covenant "between me and the earth" (Gen. 9:13).

The scope of God's covenant concern is as wide as the material creation. As the flood is a divine response to man's violation of God's word, the rupture of all created relationships resulting from that violation, and the fracture of the Edenic paradise, God's intention to wash away the stain of man upon creation is a picture of the restoration of his unopposed lordship over his creation. The inclusion of the animals and the very earth within the covenant emphasizes that the scope of God's redemptive program is as wide as his creational work. William Dumbrell appropriately comments:

> The world and man are part of one total divine construct and we cannot entertain the salvation of man in isolation from the world that he has affected. The refusal to submit in Eden meant a disordered universe and thus the restoration of all things will put God, man, and the world in harmony again.[11]

Though Cosmic in Scope, God's Grace Is Humanly Particular

Noah is, as it were, a second Adam, the father of a new world. Yet the curse of the Garden has not been removed, for man is still a sin-

11. William J. Dumbrell, *Covenant and Creation* (Nashville: Thomas Nelson, 1985), 41.

ner and in revolt against God. The reign of sin and death still holds man in its grasp. While the scope of the covenant is universal, it does not promise redemption for all people. In distinction to God's common grace that protects the conditions for life in the world and thus blesses the righteous and the unrighteous alike (Matt. 5:45), God's redemptive grace is always particular. In the midst of God's stated determination to eradicate man from the earth, Genesis 6:7–8 tells us that "Noah found favor in the eyes of the LORD."[12] God's elective mercy and grace did not extend to all men, for Noah alone is spoken of as walking with God.[13]

Yet in his election of Noah we see God's plan for families in the covenant. To Noah God says: "Everything on earth will perish. But I will establish my covenant with you, and you will enter the ark— you and your sons and your wife and your sons' wives with you" (Gen. 6:18; cf. 7:1). Noah is the covenant representative not only for creation but for his household as well. God's elective favor toward the family head serves as a basis for including his entire

---

12. David Atkinson comments, "There is a richness in the words of Genesis 6:8: Noah found favour [grace] in the eyes of the LORD; whose meaning we understand best, as J. A. Motyer has suggested, by reading the translation backwards: 'grace found Noah.' God's initiative of grace towards Noah is mentioned before there is any reference to Noah's faith and righteousness (6:9). And that is important. Between the two—the reference to grace and the reference to righteousness—the editor has given another formula to indicate a development of the story. These are the generations of Noah (Gen. 6:9)—this is the emergent story of Noah. What is the significance of this? Could it be that the author is seeking to highlight the fact that the public life of Noah—who walked before God, who had a family, and who built an ark—emerges out of the secret story of Noah as a recipient of God's grace? The editor of this text has very carefully ensured that we read about the grace of God before we read about Noah's obedience of faith. And that is the pattern which again and again the Bible makes clear: 'by grace you have been saved through faith; and this is not your own doing, it is the gift of God.' " David Atkinson, *The Message of Genesis 1–11* (Downers Grove, Ill.: InterVarsity Press, 1990), 137.

13. There is a bit of theological irony here. It is common for Christians to think of redemption in man-centered terms. That is to say, we limit the recipients of God's redemptive concern to human beings. Yet the Noahic story portrays God's concern as being as wide as all creation, but not extending to each and every human being. Man is still the problem. In a real sense, the Noahic covenant stands the notion of a dualistic salvation on its head. Where the dualist seeks a salvation from the world, the Noahic covenant suggests that the world must be saved from man.

family—wife, sons, and daughters in-law—in the covenant relationship.

Sovereign Initiative, Human Response

Derek Kidner has written that the Noahic covenant "is remarkable for its breadth (embracing 'every living creature'), its permanence ('perpetual,' 'everlasting,' etc.) and its generosity—for it was as unconditional as it was undeserved." Throughout, the emphasis falls upon God's sovereign initiation, his forbearance and his love for his creatures. "Any idea that a covenant is basically a bargain is forestalled by such an opening to the series."[14]

The covenant is not contingent upon human response. Although God calls Noah into his obedient service, recommissions him as the divine image bearer, and places the obligation of covenantal care for the creation upon him, the covenant can never depend on man. From this point forward, God covenants with man not just as image bearer but also as sinner. For a creature in revolt against the divine rule all overtures of grace are in spite of his fallen nature. God preserves his creation in spite of man. And he redeems in spite of sin.

While the covenant always rests upon God's initiative and determination, God nevertheless places obligations upon man in covenant relationship (necessary conditions). Here in the Noah story, as is the case throughout the biblical story, he calls people to obey the word of God, walk in his ways, trust him, and lean upon his mercy. Again, the distinction between conditional and unconditional covenant appears less than helpful. Is the Noahic covenant unconditional? Yes, absolutely, for it is God's promise to preserve the world no matter what man does. Yet there are obligations here as well. Aside from the restatement of the Adamic mandate to mediate the divine rule, we need only recall the simple but altogether significant initial command of God to Noah: build a boat.

14. Derek Kidner, *Genesis* (Downers Grove, Ill.: InterVarsity Press, 1967), 101.

The Bow in the Clouds

Genesis tells us that from this day forward whenever a rainbow appears it will be a sign of God's promise to preserve the earth (Gen. 9:12–13). As the bow in the sky is over all creation it signifies that the entire created order is to know the blessings of the covenant. Again, all of creation is included in God's covenantal concern.

O. Palmer Robertson has called the rainbow a sign of "grace-in-judgment,"[15] for there is more than mere preservation at stake in the Noahic covenant. The remembrance of the flood as divine judgment upon man's rebellion is part and parcel to the covenant. Thus Yahweh says:

> Whenever I bring clouds over the earth and the rainbow appears in the clouds, I will remember my covenant between me and you and all living creatures of every kind. Never again will the waters become a flood to destroy all life. (Gen. 9:14–15)

The bow in the sky is thus a sign of God's grace in the midst of judgment. God judges for the sake of grace. Man's sin necessitates covenant wrath, but God, in his abounding mercy, declares that he and not man will have the last word, that grace rather than wrath will prevail.

For whom is the rainbow a sign? Interestingly, it is a sign for God (Gen. 9:15). The bow reminds God of his promise. Of course, God does not forget his promises as you or I forget where we placed our car keys. When God remembers the past, he is affirming the continuance of relationships and promises made in the past. Remembering makes the past a present reality. As a sign of God's everlasting promise, the rainbow is a pledge of divine obligation. Revelation 4:3 says that a rainbow ever hangs before the heavenly throne. It serves, we might conjecture, ever to remind God of his promise to the earth.

Yet the rainbow also functions as a covenant sign to us, guaranteeing the divine promise and the permanence of the covenant. This

15. Robertson, *The Christ of the Covenants*, 123.

is particularly appropriate in the context of the historical reality of the flood. God will not judge the world as he once did, even though we are sinners bent on the destruction of God's good gifts. Against the background of the darkness of the fall and the storm of judgment in the deluge, God puts his bow in the clouds. We are not left without a witness (Acts 14:17) that the earth belongs to God, that he will keep the story moving toward his promised redemption, and that he will uphold his word for his creation. The bow reminds us that God is ever faithful to his world. He has not abandoned the work of his hands. God's creative blessing holds even though, and in spite of the fact that, man is a broken bearer of the divine image.

In its redemptive manifestation the covenant carries the idea of a peace treaty. The enmity that characterized the former relationship between the parties of the covenant is set aside by God's grace. This may be suggested in the Noahic covenant by the fact that the word for "rainbow" is the usual word for an offensive weapon of war, a battle bow.[16] It is quite possible, therefore, that the symbolism of the rainbow speaks of the fact that God has laid down his weapon of war and thus has put away the wrath that had led to the judgment of the flood.

As a peace treaty, the covenant is a bond of reconciliation between God and the faithful seed, and between God and the earth. A fundamental element of ancient Near Eastern covenant treaties was the blood oath. Thus a covenant treaty was a solemn promise of peace that was confirmed by oath and sealed by blood sacrifice. In the typical covenant cutting ceremony an animal was sacrificed, and its dismembered pieces were laid out in two parallel lines creating an aisle between the pieces. Then the parties to the treaty would walk the length of the aisle, enacting their oath, in effect: May I become like these animals if I do not keep my word. Since the pledge calls down

16. In fact, other than its use in reference to the rainbow of the Noahic covenant, the word *bow* in the Old Testament always refers to a weapon of war or a dispenser of wrath. When used in reference to God, the bow appears in the context of the manifested glory of God that threatens human undoing (Ezek. 1:28) and in the context of covenant curse. Lamentations 2:4 speaks of God's judgment on Israel when he sent them into exile as God "stringing his bow."

a penalty upon oneself for failure to keep the covenant, it is called a self-maledictory oath.

The divine oath of self-malediction will become an explicit aspect of the covenant in Genesis 15 when in the form of a smoking firepot God passes through the bloody aisle while his covenant partner sleeps. Although the idea no longer has a strong following, older commentators often saw hints of the self-maledictory oath in the rainbow. According to this interpretation the rainbow is God's oath, his pledge unto death that should man break the covenant peace, God himself will suffer the curse of the covenant. One could say that in the flood, God's bow was aimed toward the earth in judgment. But once God placed his bow in the sky, the plane of the earth becomes the bowstring and the weapon is now pointed upward toward God, and thus God himself becomes the recipient of threatened covenant curse.

It would be nice to find a self-maledictory reference to Christ in the rainbow—the bow is aimed, as it were, toward the cross, where God takes the curse of the covenant upon himself. The real issue, however, is not discovering veiled references to Christ in the Noahic covenant, but rather discerning its contribution to the redemptive drama of Scripture.

The Redemptive Focus of the Noahic Covenant

The common but unfortunate practice of thinking of redemptive history as beginning with Abraham and Sarah comes from a tendency to think of redemption in purely elective and man-centered terms. Certainly, the Noahic covenant is not about justification; but justification is not all there is to redemption. And the Noahic covenant is an essential stage in the drama of redemption and an important link in the biblical pedagogy concerning God and his redemptive ways.

As we have seen, God's preservation of the seed promise is a crucial element of this redemptive purpose. God's preservation of the material world tells us the scope of this redemptive concern, that creation—not just man—will be addressed in the redemptive drama. What we have called God's common grace, his preservation of the

98

structures and patterns of creation, is an expression of his fatherly favor. God's judgment upon sin by the flood is an expression of his fatherly care as well, for it serves the ultimate end of grace. What is revealed in the Noahic covenant is not an explicit emphasis upon election or justification, but God's common grace, his preservation of creation, his maintaining its integrity. This common grace serves God's ultimate redemptive purpose and thus is part of that purpose— even without election and justification. While common grace does not of itself redeem, it demonstrates the character, love, and faithfulness of the God who does redeem. As David Atkinson puts it so well: "The story of the flood is the story of God's sovereign judgment on a world that has lost its moorings. The story of Noah is at the same time the story of God's intimate, compassionate, and faithful love."[17] For this reason, if for no other, the Noahic covenant is redemptive.

The character of divine grace begins to take revelational shape here as well. As a divine favor that comes unexpected and undeserved, grace is the surprise of the gift of life and meaning when only death is owed. As the rainbow symbolizes God's faithfulness to his redemptive promise, it also symbolizes that God's covenant of grace will embrace all of creation.

Yet the joy evoked in such a revelation calls man anew to his responsibility in God's world—as grace always does. Such is the dignity of humanity that God has entrusted us with the care of this earth and its inhabitants. God upholds his covenant word for his creatures even in the midst of a disordered and fallen world. And he calls us to faith and obedience in the midst of and in the service of such a world.[18]

---

17. Atkinson, *The Message of Genesis 1–11*, 139.

18. "The life of faith is lived in a world of ambiguity and tension. Genesis 3 comes after Genesis 2: the created world is fallen, Adam is expelled from the Garden, but life goes on. Cain is punished by God, yet protected by God. The story of the flood itself is a story of mercy and rescue in the very place of judgment and destruction. And now, perhaps more clearly still, in chapter 9, Noah is given God's blessing, but God's law is, so to speak, an 'accommodation' of God's perfect will to the conditions of a very-far-from-perfect world." Ibid., 154.

6

ABRAHAM

God Narrows the Seed to Redeem the World

God's original promise to Adam and Eve had been continually threatened by human unbelief and apostasy.
However, God had maintained his commitment to
redeem his world in the Noahic flood. In the Noah narrative, God
redeemed and preserved his creation in spite of man, and in a reaffirmation of his covenant he reinstituted his creational expectations,
even though man is a sinner. Even though Noah ran to sin as soon
as the boat docked, and even though the nations conspire against
God—seeking life in the world without God and his rule, as Adam
and Eve had done before them—now God takes another step forward in his plan: he calls Abraham.

Up until the call of Abraham, God had been working on the plan-
etary scale. And in the Babel story, God forced man to the ends of
the earth (Gen. 11:4, 8–9). But at the outset of the next narrative, God
abruptly narrows the scope of his action by concentrating upon Abraham and his descendants. Out of all the Semitic peoples (the children of Shem), God chooses the people of Abraham to carry out his
will in the world.

100

SAME REDEMPTIVE PURPOSE, REVISED STRATEGY

A Fresh Start

We need to appreciate that with the election of Abraham God is beginning a new work. There is a real sense in which it is unrelated to what precedes. According to the apostle Paul, the election of Abraham involved the calling into existence of the nonexistent, a calling of life from death, tantamount, therefore, to a new creation (Acts 4:17).

As in Genesis 1, divine speech initiates the call in Genesis 12:1. God is calling a new phase of history into being, just as he called the universe into being. The covenantal pattern that we have previously noted is seen here. Redemption, like creation, begins by divine initiative. "Always in Biblical revelation God does the choosing and the human side of the relationship must obediently respond."[1]

Not a Fresh Start

Likening the call of Abraham to a new creation should not, however, lead us to overemphasize fresh start in Genesis 12. We overemphasize its distinction when we treat Genesis 1–11 as simply a preface to redemptive history rather than as theologically integral to it. Such an approach anthropocentrizes the story of redemption—it represents it as exclusively man-centered. It ignores the creation-wide sweep of God's action and concern. Limiting God's concern to man inherently devalues the integrity of the creation story, the historicity of the Adamic fall, and the cosmic scope of God's historical action.

Liberal and conservative approaches to Genesis 1–11 unfortunately share this propensity to reduce the witness of the Book of Genesis to strictly human and existential concerns. Classical critical scholarship maintains that an older, more primitive, nature-centered religion described in Genesis 1–11 is replaced by a person-centered religion, beginning with the patriarchal narratives, which revolves

---

1. Dirk P. Bergsma, *Redemption: The Triumph of God's Great Plan* (Lansing, Ill.: Redeemer, 1989), 58.

around human history. Yahweh the God of human history is set over against the ancient earth deities.

Conservatives tend to elevate individual redemption to the *sine qua non* of the Christian religion. Whatever fails to serve that focus is considered of little consequence. We begin to tell the real story, the story with which we can personally identify, with Abraham. Salvation focuses exclusively upon Israel and the church.

Both approaches limit the Christian faith to human experience or to a redeemed community. They both issue, interestingly, in the same result: the broader acts of God in creation and history fade into irrelevance. When we limit our religious vision to humankind, we separate the divine from creation and universal history. What is not divine is relativized, secularized, even vilified. And when this happens, there remains to us no satisfactory way to relate redemption to the real world of pots and pans. Redemption becomes, in the day-to-day world, more of a curse than a blessing.

One way to make sure that we do not overemphasize the fresh start with Abraham is to note the continuities between the patriarchal narratives and the preceding story. Like the patriarchal stories, the first eleven chapters of Genesis present a historical narrative in which events and persons are portrayed as being intimately connected with the mundane world. The text gives no reason to consider the story before Abraham a collection of stories whose meaning must be found elsewhere than in their narrative portrayal in the work-a-day world.

Furthermore, the new beginning of Genesis 12 fits into the pattern of beginnings that has already been established in Genesis and will continue into the Book of Exodus. God begins again with Abraham, as he did with Noah, and as he will later begin with Israel in Egypt. This demonstrates that God's new beginnings are not radical rejections of all that has gone before. The terms of God's previous covenant relationships still hold.

Most importantly, the patriarchal story assumes the covenantal development of the first eleven chapters. It makes historical sense in terms of and as part of the one unfolding story of the seed and the divine mission in Genesis. The purpose for the election of Abraham conforms to the one redemptive purpose of God since the fall.

God's Response to Babel

The call of Abraham is a response to the historical necessity of the confusion at Babel (Gen. 11), which is itself a crucial link in redemptive history. The Babelite search for a purely human greatness absent from God had moved Yahweh to scatter the family of man over the face of the earth. Yet this action presents a problem. In the Noahic covenant of Genesis 9, God reveals that his covenant concern stretches over the entirety of creation. His covenant is a covenant of life, a covenant between God and the earth, and thus the scope of God's redemption is going to be as wide as all creation.

How can a particular God, a personal God, a God with a name, a character, a God who means to work redemptively in history, now achieve a worldwide result? How can he be known by a human population that is now divided, diverse, dispersed by his own action (Gen. 11:8)?

The call of Abraham is God's missional answer to this problem. The name given to Abraham, the fame he is to acquire, the reputation his posterity will achieve, all constitute an intentional divine counterpoint to the influence sought by the Babelites. They sought to build God out of the world by their nation building. God, however, will build a nation that will represent him in the world. God's election of Abraham and inclusion of him within his redemptive purpose is the divine solution to this dilemma. Abraham is elected into the missionary service of Yahweh.

With the Abrahamic covenant, God is creating a particular people who will carry forward God's gracious concern for all creation and serve the universal history of humankind. The election of Abraham is not God turning his back on creation or universal history for the sake of salvation history but rather his forwarding it.

GOD'S SOVEREIGN RIGHT TO CHOOSE

One of the most prominent ways in which God displays his sovereignty throughout Scripture is by exercising his indisputable right to make choices. Human beings share this ability to a limited degree, but only the sovereign Lord of the universe experiences complete freedom as he chooses to embark upon, or desist from, a certain choice or action. Bound only by his holy character—for God is always true to himself—the sovereign King of creation and Lord of the covenant exercises his sovereign right in the elective choices he makes, to lavish his redemptive grace upon one and not another.

Many Christians, curiously, claim not to believe in the doctrine of election. They earnestly believe that the doctrine is nowhere to be found in the Bible, that the idea of election is the product of a sectarian mind, a conclusion of systematic theology that we are free to dismiss either as biblically unnecessary or as wrongheaded.

Yet election is not a theological term but a biblical one. Indeed the doctrine of election does not require that we draw the synthetic inferences required, by contrast, for a doctrine such as the Trinity. God's sovereign right to choose the recipients of his redemptive grace drips from the pages of Scripture.

The verb *to elect* means "to choose." The doctrine of election is that God applies his redemptive favor to those he sovereignly chooses. The Book of Deuteronomy witnesses to God's sovereign right to choose those he will redeem:

> Because he loved your forefathers and chose their descendants after them, he brought you out of Egypt by his Presence and his great strength. (Deut. 4:37)

> For you are a people holy to the LORD your God. The LORD your God has chosen you out of all the peoples on the face of the earth to be his people, his treasured possession.
>
> The LORD did not set his affection on you and choose you because you were more numerous than other peoples, for you were the fewest of all peoples. But it was because the LORD loved you and kept the oath he swore to your forefathers that he brought you out with a mighty hand and redeemed you from the land of slavery, from the power of Pharaoh king of Egypt. (Deut. 7:6–8)

> To the LORD your God belong the heavens, even the highest heavens, the earth and everything in it. Yet the LORD set his affection on your

forefathers and loved them, and he chose you, their descendants, above all the nations, as it is today. (Deut. 10:14–15)

. . . for you are a people holy to the LORD your God. Out of all the peoples on the face of the earth, the LORD has chosen you to be his treasured possession. (Deut. 14:2)

To be sure, there is an inexplicable mystery here. Why would a benevolent God not save everyone? The answer these texts give is simply that God redemptively loved Israel and not the Egyptians.

Yet, we may further observe, however contrary it is to our Western cultural commitment to egalitarianism, that to insist on a universal application of grace is to violate the character of grace. God's redemptive grace is a gift, a completely unearned divine favor given out of love.

The giver is always sovereign in the giving of a gift. That is to say, the giver is free to give and free not to give, and he gives the gift to whomever he chooses. The words *obligation* and *gift* mutually exclude one another. The common rejection of the doctrine of election in favor of a universally dispensed grace not only denies God the divine prerogative to choose whom he will redemptively love but also makes God's grace a necessary structure of the world, like gravity or photosynthesis, to which all people are entitled. If grace is an obligation, a structure or an entitlement, it is no longer a gift, and no longer grace.

Redemptive grace is always unexpected, beyond the norm, and out of the ordinary. Grace can never be taken for granted, assumed, or presumed upon. God is never obligated to redeem.

By his sovereign election, God has included some people within his historical purpose of redemption. By his elective love, God chose Seth's rather than Cain's line to pursue his purposes, even though the sin of the Garden certainly corrupted Seth's seed as completely as it did Cain's. By God's sovereign choice, he chose Noah and his son Shem, rather than Shem's brothers and their progeny, to move his plan forward. And it is by nothing but sovereign grace that God chooses Abraham to be the father of all who would believe. William

J. Dumbrell appropriately comments: "The absolutely free and unconditioned nature of the choice of Abraham is emphasized, and thus the presence of the divine will as the power which shapes and directs all history is at this point made perfectly clear."[2]

ABRAHAM—A MODEL OF GODLINESS?

Abraham was a "towering figure in biblical history."[3] No other Old Testament person besides Moses is mentioned in the New Testament as often as is Abraham. What is more, references to him frequently draw attention to God's gracious redemption. Mary the mother of Jesus anticipates his birth as evidence of God's faithfulness in "remembering to be merciful to Abraham and his descendants forever, even as he said to our fathers" (Luke 1:54–55). Paul identifies believers in Christ as children of Abraham. "If you belong to Christ, then you are Abraham's seed, and heirs according to the promise" (Gal. 3:29), for Abraham "is the father of all who believe" (Rom. 4:11).

Despite such an obvious link between Abraham and redemption we must remember that God's choice of him, and through him Israel as the people of God, was not based on any righteousness on their part. It was a pure act of divine grace. Abraham did not come from a good, Bible-believing home (Josh. 24:2–3). His father, Terah, and his ancestors worshiped a whole pantheon of gods, of which the sun was probably the chief god. It is possible that Abraham may have remained a follower of his father's religion for some time even after he responded to the call of the one true God. After the rescue of his nephew Lot, Abraham did confess Yahweh to be "God the Most High, Creator of heaven and earth" (Gen. 14:22). Yet as we know, all of the patriarchs and their families (like Israel later, and indeed like us as well) struggled with the idolatrous pull to follow other gods.

2. William J. Dumbrell, *Covenant and Creation* (Nashville: Nelson, 1984), 58.
3. Bergsma, *Redemption*, 57.

We must remember that there is historical progression in God's dealing with his people. The faith "once delivered to the saints" (Jude 3) was not delivered all at once. Abraham had no Scriptures, no church, no seminary, no General Assembly, psalters, theology books, or sacraments. And Moses, the human author of the first five books of the Bible, the Pentateuch, would not even be born for at least four hundred years. All Abraham had was the call of a strange new God, a call that he often did not appear to understand. Yet he believed, and that belief was accounted to him as righteousness. He became the friend of God.

We should not, therefore, read back a knowledge of later revelation into Abraham. He might have known more—perhaps far more—of God and his ways than is revealed in Genesis. But it is also possible that he did not. While Abraham grew in his personal knowledge of God's faithfulness, the vast majority of God's redemptive plan awaited future revelation.

The point to glean here is that our doctrinal orthodoxy does not save us. Certainly, Scripture puts great emphasis on right doctrine. As a theologian, in the doctrine business, so to speak, I have no interest in depreciating the importance of right belief. But doctrine, even orthodox doctrine, is not the final test of Christian faith. One might be most rigorous in biblical and creedal orthodoxy but spiritually dead. Theological acumen and doctrinal knowledge are no measure of godliness. And as with Abraham, God's choosing and saving us does not require us to have first attained complete theological proficiency.

When God called Abraham to leave Mesopotamia, Hebrews 11:8 tells us, Abraham "obeyed and went, even though he did not know where he was going." Abraham responded to the naked word of God. He believed in God and his promise. Whatever else he might have believed about angels, heaven and hell, or issues pertaining to the end of all things, however mistaken or ignorant he might have been about these or others issues, he was redeemed by the grace of God and only by that grace.

107

THE CALL OF ABRAHAM

The Missional Purpose of God's Covenant with Abraham

Even though the word *covenant* (Hebrew: *berith*) does not appear in connection with Abraham until Genesis 15:18, God's call in Genesis 12:1–3 expresses the heart of the Abrahamic covenant.

> The LORD had said to Abram, "Leave your country, your people and your father's household and go to the land I will show you.
>
> I will make you into a great nation
>   and I will bless you;
> I will make your name great,
>   and you will be a blessing.
> I will bless those who bless you,
>   and whoever curses you I will curse;
> and all peoples on earth
>   will be blessed through you."

Most commentators today agree that the New International Version above is somewhat insensitive to the syntax of the passage. The text begins with an imperative, a divine command for Abraham to uproot himself from his father's house and homeland. Then follows a string of three subordinate clauses, three divine volitional declarations:

- I will make you into a great nation.
- I will bless you.
- I will make your name great.

The final clause of Genesis 12:2 is the problem. While the NIV translates it as "and you will be a blessing," it is actually a purpose clause. Thus it would better be translated "so that you will be a blessing." In light of this, we see that the three promises are God's enabling provision for Abraham that equip him for his mission to be a blessing.

The third verse displays a similar structure: subordinate clauses (only two this time) followed by a purpose clause:

108

- I will bless those who bless you,
- but whoever curses you I will curse,
- so that by you all the peoples on the earth will be blessed.

These purpose clauses function as the two primary clauses in the text:

- so that you will be a blessing
- so that by you all the peoples on the earth will be blessed.

All of this underscores the main point of this chapter: that by narrowing his concern to Abraham, God is not turning his back on all others. God's election of Abraham is not a parochial dismissal of his former cosmic concern. It must be remembered that the God who calls Abraham is the God who has called the creation into existence and who has called all humankind to reflect his character and steward his creation. That sovereign kingly call is not being surrendered here. Rather, the relation between God and all the families of the earth will now depend on Abraham and his descendants, his seed, mediating the blessings of the covenant to all. God calls Abraham and his descendants to serve the well-being of all, by being the people of God, by being the kind of community that all men are called to be by their Creator.[4]

God Promises to Abraham What He Opposed at Babel

By divine promise, Abraham will become a great nation with a great name. The *name* positively echoes the faithful line of the Sethites who called upon the name of the Lord (Gen. 4:25–26). It negatively echoes the concern of the people of Babel to make a name for themselves (Gen. 11:4–5).

Babel stood in stark contrast to the beginning of the biblical story, showing just how radically wrong humankind had gone. Their self-aggrandizement ignored the God who began his journey with the human race by saying, "Let us make man in our image" (Gen. 1:26).

4. See Deut. 4:5–8 in this connection.

Created to reflect God's ways in the world, the people at Babel sought a world that bore only the name and reflection of man.[5]

God's intention to give Abraham a great name contrasts vividly to his opposition to human attempts to make a name for themselves. Abraham's greatness will be conferred by divine grace, not wrested from the world as the Babelites attempted to do. Blessing will come only from the Word of God.

Further, the contrast between fearful human attempts to safeguard their unity in one place via a walled city, "lest we be scattered over the face of the whole earth" (Hebrew: *erets*) and Abraham's willingness to follow God's call to leave his own place and people and go to a land (*erets*) he does not yet see, is also significant. The Babelites sought to absolutize place and people, land and blood, territory and tribe, secure space and common speech. God calls Abraham to break all the attachments, which in the ancient world were thought to give solidarity, protection, and purpose to existence.

God graciously promises to Abraham the very things Babel coveted and was denied—name, family, and land. But these blessings he deems merely instrumental to the covenant relationship. They cannot be taken as the substance of the covenant or as its goal. In important ways, the biblical story will transcend and relativize both blood and land.[6] It will be important for Israel to understand that these blessings constitute not its divine prerogatives but the instruments of its worldwide mission.

SEED, LAND, AND BLESSING

God's promises to Abraham in Genesis 12:1–3 include four elements (three promises and a purpose statement).

---

5. Dumbrell suggests that the Babel story should be read as constituting the logical end of the spread of sin reported in Gen. 4–11. "Babel expressed a naive and total confidence in what human achievement could effect. It looked for one world, one common language family, one common social and economic platform from which human association could proceed. In short, it was the beginning of the utopian humanistic dream to which mankind has always subsequently aspired" (*Covenant and Creation*, 63).

6. Although, as we will see, the concerns of land and progeny play pivotal roles in the covenant ceremonies of Gen. 15 and Gen. 17.

- seed or offspring
- land, namely, the land of Canaan (more explicit in Gen. 12:7)
- Israel will be blessed
- Israel will be a blessing to all nations

These four elements reappear as God repeats the promises of the covenant to the patriarchs: again to Abraham (Gen. 22:17–18), to Isaac (Gen. 26:3–4), and to Jacob (Gen. 28:13–15).

The Promise of a Seed

Abraham's wife Sarah was barren (Gen. 11:27–32). Yet God promises Abraham that he will be the father of a great nation, a nation whose numbers will be as numerous as the dust of the earth (Gen. 13:16; 28:14).

As we know, the promise of a seed is not new in Genesis 12. The seed promise began when God cursed the tempting serpent:

> And I will put enmity
>> between you and the woman,
>> and between your offspring and hers;
> he will crush your head,
>> and you will strike his heel. (Gen. 3:15)

God made this Garden promise to all people, to all creation. It extended hope to all that the problem of sin will be dealt with, that the absurdity introduced into God's creation by Adam and Eve will be removed, done away with.

As a means toward the fulfillment of that promise, God now focuses on a particular individual. He chooses one person out of the nations that had developed from Noah's son Shem. God would now keep his promise to raise up a seed of the woman through the line of the Shemite Abraham. This seed, stretching back through Shem to Noah, from Noah to Seth, and from Seth to Adam, will be the divine vehicle for bringing redemption to the world, a vehicle that will ultimately bring forth a Messiah, a Savior.

Thus the goal of the seed promise goes beyond the birth of Isaac, the child according to the promise. It even goes beyond the birth of the nation of Israel (the larger concern of the Book of Genesis). In light of the reality that it is through Abraham and his descendants that God plans to bring redemptive blessing to all the nations of the world, and that that redemption takes place only in Jesus Christ, we are, of course, right to see that Genesis 12 refers ultimately to Jesus.

Abraham's immediate concern, when he receives the promise, is not the Messiah. It is clear, from the rest of the chapter, that Abraham receives the promise as a promise of reproductive fertility. What he hears is that he is going to be a father. He does not see Jesus; he sees Isaac.

Yet the seed promise in Genesis 12 is more than merely a promise of reproductive fertility. God promises not merely that Abraham will be a father, that a seed will come from him, but that he will be the father of a nation. The word used is not *zera* ("seed"), but *goy* ("nation").

A nation is more than just people, a mere collection of individual persons, even persons who share a common ancestor. A nation is a people bound together by geography, speech, religion, and culture. A nation is characterized by common descent, history, and experience. And often a nation shares a common political structure. A nation has a recognizable character and presence in the world beyond its individual citizens, a character that gives identity to its individual members, and in terms of which those members are known by others.

In short, a nation is a cultural force within the world. Abraham will do more than be a father. He will be the progenitor of a political, cultural, and religious entity that will stand for the kingdom of God in the world.

By his calling of Abraham, God begins the business of nation building, the formation of a nation that, unlike the Babelite search for a human presence without God, will derive its character and reason for being from the redemptive purpose of God. Four key elements of nationhood appear here. With the seed promise, God inaugurates a common people, a population. The Abrahamic covenant also des-

112

ignates a territory, a geographical location. This covenant also indicates implicitly the new nation's leadership, some person or group who will provide direction and governance. As the Lord of the covenant, as the speaker of the divine word and King of creation, as Abraham's Redeemer, Yahweh himself is King over the nation that will come from Abraham's loins. Covenant leadership will develop in priestly, prophetic, and political-monarchial directions as the issue of covenant mediation will diversify in later covenant history. Finally, God will furnish this nation a common rule, or constitution. Abraham and his descendants are called to walk in the way of the Lord, to keep covenant (Gen. 17:9; 18:19). The specifics of this rule will await its expression in the law at Sinai.

The Promise of the Land

Implicit in Genesis 12:1–3 is the promise of a land, for Abraham is called to the land that Yahweh will show him. God later states the land promise explicitly: "To your offspring I will give this land" (Gen. 12:7). After the seed promise—the particular theme of Genesis—the promise of the land is the second most frequently repeated of the Abrahamic promises, appearing twelve times in Genesis alone. The patriarchs will receive only a general description of the borders of the promised lands: a land west of the Jordan River and extending from the Negeb to the Euphrates (Gen. 15:18). A detailed description of the land's borders will await the conquest of the land, some four hundred years after the patriarchs.

God does not fulfill the land promise in the lifetimes of any of the patriarchs. The patriarchs lived as aliens in the land of Canaan. As semi-nomadic wanderers they left no artifacts of a material culture there. Only the revelation of the Book of Genesis bears their history.

The final words of Genesis close the patriarchal story with a brief mention of Joseph's death in Egypt. Whereas the promise of the seed shows signs of development, the promised occupation of the land seems far from realization. The reader is left wondering how it will be fulfilled.

113

Why Canaan?

Why was Abraham promised the land of Canaan rather than some other piece of real estate? If God had chosen Abraham and Israel for some pampered and coddled existence in which the nation would relate only to him and not bear an active mission toward the rest of humankind, then Canaan was an exceedingly poor choice on God's part. But it was neither a mistake nor happenstance that Canaan, the crossroads of the ancient world, was chosen to be the dwelling place of Israel.

There is nothing particularly inviting about Canaan simply as real estate. To be sure, the Book of Joshua records that when the spies surveyed the land, they returned and reported that it was a rich land flowing with milk and honey. Idyllic descriptions of the land are common throughout the Pentateuch.[7] Certainly, there were fertile areas in Canaan at the time of the conquest, and undoubtedly the land was more inviting then than it is today. But overall the climate of Canaan, then as now, was semi-arid. The encroachment of the Sahara across North Africa and into Canaan began in the third millennium B.C. And the ground is extremely rocky. An old Jewish saw quips that when God created the world he had a spare handful of rocks left over. With no particular intent he tossed them to the ground, and they covered the land of Canaan.[8]

Agriculturally, God could have done much better by the people he made for himself out of Abraham. They were not getting the choicest piece of property for their crops and herds. If that had been the goal, the Nile River valley would have been far better. Or

7. E.g., Ex. 3:8, 17; 13:5; 33:3; Lev. 20:24; Num. 13:27, etc.

8. O. Palmer Robertson, *The Israel of God: Yesterday, Today, and Tomorrow* (Phillipsburg, N.J.: P&R, 2000), 12–13, reports another Jewish fable to the same effect: "According to this legend, God at creation commissioned two storks to scatter stones over the face of the earth. These stones were divided into two bags, one for each stork. But the bag being carried by one stork broke over the land of the Bible. As a consequence, half of the stones of the world are located in Israel. It is indeed a glorious land, a land with great diversity and beauty. But many other parts of the world are much more fertile and lack all the stones found so abundantly in this land."

Noting that Israel's actual experience of the rocky and marginal fertility of the land did not always live up to the Mosaic promise of a land flowing with milk and honey, Robert-

if safety from marauding neighbors or security from social and cultural corruption had been God's intent, the island of Madagascar or Iceland would have provided security and isolation for his chosen people.

But God's choice of Canaan as a land for Abraham was intentional and central to the redemptive mission for which Abraham was chosen. What was important about this particular piece of real estate was its geographic relationship to other lands. It was a doorway to the world, on the way to everywhere else.

Bounded by the Mediterranean to the west and the vast expanse of the Arabian Desert to the east, Canaan is a natural bottleneck between Asia Minor, Asia, and Africa. It is no wonder that Canaan is the most traveled, most disputed, most fought over, and most conquered land in the history of the world. Located astride the major trade route between Asia Minor, Asia, and Africa, the land of Canaan was ideally situated to serve as a focusing point for cultural exchange. It was God's intention that Canaan would serve as a staging area for the dissemination of the faith to the heathen nations that surrounded Israel. God did not call his people to a mountain-top monastery but to a strip mall on Main Street.[9]

We Christians sometimes think of the land promise as a reward for Israel's four-century-long sojourn in Egypt or as a respite from the ardors of its wilderness wanderings after the exodus out of Egypt, a place where Israel could bathe those feet that had trudged through the desert for an entire generation. But Canaan was not a payoff or a perk of election. It was not the end but rather just a

_____

son concludes that the promise of an idyllic land was intended as a reflection of the nature of paradise, a paradise lost in the Adamic fall, but a paradise promised in the future restoration of creation. Thus the Mosaic portrayal of the land is more prophetic than immediately descriptive. "As Adam and Eve had known God's blessing in Eden, so God would bless his people in a new land. This idea of restoration to paradise provides the proper biblical context for understanding God's promise to give land to Abraham (Gen. 12:1)," 7.

9. "As a narrow land bridge connecting the continents of Africa, Europe, and Asia, this place and no other was rightly situated for the extension of God's covenant blessing to the entire world. It was for this reason that the prophet Ezekiel later declared that God's people were situated 'at the center of the earth' and that Jerusalem was set 'in the center of the nations' (Ezek. 38:12; 5:5)." Ibid., 11.

beginning. It was not an end but a means. When Israel finally entered the land under Joshua, it was beginning its mission in earnest.

The generation in the desert was going to school. Those forty years in the desert between Sinai and Canaan were crucial, not merely because they would see the passing away of the generation that had been faithless at Sinai; but because those were years in which Israel learned to live by the word, love, promise, and grace of Yahweh. Now the real work would begin, the building of Yahweh's kingdom, the shedding of Yahweh's light.

The Promise That God Will Bless Abraham

Accompanying as it does the seed promise God makes to Abraham and repeats to the later patriarchs, God's promise that he will bless Abraham does not apply to him alone but to that seed as well. The promise of blessing includes the protection of the seed[10] and God's covenant presence in the lives of the patriarchs.[11]

God seeks to be with his people, as he had been in Eden. Thus the blessing of divine protection and presence are inseparable from covenant intimacy and relationship with God. James 2:23 tells us that because Abraham believed God and in his promise, he was declared righteous in God's sight and "was called God's friend."[12] Even people outside of the covenant, Genesis records, testified to God's presence in Abraham's life.[13] The goal of this promise is that God's presence should be evident in Israel's existence. The transformation of men from hostility and enmity toward God to covenant intimacy and friendship was the ultimate goal of the Abrahamic covenant.

---

10. See Gen. 15:1; 26:24; 28:15.

11. See Gen. 26:3; 28:15; 31:3; 46:4; 48:21.

12. Cf. 2 Chron. 20:7; Isa. 41:8.

13. See Gen. 21:22 and Gen. 26:28, in which Abimelech king of Gerar and Phicol the commander of Gerar's army witness to the presence and protection of Yahweh on Abraham's behalf.

A BLESSING TO THE NATIONS

As we have observed, God promises Abraham a seed, indeed a nation, a land, and God's covenant protection and presence. He promises these blessings to Israel so that the seed that comes from Abraham will in turn be a blessing to all. It is right to see this as a messianic promise, for ultimately Jesus—God come in the flesh to take away the sin of the world—is the seed *par excellence* (Gal. 3:16).

But a strong missional declaration is also being made here about Israel. God is calling Israel to be a missionary nation. He intends its life among the nations to demonstrate its allegiance to Yahweh, and thus to be a beacon to others. "What is being written in these few verses," Dumbrell claims concerning Genesis 12:1–3, "is a theological blueprint for the redemptive history of the world."[14]

Far too often, books about mission begin with the missionary mandate of Matthew 28:19 and cite New Testament Scripture exclusively. The strong missional element of the Old Testament gets overlooked.

Happily, in his recent survey of biblical theology, Roger Hedlund finds a missional impulse running throughout the entirety of the Christian Scriptures. Hedlund finds it already in the Garden:

> God reveals himself to be the missionary God. In the Garden God comes seeking man (Gen. 3:8ff.). The world's religions represent man seeking for God. Here we see the reverse. In Genesis God takes the initiative. Men may seek God but they also flee from him. Adam tried to hide from God. But God entered the scene of Adam's disobedience. God, someone has said, was the first missionary. He came, he sought and he found, and he provided salvation for his lost creature (Gen. 3:8). Man is not left in his predicament. God provides the remedy (Gen. 3:15) for the human race. This is the gospel of the Garden.[15]

Israel's birth certificate bears the mark of divine purpose. Yahweh has elected it for service. Abraham is to be the father of a chosen peo-

---

14. Dumbrell, *Covenant and Creation*, 66.

15. Roger E. Hedlund, *The Mission of the Church in the World: A Biblical Theology* (Grand Rapids: Baker, 1991), 24–25.

117

ple, a people chosen for a purpose, chosen to participate in God's mission of redemption. Israel is elected to be God's channel of blessing to all nations. Again, the three promises given to Abraham in Genesis 12:1–3 (a seed, a land, and God's covenant blessing) are given for the sake of the fulfillment of Israel's missionary mandate. The goal of God's covenant with Abraham is that people from every nation, not just Israel, will be redeemed. The Old Testament is a missionary book because Yahweh is a missionary God.

COVENANT PROMISE, COVENANT RESPONSE

The seed and land promises offer an opportunity to observe something of the dynamic of covenant promise. God's promise does not annul human agency and responsibility. While the promises of the covenant are divine promises, this does not suggest automatic fulfillment, as if they are to transpire apart from human involvement. Stating it crudely: the fulfillment of divine promise does not fall out of the sky.

In his relationship to his covenant people, God's initiation, his gracious promise or action toward his people calls for our response. The complement of divine grace and promise is not human passivity, a *let go and let God* attitude. Grace always calls to action, to response.

The seed promise to Abraham exemplifies this dynamic of human involvement in divine promise. At one hundred years of age and ninety, Abraham and Sarah were well beyond their childbearing years when Isaac was born. While this child's birth was a minor miracle, it was not a virgin birth. Isaac, the child of the seed promise, would not have been born unless Abraham and Sarah responded to the promise in an appropriate fashion.

Years later, when Israel finally enters the land under Joshua, its army must conquer in order to take possession. Thus Moses instructs the people:

> The LORD your God has given you this land to take possession of it. But all your able-bodied men, armed for battle, must cross over ahead of your brother Israelites. (Deut. 3:18)

118

The people of God are called to act in conformity to grace, in the light of grace, and in the power of grace. What we are and what we are called to do is a result of God's grace and promise. But he calls us to walk in its light, and walking is a matter of a believing conformity to his promises.

7

THE PATRIARCHS
Thwarting God's Mission to the Nations

Obviously, the call of Abraham and the promises of the Abrahamic covenant present a quite different missionary strategy from the one we see in the New Testament. In Matthew 28:19 and the Book of Acts we see a centrifugal model of mission. Beginning with a core of Hebrew disciples, Jesus sends his followers out "into all the world." Moving out from Jerusalem, the gospel goes to Samaria and then across Asia Minor, to Greece, and finally to Rome, the capital of the empire.

The model presented in the Old Testament, however, is centripetal, moving in toward a center rather than moving out from a center. Rather than send his evangelists and witnesses out to the far-flung corners of the earth, as he does in New Testament times, God set a mission station in the midst of the nations for all to see. As the caravans made their way through Canaan on the way to Egypt or Babylon or Greece, they came into contact with the people of Israel, who were called to be a living embodiment of God's grace and rule.

120

YAHWEH, THE GOD OF THE WHOLE EARTH

The Old Testament story is not the story of Yahweh, the God of Israel, but of Yahweh, the God of the whole earth.[1] For "God's activity in Abraham's election is for the good of all the nations of the earth."[2] God's covenant with Abraham (Gen. 12) reveals his purpose for creation—for all nations[3]—through Israel his mission station.[4] The story narrows to one man and one people for the sake of its ultimate expansion to all. The Lord chooses one nation, an idolatrous and degraded slave people, in order to proclaim his sovereignty and his redemption throughout the nations. He calls Israel into service of the other nations. Through Israel, he intends for those nations to know him.

God's centripetal mission strategy calls for this nation of witnesses to Yahweh to model the kingdom of God. Thus what God does with the people of Israel is, on the small scale, what he plans for all nations. Israel is the whole world in microcosm. Similarly, what God does with the land of Canaan is a microcosm of what he intends to do with the entire creation.[5]

ISRAEL, THE MISSION STATION AMONG THE NATIONS

Bound by covenant election and oath to serve Yahweh, Israel is the recipient and custodian of God's particular revelation of his redemptive ways in the world. Israel receives and mediates the record of God's redemptive acts. Thus, Israel also serves the nations as a historical and cultural channel for redemption, the divinely ordained vehicle for the mediating of God's grace to the nations.

1. Gen. 18:25; Ex. 19:5, 29; Pss. 22:27–28; 47:8; 67:4–5; 72:19; 86:9; Jer. 10:6–7; Dan. 2:47.
2. R. R. DeRidder, *Discipling the Nations* (Grand Rapids: Baker, 1975), 23.
3. 1 Kings 8:41–43, 60; Pss. 68:31–32; 86:9; 87; Isa. 19:19–25; 45:22; 56:7.
4. "The first concern of the Bible is not with Hebrews but with humanity." Roger E. Hedlund, *The Mission of the Church in the World: A Biblical Theology* (Grand Rapids: Baker, 1991), 14.
5. Gen. 18:18–19; Jer. 2:3; 4:2.

In the midst of an extremely pluralistic atmosphere, an environment of tribal deities and cults of every possible imagination, Israel is called to give witness to Yahweh. God intends Israel to live before the pagan peoples around it as a witness to God's intervention in, and sovereignty over, history.

To be sure, there is an exclusive aspect to the covenant and to election. After all, God elects Israel, not the Eskimos. And Israel is to protect its election, its uniqueness, by maintaining its separateness. But this separateness is not meant to wall Israel in, to keep it from contact with the nations. Israel's separation is not a spatial idea but rather a moral and religious one. What God does in Israel is set in the midst of the nations.[6] Thus, as Roger Hedlund writes:

> The Old Testament gives no basis for isolation from the world. The devotional life with its Godward dimension must have a collateral service dimension of life in the world. Israel was set in the midst of the nations where she did not withdraw from social conflict. The Old Testament constantly warns against syncretism (absorbing the world), but it also stands against resignation (giving up on the world). Israel was to maintain the uniqueness of her witness, and she was responsible to see that there was active witness.[7]

The privilege of knowing God in covenant relationship is the privilege of glorifying him among the nations.

ISRAEL REMEMBERS THE PROMISES AND FORGETS THE MISSION

Repeatedly throughout its history, however, Israel forgot or ignored its covenant heritage and failed in its mission to be a light to the world. The nation forgot God's call to represent the rule of heaven among the kingdoms of the world (Isa. 42:6), to be in the world but not of the world. It was to model the kingdom of God. Instead, it tried to imitate the life and religion of the nations around it, unwilling to be different from those not called to the Lord's service.

6. Ex. 14:4; 15:14; Deut. 28:10; Jer. 22:8; Ezek. 20:22.
7. Hedlund, *The Mission of the Church in the World*, 26.

This is not to say that Israel did not enjoy the benefits of the covenant. God did not ignore his promises of covenant blessing but rather magnified them. But Israel came to take them for granted. It came to assume material blessing as its due because Yahweh was its God. It presumed upon the promises of posterity and the land, the blessing of prosperity that came with them, and the protection of Yahweh as its divine right.

Israel forgot that blood and land were covenant means rather than ends in themselves. Ignoring the missionary mandate enabled by the blessings of the covenant, Israel saw the covenant in terms of mere physical descent and divine right rather than in terms of God's larger historical purposes in the world.

Examples of Israel confusing the covenant with its instruments abound in the biblical record. After the people of Israel had returned from exile in Babylon and had been reorganized into a nation under Nehemiah and Ezra, the country's outlook became extremely narrow and introspective. It increasingly thought of itself as the only nation in the world that God cared about, rather than as belonging to him and called into his service. Israel even misinterpreted God's promise of a Messiah, and as a result, it looked for a political conqueror who would destroy the enemies of the Jewish state.

The Book of Jonah was written at this time to remind the people of Israel of their missionary calling and to rebuke them for their arrogance. Their desire for vengeance against those who had taken them into exile rendered them unfit for service.

In his experience, the prophet Jonah reenacted the experience of the people he represented. As he fled his mission, so did they. As he looked forward to seeing the Gentiles destroyed, so did they. In asking the Lord why he was sending a prophet to the Ninevite pagans, it is evident that Jonah had forgotten the purpose of the covenant. Finally, the Book of Jonah tells the story of a prophet who makes the staggering discovery that God loves the whole world and that the mission of Israel consists of its proclamation of that fact.

In a manner much like Israel during the time of the restoration, Jewish sects of the intertestamental period placed a heightened importance upon observing all the laws of the Old Testament and even tended to give that observance redemptive weight. The rigidity of groups like the Pharisees regarding legal observance was in large measure intended to guard Judaism from religious syncretism. The Pharisees also tended to consider Israel's election as the people of God in exclusionary terms (the exclusion of the rest of humankind) rather than Israel's inclusion in the covenant for the sake of God's redemptive mission among all people. The net effect of such exclusionary notions of election was a complete separation of the faithful from the world.

In Acts 10:28 Peter tells Cornelius, "You are well aware that it is against our law for a Jew to associate with a Gentile or visit him." If this were a real Old Testament injunction, it would create serious problems for God's mission of making Israel a light to the nations. Yet it is not part of the Mosaic law but merely part of the Pharisaic fence around the law. What the Pharisees missed was that election is never for private enjoyment or personal privilege. It is for service. And the service of Yahweh means glorifying his name in the world.

THWARTING GOD'S MISSION

Understood in light of God's covenantal redemptive purpose in and through Israel, the story of the patriarchs—Abraham, Isaac, and Jacob (Gen. 12–50)—is a tale of one threat to God's redemptive promise after another. Apparent obstacles present themselves repeatedly. When God called Abraham, for example, he told him to give up his country, his clan, and his home to go to an unknown, far-off land that he promised would be his. Abraham obeyed; but when he arrived in Canaan, what he found was famine (Gen. 12:10). This was an inhospitable land, a land that could not sustain him. Throughout the patriarchal narratives, drought and famine remain ever-present realities, a constant threat to mere biological survival.[8]

But the greatest threat to the promise is the patriarchs themselves. They did not seem to understand their call to be a blessing, to mediate God's gracious intention, his presence, within the world. They

8. See Gen. 12:10; 26:1; 41:56–42:2.

124

evidenced their failure to understand and comply with the divine promise in two ways. First, the patriarchs were often a curse to their world rather than a blessing, for Abraham and his descendants were frequently at war with their neighbors. Second, those elements of the promise with which they did identify (the seed, the land, God's commitment to them), they often attempted to force by their own efforts.

ABRAHAM SURRENDERS THE MOTHER OF THE PROMISE

Due to famine in the land of promise, Abraham migrated to Egypt. According to Genesis 12, the first thing he did upon his arrival was to surrender his wife Sarah into the harem of the pharaoh. Shockingly, the first incident recorded about Abraham after he received the promise is the surrender of the promised mother of a promised people to a man who was not the recipient of the promise.

This story of Abraham's deceit in Pharaoh's court is not meant to instruct us about marital infidelity (as important as that is). The story is about the threat to the promise. Abraham gives his wife to another man. Can God keep his promise? Will God keep covenant even though his covenant partner does not?

Indeed, the story underscores the graciousness of God's election of Abraham. God did not choose Abraham because of any inherent merit. Abraham fibs to Pharaoh to save his life. "Say you are my sister," he instructs Sarah, "so that . . . my life may be spared on your account" (Gen. 12:13). Far from being a morally upright person, Abraham is a liar who stands before Pharaoh surrendering his wife into Pharaoh's harem. Obviously there is no one-to-one correspondence between election and virtue or merit.

Nonelected Pharaoh is more virtuous than elected Abraham. Pharaoh asks, "Why did you say, 'She is my sister' . . . ? Now then, here is your wife. Take her and go!" (Gen. 12:18–19).

What is more, Abraham pulls the same stunt a second time (Gen. 20). This time the scene is not Egypt but Gerar. Again Abraham says of Sarah his wife, "She is my sister" (Gen. 20:2). Again Sarah is taken

125

into a harem. Again God intervenes to make sure that there is a mother to bring forth the elect people.

The same sorry plot appears yet again (Gen. 26:6–11). This time the lying patriarch is Isaac, Abraham's son. Both Abraham and Isaac take matters into their own hands. Rather than following God's lead, responding faithfully to his initiative, both try to force the fulfillment of God's promise by devious means. Both fear the power of kings more than they trust the promise of God. If there is a moral message in the responses of the patriarchs, it is the proposition that often the greatest threat to the kingdom of God is the people of God.

GOD'S REAFFIRMS HIS PROMISE WITH A SIGN

In spite of Abraham's cowardice and misguided attempts at self-preservation, God responds with a stunningly gracious reaffirmation of his promise and his sovereign agency. Genesis 15:1–21 records an exchange between Abraham and Yahweh concerning God's promise of progeny and of land. Regarding one and then the other promise, God initiates discussion by restating the promise (Gen. 15:1, 7), Abraham expresses doubt concerning first God's ability to keep his promise that Abraham will be the father of a great nation and second whether that nation will possess a land of its own (Gen. 15:2–3, 8), and Yahweh responds with a sign to strengthen Abraham's faith (Gen. 15:4–5, 9–21).

Regarding the matter of the seed, God assures Abraham that the son of promise will not be a son by adoption but a natural son from his very loins, and that the loins of Abraham and his succeeding seed will be fertile (Gen. 15:4–5). God intends the promise of a son of his own and Sarah's to be a sign to strengthen Abraham's weak faith.

To confirm his promise of the land, Yahweh offers a ritual of covenant making. As we saw in chapter 5, in standard ancient Near Eastern covenant practice five animals are cut in half and the pieces laid opposite each other. Custom dictated that the partners to the covenant would then walk through the lane formed by the pieces of meat, thereby invoking a curse upon themselves should they break the covenant (the oath of self-malediction).

126

Up to this point in the ceremony, God follows the custom. But then an absolutely unique event takes place, for only one of the covenant partners passes through the pieces, taking the curse upon himself. The other partner is completely passive, as "Abram fell into a deep sleep" (he didn't just nap off; Gen. 15:12). In his sleep, Abraham sees a smoking pot and a flaming torch pass between the pieces of slaughtered animals.[9]

What does the vision mean? It means that the covenant between God and Abraham depends on the promise of God alone. God binds himself to the promises in this ritual of confirmation.

A number of scholars have suggested that the model followed here is not the Hittite covenant form but the Royal Grant covenant model of the *kudurru* documents of sixteenth-century B.C. Babylonia. The Royal Grant covenant places greater stress on the covenant relationship as a gift given for the sake of the mediator than occurs in the Hittite model. In Abraham's vision, as in the *kudurru* documents, emphasis is placed upon the gift and the mediator as the receiver of the gift. The suggestion may be correct. Certainly, the Hittite model does not capture the entirety of the biblical covenant, and there were other models available within the culture for creating analogs to Yahweh's creative and redemptive ways.

The point here, however, is that God takes upon himself the full weight of the covenant. Abraham is not required to pass through the parts. The emphasis falls instead upon God's redemptive grace. He will guarantee the covenant and its details.

ABRAHAM AND SARAH SUBSTITUTE A SERVANT

But still Sarah remains barren. She reasons that if the ancient convention of adopting an adult servant as one's legal heir is not what God has in mind (Eliezer of Damascus [Gen. 15:2]), if God insists that the promised seed must come from Abraham, perhaps another accepted Bronze Age custom will do the trick. The child of a union

---

9. A blazing torch or fire is often associated with destruction in the Old Testament (Judg. 7:16, 20; 14:4–5; Ezek. 1:4; Nah. 2:4). Smoke too was associated with destruction and terror (Judg. 20:38–41).

with a concubine counts as an heir. She decides to lend God a helping hand by sending her Egyptian maid Hagar to Abraham. Ishmael is conceived by the union.

But again God intervenes. This is not the child of promise. God declares that Sarah will bear the child of promise. Hearing this, Abraham doubts even more, falling prostrate on his face—not in awe, as we might think, but in laughter. "Falling upon one's face" was a common idiomatic expression for laughing. "Abraham fell facedown; he laughed and said to himself, 'Will a son be born to a man a hundred years old? Will Sarah bear a child at the age of ninety?'" (Gen. 17:17). All of this sounds ridiculously implausible to Abraham. Thus, Abraham begins to plead with the Lord for what is biologically possible. "If only Ishmael might live under your blessing!" (Gen. 17:18).

Abraham laughs; and Sarah laughs (Gen. 18:12). Yahweh tells them that he will remind them of that response the rest of their days, for their child will be named Isaac ("he laughs"). In this God underscores that he is quite capable of fulfilling his promise, in spite of Sarah's barrenness, in spite of their tampering, and even in spite of their doubts.

CIRCUMCISION: THE COVENANT SIGN

Yahweh comes again to Abraham and reaffirms the covenant promises, the fact that Yahweh alone guarantees the covenant. In Genesis 17:2–21 Yahweh refers to the covenant as "my covenant" nine times. He has initiated and confirmed it, and he will establish it. The promise of a people and a land are again renewed. But then Yahweh turns his attention to Abraham's response, saying, "As for me," I keep covenant (Gen. 17:3–8). Immediately God includes Abraham in the covenant: "As for you," you must keep my covenant (Gen. 17:9–14). And as part of the stipulation of obedience, God subjects Abraham, and all of his male descendants hereafter, to the rite of circumcision. When Ishmael is born, Abraham is eighty-six years old (Gen. 16). At the time of these events, he is ninety-nine.

Circumcision was an extremely common practice in the ancient world, at least among the western Semitic peoples of Mesopotamia.

128

The Canaanite Philistines, who did not practice circumcision, stood out as exceptions. This was probably because they were not of Semitic origin but rather were a Mediterranean seafaring people who had migrated into the area. This reality gave rise to the common designation of the Philistines in the Old Testament as the uncircumcised. Egypt, along with the ancient world in general, performed circumcision as a rite either at puberty or in preparation for marriage. Abraham would have known of the rite from his two sojourns in Egypt.

People conversant with ancient Near Eastern practice and symbolism would have understood circumcision's original meaning. While scholars debate the precise meaning of circumcision in ancient Near Eastern culture, it seems natural, and fully in keeping with the story of Abraham's circumcision, to view it as a symbolic unlocking of the emergent powers of procreation and sexual potency (whatever further cultic connotations might have also been attached to the rite). The male foreskin, a symbolic barrier to fruitfulness, blocked the path of the male semen. It is quite possible that originally the rite also constituted a vestigial human sacrifice. For the sacrifice of the foreskin to the deity, the deity in turn blesses its donor with procreative fruitfulness.

In this light, the circumcision of a ninety-nine-year-old man was doubtless the occasion for great public humor. But it indicates that God means to remove the blockage of fruitfulness for Abraham and Sarah. Circumcision becomes the sign of the covenant, the sign that God would sovereignly keep his seed promise.

The rite of circumcision also becomes part of Abraham's covenant obligation (Gen. 17:9–14). Any male who is not circumcised will be cut off from the people, for he has broken the covenant. Israel is to bear the sign of the promise as their obedient response.

Thus, even as circumcision relates to reproductive fecundity, the rite begins to undergo reinterpretation right from the beginning. Stipulating that "every male among you who is eight days old must be circumcised" (Gen. 17:12), God abstracts the rite from its associations with sexual potency and introduction to puberty, reconfiguring it as a sign of his covenant pledge of fruitfulness and of Israel's dedication to Yahweh.

In the history of redemption, circumcision comes to take on a symbolism of ritual cleansing or consecration, the cutting away of that which impedes relationship and holiness.[10] As a covenant sign, circumcision was not intended as a racial badge. Indeed, the non-Israelite who became a believer in Yahweh was also to be circumcised (Gen. 17:12). Nor was circumcision ever meant to mark automatic inclusion in the covenant. Thus Moses, in the plains of Moab, admonished Israel to circumcise the foreskin of their hearts and to be hardened against God no more (Deut. 10:16). Later Moses promised that God would circumcise the heart of Israel so that they would love the Lord with all their heart (Deut. 30:6). True inclusion in the covenant came not to those who merely went through the formality of the circumcision rite but to those who bore it as a symbol of living faith in the God who set Israel apart for his service.[11] The outward rite of the covenant symbolized the gracious promise of God to the seed and the inner purification necessary for the life of covenant mission.

GOD'S POWER AND FAITHFULNESS PREVAILS

The threat to the seed promise continues throughout the book in the recurring problem of the barrenness of the patriarchs' wives. God had promised to make Abraham a great nation. Yet we do not see Abraham, or Isaac, the first son of the promise, fathering sizeable families from which a great nation might be expected to come. Each of the patriarchs' wives is for a time unable to bear children.[12] Abra-

10. See O. Palmer Robertson, *The Christ of the Covenants* (Grand Rapids: Baker, 1980), 150ff.

11. Gal. 3:7, 9; cf. Rom. 9:8. As one might expect, as Israel came to assume upon the blessings of the covenant, it also presumed upon the validity of the covenant rite as well. Israel proudly identified themselves as the circumcised and trusted in the external form to make them right with God. In John 8:39–41 Jesus had to warn his generation that physical descent from Abraham did not guarantee relationship with Abraham's God.

12. Sarah (Gen. 11:30; 15:2–3; 16:1); Rebekah (Gen. 25:21); Rachel and Leah (Gen. 29:31; 30:9, 17).

ham and Sarah have to wait twenty-five years for a son. Isaac and Rebekah are married twenty-one years before giving birth to the twin sons Jacob and Esau. Jacob eventually fathers twelve sons, from whom the twelve tribes of Israel will come, but only after he and Rachel also endure a period of childlessness.

In this threat to the seed we may also recognize a challenge to God's sovereign power and authority and the patriarchs' trust in him. Yahweh is pitted against the idols of the day. The testing of the patriarchal faith took place within the context of the polytheistic pantheon of the ancient Near East. Many of the pagan gods, especially those best known and most revered, were fertility deities. The barrenness of the patriarchs was a test of Yahweh as well as of the patriarchs. Other gods promised fertility. Could Yahweh fulfill his promise? Might the patriarchs begin to seek other gods?

By the end of Genesis, God has fulfilled his promise to Abraham that he would be the father of a great nation. Joseph and his brothers bore so many children that seventy people went down into Egypt. In the opening words of the Book of Exodus, Moses records that 430 years later, the land of Egypt is "full of them."

Genesis 12–50 is in some ways a disappointing narrative. The stories of the patriarchs refuse to conform to our expectations regarding founding fathers. It is not the sort of story a people would write for themselves. Far from being romanticized or idealized figures, all the patriarchs, from Abraham to Isaac, Jacob to Joseph, are presented as sons of Adam in all their pride, shortsightedness, treachery, greed, ignorance, and self-centeredness.

Were the patriarchs faithful to Yahweh? Often, no. But God was faithful, and that in the end is the story of Genesis. What Moses is teaching Israel in the book of beginnings is that the patriarchs are not the heroes of the story of Israel. Ultimately, the story is not about them. The patriarchs do not carry the story. Rather, the story carries them. The drama keeps coming back around to Yahweh, and to his faithfulness in spite of the faithlessness of his covenant partner. The divine purpose cannot be defeated by sin, even the sin of the covenant vassal.

8

SINAI
God Covenants with His Chosen People

Human beings are a forgetful species. Husbands forget anniversaries. Teenagers forget to take out the trash. We forget the names of people we went to school with. And no matter how hard we try, we can't remember where we put Jimmy's birth certificate.

But the omniscient, ever-faithful King of the universe does not forget. The only wise God does not suffer from absentmindedness. Nor does he pace the celestial precincts, trying to recall Old-What's-His-Name. And although four centuries had passed since Joseph, the last of the patriarchs, buried his father, Jacob, in Egypt, God had not forgotten his promises to Abraham.

YAHWEH REMEMBERS HIS PROMISES

Yahweh had indeed fulfilled his seed promise in Egypt. Jacob's children multiplied into a nation, such that the pharaoh began to fear their numbers. Thus he sought to control them by enslaving and employing them as a slave-labor force (Ex. 1:8–14).

Seeing his family multiply over three generations, Joseph had assured his brothers of the promise just before his death: "God will surely come to your aid and take you out of this land to the land he promised on oath to Abraham, Isaac and Jacob" (Gen. 50:24). God had promised the patriarchs not only a great nation but also the land of Canaan. But 430 years had passed, and God had not come. Israel remained enslaved in a land not its own.

Had God forgotten his promise? Most certainly not. Exodus 2:23–24 tells us: "The Israelites groaned in their slavery and cried out, and their cry for help because of their slavery went up to God. God heard their groaning and he remembered his covenant with Abraham, with Isaac and with Jacob."

The story of Exodus links directly to the patriarchal drama of Genesis. The God who calls Moses introduces himself as the God of Abraham, Isaac and Jacob (Ex. 3:6). Moved by the plight of his people, he has resolved that the time of their deliverance has come.

> I have indeed seen the misery of my people in Egypt. I have heard them crying out because of their slave drivers, and I am concerned about their sufferings. So I have come down to rescue them from the hand of the Egyptians, and to bring them up out of that land into a good and spacious land, a land flowing with milk and honey. (Ex. 3:7–8)

Yahweh is inaugurating the next stage of his covenant plan.

A DRAMA STARRING YAHWEH, MAJESTICALLY PRESENT WITH HIS PEOPLE

The Book of Exodus stresses the personal but also quite terrifying presence of God with his people. Yahweh meets personally with Moses in the theophany of the burning bush (Ex. 3), and he promises Moses that he will accompany him when he returns to Egypt (Ex. 3:12). Yahweh is said to appear to Moses (Ex. 3:16; 4:5). The plagues upon Egypt testify to the presence, sovereignty, and power of God (e.g., Ex. 7:17; 9:14; 10:2). So undeniable was God's presence in the exodus that Israel and Egypt recognize that he is the one who is fighting for Israel (Ex.

133

14:14, 25). In their sudden deliverance from Egypt through the sea and their long wilderness years, the people of Israel witness Yahweh's majestic presence as he leads them in a pillar of cloud and a pillar of fire (Ex. 13:21). God inaugurates the covenant at Sinai in another theophany, this time in thunder and lightning, smoke and fire (Ex. 19). Finally, the astounding and gracious presence of God with his people is formalized in the tabernacle over which the cloud of his glory settles.

Even though we rightly associate the name of Moses with this episode of covenant history, as its principal covenant mediator, the covenant, as always, belongs to God. It is first and foremost Yahweh who is present and active in the events. Without God's initiation, involvement, and condescension to dwell with his people and to reveal himself to them, there would be no story to tell.

YAHWEH CALLS ISRAEL AT SINAI

In fulfillment of his promise to Abraham that he would give them a land of their own (Gen. 12), and to Moses in revealing to him the divine name (Ex. 3), God brings Israel out of Egypt, through the sea, and finally to Mount Sinai.

While Israel camps at the foot of the mountain, Moses ascends its heights. And there God repeats his historical promise to the patriarchs and expresses his love for Israel:

> Then Moses went up to God, and Yahweh called him from the mountain and said, "This is what you are to say to the house of Jacob and what you are to tell the people of Israel: 'You yourselves have seen what I did to Egypt, and how I carried you on eagles' wings and brought you to myself. Now if you obey me fully and keep my covenant, then out of all nations you will be my treasured possession. Although the whole earth is mine, you will be for me a kingdom of priests and a holy nation. These are the words you are to speak to the Israelites.'" (Ex. 19:3–6)

Israel's encounter with Yahweh at the mountain in the desert weaves together God's promises made to the patriarchs so long before with his chosen people's future direction and vocation.

134

The Sinai revelation constitutes one of the great defining moments in the history of redemption. William J. Dumbrell overstates it only slightly in saying that "the history of Israel from this point on is in reality merely a commentary upon the degree of fidelity with which Israel adhered to this Sinai-given vocation."[1]

Sovereign Initiative and Redemptive Grace Ground the Covenant

God's words to Moses here, "the words you are to say to Israel," constitute Israel's calling as a nation into the covenant and lay the charge of that nation's divine calling upon it. But before laying the charge, God reminds Israel of his action on its behalf. He has rescued it out of Egypt ("you have seen what I did to Egypt"). He has protected it through the hardships of the wilderness ("I carried you on eagles' wings"). And he has chosen it to be his people (I "brought you to myself"). Indeed, before we come to God's giving the law, half of the Book of Exodus has recorded God's blessing and protecting Israel and his fulfillment of the promise that he would rescue it out of Egypt. "It is a story, in other words, of God's grace in action."[2]

Sovereign grace always goes before human response in the covenant. Indeed, in order to understand the contours of the Mosaic covenant, we must grasp and fully appreciate the historical and canonical context of Exodus 19–20: The calling of Israel depends upon the grace already given.

Thus, in light of God's gracious action already undertaken on Israel's behalf (Ex. 19:3–4), God lays out Israel's threefold vocation, its calling as a nation before the Lord (Ex. 19:5–6). Exodus 19:5 begins with "now," in the sense of "therefore." Yahweh calls Israel to be a treasured possession, a kingdom of priests, and a holy nation. The "if" clause signals that the vocation and obedience to which God calls his people are always responses to his gracious, elective action. Sinai can be appreciated only in that light.

---

1. William J. Dumbrell, *Covenant and Creation: A Theology of the Old Testament Covenants* (London: Paternoster, 1984), 80.
2. Christopher J. H. Wright, *Knowing Jesus Through the Old Testament* (Downers Grove, Ill.: InterVarsity Press, 1992), 192.

Why Israel?

The grace that undergirds the narrative in Exodus (indeed, the entire history of redemption) gives us a clue to why God elected this nation. After all, he could have chosen another. Imagine if God had chosen the Egyptians rather than Israel. Egypt's ancient history and prestige in the world would have made a great beginning for God's mission to the peoples of the earth. A pyramid would have offered a wonderful location for a gigantic sign saying *Yahweh Saves!* God could have chosen the Babylonians or the Assyrians as his people. The military acumen of either would have all but assured the domination of the entire world. Or God could have elected the Greeks. Their philosophy and science would have contributed a natural complement to God's redemptive revelation. If God had waited a number of centuries, Roman political administration and genius for law certainly would have aided God's mission. It would seem that under any of these choices, the divine agenda would have faired far better and been expedited more effectively than God's choice of a no-account slave people.

Why then choose Israel to be a treasured possession, a kingdom of priests, and a holy nation? Why choose this people to represent him in the earth, to stand before him on behalf of all the nations? Why choose this nation to live out his kingdom word and mediate the blessings of the covenant?

God's choice of Israel patterns his choice of the patriarch Jacob. By any worldly measure of preference, Esau would seem the better choice as the larger and stronger of the twin boys, the elder, and thus the natural inheritor of Isaac's estate. Yet God chose Jacob—Jacob the liar, Jacob the loser—rather than his brother Esau. Like Jacob, Israel was, as nations go, a loser, homeless and powerless.

We cannot answer the question with finality, for God's elective choice is always his free and sovereign act. "I will have mercy on whom I will have mercy, and I will have compassion on whom I will have compassion" (Ex. 33:19). Yet choosing such a people held definite advantages. It allowed God to mold it like a lump of unformed clay and then build it into a nation, a nation that would not be constantly tempted to idolize some glorious past or honored traditions or to cite some hall of heroes as the source of its nationhood. It would have to look to Yahweh. In electing a despised, homeless, slave people,

> God chose the foolish things of the world to shame the wise; God chose the weak things of the world to shame the strong. He chose the lowly things of this world and the despised things—and the things that are not—to nullify the things that are, so that no one may boast before him. (1 Cor. 1:27–29)

Everything Israel is or will be is the result of his grace.

A People with a Mission

God chooses Israel out of nothing but his good pleasure, to the exclusion of all merit, for indeed there is no merit in Israel. He calls it into relationship, to live in the light of his grace, to live as a member of his gracious household, in obedient service. Israel's adoption, the product of a thoroughly unearned grace, comes with responsibilities, a call, a vocation. God calls Israel to be a treasured possession, a kingdom of priests, and a holy nation.

If God considers Israel a treasured possession, does this not belie his concern that Israel serve the nations? In calling Israel his treasured possession, God is not saying that only Israel is his or that he cares only for Israel. Rather he is saying that if Israel obeys his word, it will enjoy a special relationship to him and a special status within the world.

We see something similar when David commits his country's resources to the building of a temple to the Lord (1 Chron. 29). Although David is the king over all of Israel and thus in charge over all its resources, he speaks of devoting his "personal treasure" to the work (1 Chron. 29:3). While all nations are Yahweh's, Israel is in a special sense his personal possession by virtue of his promises to Abraham and the patriarchs and his rescuing it from Egypt.[3] But he has separated Israel—distinguished it—from the whole, for the sake

3. Cf. Deut. 7:6; 14:2; 26:18; Ps. 135:4; Mal. 3:17.

of the whole. As with David's personal fortune, Israel is not an end in itself but a means to God's ends. Its uniqueness among the nations of the world stems from its calling to an identity and role in relationship to them.

Thus, God's Sinai covenant with Israel (Ex. 19) harks back to his promises to Abraham (Gen. 12). Yahweh is reminding Israel that he is not a deity restricted to a particular territory or tribe. Rather, "the whole earth is mine."[4] God's selection of one people out of all the earth, while maintaining his sovereign rights over all nations, leads to the conclusion that the election of the one is for the blessing of all. Israel's calling is a means toward the end of universal blessing.

It is in this light that the call to be a kingdom of priests and a holy nation is to be understood.[5] The calling to be a kingdom of priests and a holy nation tells Israel how it is to fulfill its calling to be a blessing to the nations.

As a kingdom of priests, Israel is called to represent the nations before God, to mediate God's redemptive purpose in the world. A priest stands between God and the people, representing each to the other. The fundamental purpose of priests in Israel was to represent the people before God through their sacrificial and intercessory ministry. Yahweh here summons Israel as an entire nation to act as a priest, a covenantal mediator between him and the rest of the world. In this priestly service, he expects Israel to pray for, love, minister to, and witness to the nations.[6]

To fulfill such a mandate, Israel must also be a holy nation. To be holy is to be separate from but not separated from. God means Israel

4. Cf. Ex. 9:29; Deut. 10:14–15.

5. Dumbrell's suggestion that Ex. 19:4–5 is a virtual restatement of Gen. 12:1–3, and thus that the Mosaic covenant is a restatement and expansion of the Abrahamic promises of Gen. 12, seems correct. See *Creation and Covenant*, 89–90.

6. A vivid example of this outward-looking priesthood, especially its intercessory function, can be found in Gen. 18, in which Abraham interceded before the Lord on behalf of the city of Sodom. From that story Christopher J. H. Wright concludes, "We are to intercede even for those we know are facing God's judgment. We are also to proclaim that judgment, but in the hope of repentance and reprieve, in the spirit of Abraham, and not of Jonah." *An Eye for An Eye: The Place of Old Testament Ethics Today* (Downers Grove, Ill.: InterVarsity Press, 1983), 126. Cf. Jer. 29:7; 1 Tim. 2:1–4.

to be distinct, distinguishable, different—but distinct in the midst of the nations, distinct even for the sake of the nations. What makes Israel distinct is its orientation to Yahweh, who is holy. God's holiness is a matter of his distinctiveness as the transcendent Creator of all and his moral purity. Elected into redemptive relationship with Yahweh, called to dwell with the Holy One of Israel, Israel is charged to live out Yahweh's moral character in a life of righteousness and justice such that its national and cultural life is a testimony to the moral character and redemptive love of God. In short, what God is should be seen in how Israel lives. As a nation among the nations, Israel gives living embodiment of God's rule, a flesh-and-blood example of what it means to serve God with full devotion. God intends it to be a model, an example, a pattern among the nations.

THE FORMAL STRUCTURE OF THE COVENANT

Covenant is a pervasive theme in the Old Testament. With the word *covenant* (Hebrew: *berith*) appearing 286 times, and covenant themes and catch words everywhere present, we may surmise that even though Scripture never offers a technical definition, the biblical writers were employing a concept familiar in the ancient world.

But just how common an idea covenant was in the ancient Near East, and exactly how covenant functions in the biblical materials became clear only quite recently. In the 1950s G. E. Mendenhall and others began studying the vast field of oriental law and political treaties of the Late Bronze Age (1500–1200 B.C.) with a view of shedding some light on the cultural context of the Old Testament understanding of covenant. They discovered that covenant served as an extremely common and important means of determining and regulating tribal and national relationships.

In the dog-eat-dog world of tribal conflict and nation building, the formation of political alliances was a common and often necessary strategy for self-defense for marginal peoples and petty kingdoms. In these alliances the parties would promise military or substantial aid to one another when such help was needed. Parity covenants thus were formalized, treaty-bound relationships in which two tribes or kings pledged themselves to mutual defense and economic assistance. A biblical parallel is the friendship covenant, of which the covenant between David and Jonathan is a notable example (1 Sam. 20).

The Hittite Suzerainty Treaty

However, scholarly studies focusing on the treaties of Hittite kings proved far more important for the biblical conception of covenant. At the height of their power (c. 1400 B.C.) the Hittites controlled a vast empire throughout Asia Minor, and they regulated the relationships between themselves and their subjugated states (vassals) by treaty arrangement. The Hittite king would offer to protect a people in exchange for their support and tribute. This was the only choice open to many small tribes that found themselves caught between larger powers. Such treaty relationships provided them a means of security in a world in which a small nation or tribe endured the continual threat of annihilation.

Named after the Hittite king, the suzerain, these treaties have come to be known as suzerainty treaties. They provide an illuminating parallel to the covenant between God and his people in the Old Testament. Unlike the parity treaty, a voluntarily entered relationship between equals, the suzerainty treaty featured a relationship between a lord (the Hittite king or empire) and a vassal (a lesser group or nation). One party of the relationship was clearly the superior, and the other was dependent. Furthermore, the suzerainty treaty was a virtual statement of imposition from the suzerain to the vassal, enacted upon the instruction of the Hittite king and only at his good pleasure. Although decidedly one-sided in its initiation, the treaty stipulated responsibilities for both parties.

Mendenhall noted that suzerainty treaty texts tended to follow a fairly fixed formula containing six components. Each contained, first, a *preamble* identifying the parties participating in the treaty, or simply the suzerain. Next usually followed a *historical prologue* that reviewed any former relationships between the two parties. It recounted the suzerain's past aid to the vassal to remind the vassal of the suzerain's trustworthiness and the debt of loyalty he owed to the suzerain.

140

Third, the treaty would list the *stipulations* or requirements that would regulate the relationship between the parties. Usually these would concentrate upon the responsibilities of the vassal. Beyond the general obligation of loyalty to the suzerain, it included an itemized list of specific stipulations. These might concern boundaries, throne successions, tributes and taxes, concubines for the king's harem, and young men for the king's army.

Fourth, the treaty would specify some provision for safeguarding the document, as well as for an annual *public reading* of the treaty, usually on each anniversary of its enactment. The public reading would ensure that all parties remained aware of their obligations. Often two copies of the document were prepared, each party then securing one of the copies to *deposit*, perhaps, in the temple of their deity. Fifth, the usual Hittite treaty was notarized by an appeal to the respective deities of each party. In an oath ceremony, each party would swear before his god to keep the stipulations of the treaty, thus invoking the gods as *witnesses* to the treaty. Finally, the treaty often enunciated the blessings or benefits that would accrue to the vassal upon the successful satisfaction of stipulated requirements, and curses or penalties the suzerain would exact upon the vassal for failure to comply with the treaty.

Parallels in Exodus 20

Mendenhall's claim that Exodus 20 evidences most of these elements seems accurate.[7] Exodus 20:2 constitutes a preamble, with its self-identification of Yahweh, the covenant Lord, as the God of Israel, along with a review of the immediate antecedent history of God's mighty work of liberating Israel from Egypt.[8] This historical prologue is nothing less than a declaration of God's sovereign right to call Israel to keep the law that follows. As with the suzerainty treaty of the Hittite king, this statement does not invite the vassal into relationship. Rather, the relationship is established by God's sovereign

---

7. G. E. Mendenhall, "Covenant Forms in Israelite Traditions," *Biblical Archaeologist* 17 (1954): 58.

8. John Bright, *A History of Israel* (Philadelphia: Westminster Press, 1959), 115.

redemptive action in fulfillment of his promise to Abraham to create a people and bless that people by his protection and presence.

The Ten Commandments (Ex. 20:3–17) that follow the historical prologue constitute the covenant stipulations God lays upon Israel, his vassal. These commandments are meant to demonstrate Israel's loyalty, and of course its obedience, to its covenant Lord. We may extend the stipulation section of the Mosaic covenant through Exodus 23:19, as Exodus 21–23 offer an explication or application of the fundamental ten stipulations.

Scripture's provision for public reading of the covenant document appears in Exodus 24:1–11. The deposit of the tablets within the ark of the covenant (cf. Ex. 25:16) could be an analog to the Hittite treaty as well. Deuteronomy 31:9–11 requires regular public reading of the covenant. Exodus 23:20–23 lists blessings and curses that would follow obedience or disobedience to the covenant. These receive lengthy and detailed exposition in Deuteronomy 28.

Nothing in the Mosaic covenant offers any real parallel to the invocation of deities to witness the covenant. But this absence is understandable given the nature of the biblical materials. After all, God has no greater than himself by whom to take an oath. He is his own witness (see Heb. 6:13–18). Seeking a possible analog to the Hittite treaty structure here, some interpreters have cited Exodus 24:4, the erection of the twelve pillars, while others have seen the blood ritual of Exodus 24:4–8 as double oath, involving both Israel and the Lord.[9]

---

9. Josh. 24 records a covenant renewal ceremony that also bears a number of striking parallels to the Hittite treaty: (1) preamble (Josh 24:2a: "This is what Yahweh, the God of Israel, says"); (2) historical prologue (Josh. 24:2b–13: a recounting of the highlights of God's redemptive acts in the exodus, wilderness, and conquest); (3) stipulations (Josh. 24:14–15: the requirement that Israel serve Yahweh only and throw away all their idols [note the repetition of the command "serve the LORD" in Josh. 24:14–22]); (4) provision for deposit and public reading (Josh. 24:26: Joshua recorded the covenantal proceedings in order to remind Israel of the covenant); (5) witnesses (in Josh. 24:22 the people are charged as witnesses against themselves, and in Josh. 24:26–27 Joshua set up a stone as a witness to the people's commitment); (6) blessings and curses (Joshua warns the people in Josh. 24:19–20 of the disasters that await them if they forsake Yahweh. Although blessings are not explicitly mentioned, the continued blessing of living in the land is implied in keeping the covenant).

God's covenant certainly predates the Hittites. They did not invent the idea. As we have seen, God called Adam into covenant relationship, Noah to be a covenant bearer, and Abraham to be the father of a covenant people. Yet when the Hittite treaty is invented, the Lord employs it as a teaching analog for his people. Just as with circumcision, God appropriates existing concepts, forms, and customs for his revelational and redemptive purposes. The plundering of the Egyptians did not end with Israel's exit from the pharaoh's land. As a commonly known convention of the ancient world, the Hittite treaty offered a strategic model for God to apply to his covenant, saying in effect: You see that Hittite treaty? My relationship is like that.

Implications for Understanding the Covenant

From this parallel between the biblical covenant and the Hittite suzerainty form we learn a number of things. First, it illuminates the relationship between covenant and law. Law is a function of the covenant. While it can be expressed in the legal language of obligation, benefits, and penalties, the covenant relationship nevertheless precedes the law.[10]

Second, although Israel enjoys a life of particular blessing and privilege before Yahweh, it is bound to him by a covenant oath articulable in legal language. In short, a covenant is a relationship under sanctions or obligations. Thus the Mosaic covenant subjects Israel as vassal to the kingship of Yahweh. But we may observe that this legal, even contractual relationship, "subjects" Yahweh to Israel as well, to fulfill his promised role as covenant overlord to his people.

Third, the Hittite treaty form reminds us of the importance of historical actions and context to covenant relationship. Without the action of the suzerain recited in the historical prologue, the bond between lord and vassal is void. Thus the frequent biblical recitation of God's mighty deeds in the history of his people (e.g., Ps. 78, 89, 104, 105, 136; Amos 2). People sometimes think that history is unimportant in biblical religion, that what matters is its ethical teaching

---

10. O. Palmer Robertson, *The Christ of the Covenants* (Grand Rapids: Baker, 1980), 170.

or its affirmation of the believer's immediate and present relationship with God. To be sure, moral imperative and personal relationship are crucial to the Christian faith. But without the historical action of God, the bond that creates relationship and the ethical command that regulates relationship are invalid. In biblical religion, as in the Hittite treaty, historical action always anchors relationship and obligation.

Fourth, the Hittite parallel alerts us to the importance of covenant renewal. The recitation and confession of the constitutional events of covenant history remind the people of God's covenant bond upon them, calling them to renewed commitment to their vocation as the mediator of his redemptive ways in the world. This renewal of the covenant restates the obligations of the covenant. It also reminds them of the blessings and curses that always accompany covenant relationship. Israel will retain God's blessing only if they gratefully acknowledge him as their source, and if the life of the people reflect God's character. Blessings will be lost if Israel forgets the suzerain to whom it owes allegiance.

Israel More Than a Vassal

While the Hittite treaty parallel suggests a fundamental suzerain-vassal relationship between God and his people, it would be a mistake to limit our understanding of the covenant to the suzerainty treaty. Even as the Old Testament uses elements of the Hittite treaty as an analog for God's covenant with his people, it also expands the form and breaks from it. The Hittite treaty is no more than an analogy, an accommodation. There is more to the biblical reality of covenant than a political treaty can bear.

To be sure, Israel is God's vassal, and he is the great King. Thus the covenant is a lord-servant relationship. Israel is legally bound to the service of Yahweh and to all the contractual obligations he sets upon it. Failure to comply with stipulated requirements constitutes a breach of the covenant and thus merits covenant curse.

Yet the Hittite model does not exhaust the covenant. The Old Testament employs a rich variety of other imagery to describe the

144

covenant relationship between God and his people. Israel is more than a vassal, defined merely by legal or contractual obligations. The Book of Exodus also employs kinship terminology and family terms in its covenant description. Israel has been adopted into a filial relationship with Yahweh, a family relationship ("This is what the LORD says: 'Israel is my firstborn son'" (Ex. 4:22; cf. Deut. 8:5; 26:18). Israel is not only a servant of Yahweh but also a son to Yahweh.

God is not only the suzerain, the great King; he is also Father to his people. Israel's Redeemer (Ex. 6:6; 15:3; 20:3; Deut. 7:8), the one who keeps his covenant word made to the patriarchs, is also the one who brings Israel into sonship by adoption, as its next of kin who "intervenes as father to demand the return of his son from a tyrant who has enslaved him."[11]

> The canonical portrayal of God's love for Israel is that of a father's care for his son. He exalts them before the Egyptians as his "firstborn" (Ex. 4:22). He carries them out of Egypt "on eagles' wings" and brings them to himself (19:4). Like a caring parent he meets their needs (Deut. 32:10–14) yet teaches them by his fatherly discipline (8:1–5).[12]

Such terminology colors the mighty deeds of God as surely as does the language of legal obligation. While we may never discount the legal language of king and servant is present in Exodus and throughout all of Scripture, we must also qualify this imagery of transcendence and formal obligation by the familial language of Scripture if we are to understand God as the covenant Lord and the role of the law in the covenant.

Treaty models emphasize the distance between the suzerain and the vassal, retaining formality in the relationship as it concentrates on contractual obligations. The language of family, however, emphasizes personal relationship and the presence of the father/husband with the son/wife. To state it theologically, the Hittite treaty points

11. Dumbrell, *Covenant and Creation*, 100.
12. Willem Van Gemeren, *The Progress of Redemption: The Story of Salvation from Creation to the New Jerusalem* (Grand Rapids: Zondervan, 1988), 146–47.

toward transcendence (distance), while the familial model points toward immanence (presence).

The prophets will later employ the imagery of marriage to describe the covenant. Israel is Yahweh's covenant wife (e.g., Hos. 1–3; Jer. 2–3; Ezek. 16; Isa. 54). Her failure to keep the covenant is not merely a legal failure but adultery against her beloved.

Familial relationships include legal requirements but are always more than those requirements. In a merely contractual relationship, when one party fails to live up to his or her contracted obligations, the contract is broken, penalties are incurred, and the contract might be dissolved. The biblical covenant, however, shows far more depth and flexibility. Legal stipulation fails to capture a relationship. Covenant, however, is person-oriented or relationship-oriented, for it arises out of a desire for the relationship itself. A ticking off of terms in a checklist fashion can reveal a broken contract, and the point of contract breach can be clearly identified. A covenant too can be broken, but the point at which this transpires is less clear, because in a covenant the focus is not the itemized list of stipulations but the quality of the relationship.

As the Book of Hosea makes eminently clear, if Israel's relationship to God were merely legal or contractual, that relationship would have been dissolved due to her many adulteries with the idols of the ancient Near East. Because the commitment and longsuffering of Yahweh, Israel's covenant husband, goes far beyond any obligation of a Hittite treaty, the covenant is not dissolved, and God calls his people to repentance and covenant renewal.

The suzerainty treaty focuses on obligations. They are, from the suzerain's point of view, the very reason for the treaty. The biblical covenant also features obligations, but by contrast, they are not ends in themselves but rather signs or tokens of covenant loyalty to the other party, meant to illustrate or embody the relationship between God and his people. In a purely political or legal contract, the stipulations are the center of the arrangement. In the biblical covenant, the relationship is central and prior to stipulations. The stipulations exist to serve the relationship.

Indeed, in the covenant renewal ceremony of Joshua 24 the fundamental principle of serving the Lord stands above the stipulations of the Ten Commandments to which the ceremony looks back. We might say that the one great stipulation is the call to love the Lord (e.g., Deut. 6:5). Jesus confirms this when he identifies the "first and greatest commandment" as "Love the Lord your God with all your heart and with all your soul and with all your mind" (Matt. 22:37–38).[13] The first issue in the biblical covenant is always loyalty, allegiance, love. In its detailed stipulations, the law is an exposition of what a bonded relationship of absolute dependence and love looks like. "These commandments that I give you today are to be upon your hearts" (Deut. 6:6).

Thus we return to the fact that Yahweh elected Israel into redemptive relationship, to be his treasured possession, a kingdom of priests, a holy nation: living out his moral character in response to his commands, as a witness to the watching nations, giving winsome expression to her relationship with him, and to his redemptive concern for his world.

---

13. To which Jesus immediately adds: "And the second is like it: 'Love your neighbor as yourself.' All the Law and the Prophets hang on these two commandments." Together, the love of God and the love of neighbor capture the essence of the Ten Commandments. We often speak of Jesus' citation of these two laws as a "summary" of the Decalogue. And so they are, but it would also be legitimate to say that the Decalogue is something of an expansion of the more fundamental law of love, which is so perfectly encapsulated by Jesus in Matthew 22.

9

THE LAW
Transcribing God's Character in the World

I n Yahweh's mighty deeds in Egypt, through the sea, and in the
wilderness, he has declared himself Israel's Redeemer. He has
now called Israel to be his treasured possession, a priestly and
holy example to the nations. In the exodus story, the giving of the
law immediately follows.

GOD'S CHARACTER DISPLAYED IN HIS ACTS AND EXPECTATIONS

Law Presupposes Historical Action

God's historical action and his law go hand in hand for Israel. The
two together form a picture of God's character and ways and his
expectation of his people. They tell Israel who God is and who Israel
is to be in response.[1] No text in Scripture proclaims this point more
clearly than Deuteronomy 10:12–19:

1. "What God is like is to be seen in what he does or has done. That was an axiom of
Israel's belief about God's self-revelation. Therefore, history became something of an eth-

And now, O Israel, what does the LORD your God ask of you but to fear the LORD your God, to walk in all his ways, to love him, to serve the LORD your God with all your heart and with all your soul, and to observe the LORD's commands and decrees that I am giving you today for your good?

To the LORD your God belong the heavens, even the highest heavens, the earth and everything in it. Yet the LORD set his affection on your forefathers and loved them, and he chose you, their descendants, above all the nations, as it is today. Circumcise your hearts, therefore, and do not be stiff-necked any longer. For the LORD your God is God of gods and Lord of lords, the great God, mighty and awesome, who shows no partiality and accepts no bribes. He defends the cause of the fatherless and the widow, and loves the alien, giving him food and clothing. And you are to love those who are aliens, for you yourselves were aliens in Egypt.

The ethic of the law presupposes God's historical action, an action that calls Israel to mimic him, to transcribe his ways into righteous behavior.

Law Shows How to Transcribe God's Character in the World

As in the Garden of Eden, God calls Israel to image God, to represent his character and rule in the world. The God who fashioned the very heavens called Abraham and his descendants to embody his covenant love and historical action, love and action that pursue justice and cherish righteousness, to be his vehicle of bringing blessing to the nations. The law tells Israel how to live as God's image bearers, what it means to be a kingdom of priests and a holy nation. Israel's keeping the covenant, conforming to its stipulations, embod-

---

ical 'copy-book,' because it showed God in action. For example, God has just freed Israel from slavery. So that same justice and mercy was to be reflected in Israel's own treatment of slaves and other vulnerable people in their society: 'Do not oppress an alien; you yourselves know how it feels to be aliens, because you were aliens in Egypt' (Ex. 23:9; cf. Ex. 21:2–11, 20f, 26f; Dt. 15:15)." "If Israel were to lose sight of what God had done for them, it would inevitably lead to failure to obey his law. They would lose both model and motive." Christopher J. H. Wright, *An Eye for an Eye: The Place of Old Testament Ethics Today* (Downers Grove, Ill.: InterVarsity Press, 1983), 26, 29.

ies the covenant so that the nations will witness Yahweh's will and grace. Israel can fulfill its calling only if it lives according to the law.

The great contribution of the Sinai covenant to the ongoing covenant story is the revelation of God's demands for Israel's obedience. The patriarchs knew that they were to obey the Lord (Gen. 17:9: "As for you, you must keep my covenant"; cf. Gen. 15:6; 22:1–11). Now at Sinai, however, the precise terms of Israel's obedience are made plain.

LAW IN THE CONTEXT OF REDEMPTION AND COVENANT

Keeping the Law Is Not an Alternative Way to God

The law did not appear on the scene as a new or alternative way to God. It is imperative that we see that in the giving of the law we witness the same relationship between grace and obedience that God has maintained from the beginning. O. Palmer Robertson insistently writes:

> The concrete externalization of covenant stipulations written on tablets of stone never was intended to detract from the gracious promise of the Abrahamic covenant, as Paul argues so aptly. The covenant of law, coming 400 years after promise, could not possibly disannul the previous covenant (Gal. 3:17).[2]

God did not send Moses to Israel with a new method of forging relationship, one that would set aside the grace of God's promises to Abraham, a plan that said in effect: If you keep the law, I will save you. It is precisely the other way around. Obedience flows from grace; it does not buy it. The exodus precedes Sinai. Before he gives the

---

2. O. Palmer Robertson, *The Christ of the Covenants* (Grand Rapids: Baker, 1980), 174. Robertson goes on to say, "The covenant of law is related organically to the totality of God's redemptive purposes. To speak of an organic relationship is to suggest a living, vital inter-connection as over against an isolationistic compartmentalization. The clear enunciation of the will of God at the time of Moses did not appear as something novel in the history of redemption. At the same time, law did not disappear after Moses. Law functioned significantly in the period preceding Moses, and law functions significantly in the period succeeding Moses" (175). "Law simply becomes predominant under Moses" (177).

first commandment, and on the basis of his mighty saving acts recorded in the previous chapters, Yahweh identifies himself as Israel's Redeemer (Ex. 20:1–2). The list of commands thus begins with an implied "therefore." Because God has redeemed Israel and made it his own, it must walk in his ways.

The law does not create relationship. God calls Israel to keep the law, not in order to become God's people but because they already are God's people (Ex. 19:4; 20:1–2). As he created Adam to obey his word, Yahweh redeems Israel to obey his word. There is no question of merit in either case. "The law of God is not a system of merit whereby the unsaved seek to earn divine favor but a pattern of life given by the Redeemer to the redeemed so that they might know how to live for his good pleasure."[3]

Divine initiative and human response constitute the pattern throughout all of Scripture. "Love each other as I have loved you" (John 15:12). "We love because he first loved us" (1 John 4:19). The biblical call to obey the Word of God, to keep his law, is a call to respond to his love and redemption.

I cannot say this strongly enough. The law was never intended to be a means of earning salvation. Rather, God gave it to guide Israel in living in a way that would please their Redeemer. Far from setting aside the promise of grace, the law was given to those who had been saved by grace in order to show them how to live in that grace. Thus Sinai does not bring fresh bondage but rather proof that the old bondage had been broken. In fact, we can speak of the law as a further act of grace, a gift to God's people that serves his covenantal and gracious purposes. Thus the call of the law is to translate God's grace into action.

Keeping the Law Nourishes the Covenant Relationship

The law is the divinely intended means by which the covenant is nourished and maintained. The law shows the people of God the con-

3. J. A. Motyer, "Biblical Concept of Law," in *Evangelical Dictionary of Theology*, ed. Walter E. Elwell (Grand Rapids: Baker, 1984), 624.

duct fitting for God's covenant community. In obeying the law, Israel actualizes in human life its covenant relationship with Yahweh.

Israel was to look upon the law as a gift, not a burden. The law was a delight because it aided the covenant relationship. The relationship was not a matter of external or mechanical rules but a personal relationship with a God who is not only the sovereign King of the universe but also a father who has promised himself to his covenant people. Thus when an Israelite son asked his father what the law meant, the answer was the story of the exodus and the fulfillment of covenant promise, "the old, old story of God's saving love and deliverance. The very meaning of the law was to be found in the Gospel."[4]

"Oh how I love your law! I meditate on it all day long," sings the author of Psalm 119. God's law is a delight (Ps. 119:70, 92), a source of comfort (Ps. 119:52), an object of love (Ps. 119:97), a means of peace (Ps. 119:165), a vehicle of liberty more precious than silver (Ps. 119:72), the truth of God (Ps. 119:151, 160), and a source of light and understanding by which to make one's way in the world (Ps. 119:105, 130, 144). In shorter compass but in language no less exalted, in Psalm 19 David describes the law as perfect, trustworthy, right, radiant, pure, sure, and righteous. Such a law is "more precious than gold, than much pure gold," and "sweeter than honey, than honey from the comb."

To meditate upon the Lord in the Psalms is to meditate upon his instruction. To know God as Savior is also to know him as lawgiver. To walk securely and confidently in the world is to walk in the way of the Lord.

HOW CAN LAW AND GRACE GO TOGETHER?

Evangelical Christians do not customarily think of Old Testament law in these terms. To speak of the law in the glowing, even affec-

---

4. Christopher J. H. Wright, *Knowing Jesus Through the Old Testament* (Downers Grove, Ill.: InterVarsity Press, 1992), 193.

tionate terms of the psalmist seems strange to us moderns. What leads us to suppose that law must oppose or abrogate grace?

We Mistakenly Identify the Pharisees with the Old Testament Saints

We can make the mistake of supposing that the Pharisees of the New Testament truly represent Old Testament religion and that when Jesus criticized them, he was denying any value to the law. But to Jesus, Pharisaic Judaism was a wild root, one not planted by God, for it was blind to the real intent of the law (Matt. 15:13).

We Misconstrue Freedom

As post-Enlightenment, Western people, we tend to think of law as a coercive force, a destroyer of freedom. Anything that limits free choice (the right to do as we please, or even the right to choose the contrary) is considered oppressive and inhumane. Freedom within the biblical mind, however, is not lack of restraint, the right to do or be whatever one individually wishes. This is, instead, the way of the fool.

Whereas freedom in modern liberal culture is the right to choose to disobey without penalty, Scripture views freedom as the right to obey. Real freedom is the right to be properly related to God, to other human beings, and to the world about. In Psalm 139 David pleads with God: "Search me, O God, and know my heart; test me, and know my anxious thoughts. See if there is any offensive way in me, and lead me in the way everlasting." In Psalm 19 he says,

> By [your ordinances] is your servant warned;
>> in keeping them there is great reward.
> Who can discern his errors?
>> Forgive my hidden faults.
> Keep your servant also from willful sins;
>> may they not rule over me.
> Then will I be blameless,
>> innocent of great transgression. (vv. 11–13)

Far from bringing bondage, the application of the law to one's life brings liberty.

How can law—which is obligatory and restrictive in its very nature—bring liberty? By telling us exactly what is expected of us. By laying out the rule by which he expects his people to live, God removes the anxiety and fear that always attend not knowing. Unlike the potentate or the incompetent parent, God's rule is not bent by meanness or caprice, self-interest or vacillation. Unlike the law of fallen man, which often merely reflects the senseless world we make for ourselves, the law of God is a joy because it makes sense of the world. Knowing what is demanded of one is liberating. Never knowing how to satisfy someone produces slavery. As a morally sensitive God, he tells us what constitutes a moral life.

We Have Inherited a Faulty View of the Law

Our Protestant heritage partly explains our particularly negative attitude toward the law.

In the early sixteenth century, Martin Luther castigated the late medieval church for losing all appreciation of redemption by the gracious activity of God in Jesus Christ. In its place, the Roman church had set up a complex system of salvation by legalistic observances, prayers to saints, rosaries and masses, pilgrimages, and the buying of indulgences. By such things, people hoped to earn salvation. This system filled the young monk with anxiety, for it made God a distant monarch at best and an uncaring and calculating accountant at worst.

Through his study of the Book of Romans, and later Galatians, Luther concluded that salvation is by grace alone (*sola gratia*), not by law keeping or supposedly meritorious cultic observances. Salvation comes to fallen humanity through the merit of Christ's sacrificial death rather than its own efforts.

In his rediscovery of the biblical doctrine of grace, Luther tended to denigrate the law, undoubtedly in reaction to the teaching of the medieval church. He removed law from the center of his understanding of redemption, leaving little room for the law in the life of faith. Luther held that the law is the will of God, revealed first as a natural law known by all. But since the fall, humankind has become incapable of keeping its righteous demands. From this point on the revelation of the law presupposes sin and functions in relation to sin. The law views man as sinner.

Luther believed, therefore, that the law has two primary applications. First, the law is revealed in creation and human institutions, written upon the heart and codified in the laws of men. As such the law works as a civil fence against sin, restraining the wicked and providing the necessary social order for life in the world and the proclamation of the gospel. By making some actions or modes of behavior illegal and liable to penalty, the law urges fallen human beings to function in a socially acceptable way.

Second, the law defines sin and thus convicts man of his sinfulness. It also makes man conscious of his inability to fulfill its demands. Thus it teaches fallen man of his need, his need for a savior. Luther called this the pedagogical use of the law, for the law teaches us our need for Christ and leads us to his grace.[5]

In both uses Luther cast law in fundamentally negative terms. Law names sin as sin and works as a principle of civil restraint. The law also functions negatively in the Christian life. While the holy life arises spontaneously from the heart of the believer and not from the urging of the law, the law continues to help the Christian recognize and confront sin in his life and to keep him from losing sight of his justification by grace through faith.

In the second generation of the Reformation, John Calvin insisted that the law plays a more positive role in the Christian life than Luther was willing to acknowledge. Though he appreciated the fact that Luther wanted to get away from legalism and the medieval notion of salvation by meritorious works, Calvin noted that the Bible (New Testament as well as Old) also viewed law as positive instruction to the people of God. Scripture has a negative attitude toward legalism, but it is positive toward law. While negative toward moralism, the Bible certainly favors morality.

5. *Luther's Works*, ed. Jaroslav Pelikan et al. (Philadelphia: Fortress, 1973), 26:274–75.

To address these concerns, Calvin spoke of the third use of the law. The proper or Christian use of the law is to provide a lamp for the feet and a light to the path of life (Ps. 119:105). Once we are delivered from the false idea of law keeping as being redemptively meritorious, we can then embrace the biblical idea of the law as the expectation of our heavenly Father for his children.

This difference between the two Reformers stems from the fact that Calvin sought to ground the law in creation, whereas Luther viewed the law solely in reference to sin. The law for Calvin is God's common grace to man as creature. Thus the law provides a description of the moral life, and it addresses man not first as sinner but as a creature of God.

Calvin affirmed Luther's notions about the law as a social fence against sin and the law as a tutor leading the sinner to Christ. But Calvin interpreted the first use of the law positively, as a manifestation of God's common grace. In spite of man's sin, God upholds his world and his word for it. Thus the good order of creation imposes itself upon the sinner. Calvin reinterpreted the second use positively as well: the law serves not merely a pre-Christian function, solely as introductory to grace. In urging moral behavior and condemning sin, the law—as a law of repentance—continually reminds the believer that he needs grace and must depend upon Christ.[6]

With these three positive uses of the law, we can see that Calvin thought of the law as something of an operator's manual for the covenantal machine. The Heidelberg Catechism, a Reformation-era catechism that came out of Germany, spoke of the law as a guide, a rule of gratitude, a map to the healthy and obedient life. We are not saved by works, but we are certainly saved for works. We are saved by grace alone, but the grace that saves is never alone. There must also be instruction in the life of faith.

Thus Calvin was able to integrate the genius of Old Testament piety into his understanding of the law far better than the Lutheran tradition did. Unfortunately, Luther has had far greater influence upon

6. John Calvin, *Institutes of the Christian Religion*, ed. John T. McNeill, trans. Ford Lewis Battles, 2 vols. (Philadelphia: Westminster Press, 1960), 2:5–9.

the evangelical tradition than Calvin has had. This is due, most likely, to the strength of the pietistic tradition, whose roots lay in Lutheranism.

It should be noted that the Reformed appreciation of the law in the life of faith opens us to another danger. An emphasis upon law can slide into legalism. Whenever the law is cut loose from its intended meaning of guiding and nourishing the covenant relationship, it inappropriately comes to define the community of faith and relationship with God. Legalism always defines man's life before God in terms of performance. The test of whether one is a member of the community is the doing of A, B, and C, the refraining from X, Y and Z. Even if these are moral or unhealthy behaviors, respectively, turning them into a performance test counts as legalism.

The sociological problem here is that a social convention becomes the test for inclusion. In other words, a person is accepted as a true believer if he or she refrains from certain behaviors judged as taboo by the group or engages in behaviors that conform to the custom of the group.

The far more devastating theological problem is that behavior assessed solely by whether it conforms to a formal rule becomes the actual principle of inclusion. *A true Christian would never do that. Christians do not engage in that activity.* This pushes grace all but out of the picture. Here the legalist Christian needs to heed the warning from the Lutheran tradition: apart from grace, the law kills.

Thus it is that we Christians may identify with the Old Testament saints in their understanding of and delight in the law. For all the saints, the law serves to maintain and nurture his people's relationship with God.

THE LAW: BACK TO CREATION BUT BEYOND IT

The Law Reflects Creation

The law given at Sinai harkens back to the relationship God established with Adam and creation at the beginning. God's covenantal action after the fall is designed to return fallen humanity to the

157

integrity of Eden. It is still true that man must live according to the revelation of God written in the book of nature if he is to enjoy life in God's creation. God does not give up on his first word to man. His creational law still holds.

The Westminster Confession of Faith connects the law given at Sinai with God's creational ordinances. The law God gave to Adam "continued to be a perfect rule of righteousness; and, as such, was delivered by God upon Mount Sinai, in ten commandments, and written in two tablets: the four first commandments containing our duty towards God; and the other six, our duty to man."[7]

In his sin fallen man is largely blind to and in rebellion against God's will. Yet fallen as he is, even the sinner can see something of God's original intent, his good will for man in the world. By his common grace, God's creation word breaks through and imposes itself upon a fallen humanity, for the unregenerate are not always and everywhere blind to or uncaring of that which promotes life and social harmony. It is not accidental that behaviors like murder, rape, and theft are almost universally understood as abominable acts that must be forbidden by society and punished when perpetrated.[8] Indeed, hundreds of years before Moses received the law at Sinai, Hammurabi was setting down the law for the Chaldeans (ca. 1800 B.C.). There is a considerable amount of similarity between the Ten

---

7. Westminster Confession of Faith, 19.2.

8. "Even without God's explicit verbal positivization of the creational norms for justice and faithfulness, stewardship and respect, people have an intuitive sense of normative standards for conduct. One word for that intuitive attunement to creational normativity is *conscience*. As human beings we are so interwoven into the fabric of a normed creation that in spite of our religious mutiny we conform to creational standards 'by nature,' by virtue of our very constitution as creatures. Creational law speaks so loudly, impresses itself so forcefully on human beings, even in the delusions of paganism, that its normative demands are driven home into their inmost being, are 'written on their hearts' like the indelible inscription of a law code on a clay tablet. This does not refer to some innate virtue of 'natural man,' unaffected by sin, but to the finger of the sovereign Creator engraving reminders of his norms upon human sensibilities even in the mist of apostasy. God does not leave himself unattested; he refuses to be ignored. He asserts himself in an unmistakable display of his 'eternal power and divine nature' so that we cannot fail to take note of the Creator's claims on our obedience." Albert M. Wolters, *Creation Regained: Biblical Basics for a Reformational Worldview* (Grand Rapids: Eerdmans, 1985), 25.

Commandments and the Code of Hammurabi. Both are declarations or codifications of the moral law of creation.

The Law Also Reflects Sin and Grace

However, the law given at Sinai is more than a mere repetition or republication of natural law or creation ordinance. It is God's will given in the context of grace. Sinai can be appreciated only in the context of the unfolding drama of God's response to human rebellion and his historical intention to bring redemption through the mediation of a chosen people. In order for law to graduate into the full flowering of God's creational intent for humanity, in order for the law to bless life rather than function as a principle of condemnation, the law must be appreciated in the context of grace. That is to say, the law must be received as the revealed will of a Redeemer. Again, without grace, the law only kills. Just so, without redemption, we know the Creator only as Judge, and his covenant will only as curse.

Yet it is still the case that the Ten Commandments are a restatement of God's creational law and thus binding upon man as creature. As such, the Decalogue is not merely a law for Israel but God's moral law for all men. There was never a time when the first commandment (putting God first) was not God's will for man. Nor will there be a time in the future when the sixth commandment (the prohibition against murder) will no longer be God's will.

Why Write Them?

If the Ten Commandments are a codification of a universal moral law, a law written on the heart of all men (Rom. 2:14–15), if all men have an intuitive sense of its content, then why write it down? The written law makes clear and unambiguous what is only dimly perceived and often misinterpreted by fallen human beings. A divine imperative written in clear, unequivocal terms is less likely to be misunderstood than the wordless revelation of creation. It is far more difficult to ignore a word that is external to us than a word within. The corruptions of an apostate race sear the conscience, dulling its ability to receive God's creation word. The law spoken by God, inscribed on tablets of stone and ultimately written in an authoritative canonical testimony, corrects and condemns the spiritual blindness of the rebellious heart.

TORAH: FATHERLY INSTRUCTION

While the Old Testament employs many different words that can be translated as "law," the most important is *torah*. *Torah* comes from the verb *yarah* ("to direct, teach, instruct"). It occurs 220 times in the Old Testament. The law given at Sinai is the covenant obligation of Israel or the stipulations placed upon it by God. But that law must be seen in light of the adoption of Israel into the family of God. What we have in the law is not merely a legal code, a stipulated duty that we must perform in order to be legal or to escape penalty. It also constitutes God's fatherly instruction to his children.

Surely, the note of duty, obligation, and threat is there, and we ought not to seek to lessen its seriousness. We are talking about divine command, even though that command is given in the context of grace. Yet the historical context and relational environment of God's law given at Sinai is that of redemption, grace, and adoption. It is given in the context of God's commitment to Israel, before the calling of Israel's commitment to Yahweh.

Many teenagers have heard the parental charge, "As long as you live in my house, you will live by my rules." Parents reinforce their instructions to their children with such appeals for far better reasons than their children know. We might simply cite the parent's authority as parent, and that would be sufficient. But there is more to it than that. Authority is informed by other realities. The wisdom of age, knowing what is appropriate behavior in particular situations, having the well-being of the child at heart, bearing the calling to be a parent for the sake of the child, all ground parental authority as legitimate authority. My sons need to heed my instruction because they are my children, because I am their father, and because I love them and seek the best for them. God's authority over his crea-

tures, his right to demand obedience from them, functions in much
the same way.

THE TEN COMMANDMENTS

The Heart of the Law

The heart of the law is the Ten Commandments that God wrote
with his own finger on the heights of Sinai (Ex. 31:18; Deut. 5:22).
These Ten Commandments, or ten words[9] (Ex. 20:3–17; Deut. 5:7–21),
are the primary stipulations of the covenant relationship. They provide the basic contours of the love for God and neighbor that flow
from covenant membership. Based upon the unchanging character
of God and the covenant calling to image him, these ten instructions
are eternally binding.

The Decalogue Stands on Its Own

The Ten Commandments are not the entirety of the Old Testament
law. In addition to them, Scripture lists literally hundreds of instructions, decrees, and judgments—613 in all. But Moses' observation
that "these are the commandments the LORD proclaimed . . . and he
added nothing more" suggests a finality about the Ten Commandments. That Yahweh inscribes these and no others on the tablets suggest that they have a self-contained reality. It is appropriate, then, to
speak of the Ten Commandments apart from the law that follows.

Apodictic Law

The Decalogue may be described as apodictic injunctions—short,
unconditional assertions of right and wrong set in the language of
commandment: you shall, you shall not. They are given without qual-
ification and applied to no specific social context. Thus they are not
restricted to any one time, place, or people. The Decalogue addresses

9. The term *Decalogue*, which refers to the Ten Commandments, is the Greek rendering of the Hebrew expression "the ten words" found in Ex. 34:28 and Deut. 4:13; 10:14.

humanity's fundamental covenant duty: an embodied love of God and of others.

Freeing Prohibitions

One cannot help but notice that, aside from the command to keep the Sabbath holy and the command to honor one's parents, the laws are expressed in negative terms. Prohibitions might seem limiting and restrictive, but they are not. Prohibitory statements are far broader than statements of permission. A positive command legitimates only a single behavior. In effect, declaring one behavior illegitimate affirms those actions not named in the prohibition. The purpose of the law is to avoid obstacles to covenant relationship, to avoid those errors that destroy freedom, and thus the law concentrates on those obstacles. "There is not commanded what establishes the relation to Yahweh, but prohibited what destroys it."[10]

God-Centered Focus

Separating the Decalogue from all man-made law is the fact that it is thoroughly God-centered. Christopher Wright's observation, made concerning all the ethical teaching of the Old Testament, especially pertains to the Decalogue: "It presupposes God's initiative in grace and redemption; it is framed by what he has done and will do in history; it is shaped by his character and action; and it is motivated by personal experience of God's dealings with his people."[11]

This God-centered focus is seen in the ordering of the commandments. God comes first. By putting the commandments that relate explicitly to humanity's relationship to God at the beginning, the Decalogue declares the priority of that relationship. This is not to say, however, that all other relationships are optional. Rather, the law puts at the head of the list the one relationship that informs and is necessary for all else. If man is not correctly related to God, he will

10. W. Gutbrod, "The Law in the NT," in *Theological Dictionary of the New Testament*, ed. G. Kittel and G. Friedrich, trans. G. W. Bromiley, 10 vols. (Grand Rapids: Eerdmans, 1967), 4:1037.

11. Wright, *An Eye for an Eye*, 31.

not relate to other people or the world as he should.[12] Scripture warns that worshiping a false god (idolatry) invariably issues forth in injustice in all other spheres of life.

The first commandment rejects all other gods in order to protect Yahweh's singular right to rule over his people.[13] Only Yahweh is to be worshiped because only he is God. The Bible mentions other deities, but it allows them no role in creation and no power over humanity. It undeifies them, for it accords them no reality. Only Yahweh can be addressed and related to as a person, for only he speaks and acts.[14] No other deity could issue such a law. Only a God who loves his chosen people enough to be jealous and personally offended when they worship others could give this law. Unlike the deities Israel knew in Egypt, Yahweh is no placid, peaceful, mute idol but a sovereign, holy, transcendent, and fully living personal being. And that reality, so vividly demonstrated to Israel in its release from Egyptian bondage and sojourn to Mount Sinai, makes the first commandment both reasonable and inescapable. Thus the Decalogue enjoins not only moral commitment to the values and character of God but also absolute commitment to God and his integrity as a person.

CASE LAW

Applying Apodictic Law to a Particular Historical Context

While the moral law of God holds for all people at all times, the law was also given to Israel within a particular historical context.

---

12. Wright goes on to observe that the fact that the Decalogue ends with the command not to covet brings us back full circle to the first commandment. The Ten Commandments "begin with God and end with the inner thoughts of the heart. And yet in a sense, the first and tenth commandments correspond with each other, since covetousness puts other things or people in the place God should occupy: 'covetousness which is idolatry,' as Paul said more than once (Eph. 5:5; Col. 3:5; cf. Luke 12:15–21)." *Knowing Jesus Through the Old Testament*, 210.

13. "Indeed, the whole history of Israel's cult is a struggle solely concerned with the validity of the first commandment." Gerhard von Rad, *Old Testament Theology*, 2 vols. (New York: Harper & Row, 1965), 1:120.

14. Dale Patrick, *Old Testament Law* (Atlanta: John Knox, 1985), 43; John Bright, *A History of Israel* (Philadelphia: Westminster Press, 1959), 154.

Thus after stating the law in broad, prescriptive, and principial terms, Moses begins the process of applying the Ten Commandments to the historical situation of Israel.

Israel had been a nomadic people, then a slave people, now a nomadic people again, and will become homesteaders and farmers in the land promised to Abraham. How will the nation live out Yahweh's law when it enters Canaan? Will it know how to live as the people of God rather than the servants of Egyptians, to live together ruled by Yahweh's will rather than the foreman and the whip, to live in the land of testimony to the nations rather than in a land where its story is not told?

The heart of the law is love. But love of God and neighbor and care for God's world work out differently in different contexts. Principles must be applied to real situations. Moses knew that the Word of God is not ivory tower ideology, good in theory but inappropriate to real life. Thus after a prologue that underscores the holiness of God (Ex. 20:22–26), he begins the work of application: "These are the *mishpatim*," that is, the cases (Ex. 21:1).

The case law describes how to apply the Ten Commandments (apodictic law) to particular situations or cases. As in modern case law, it therefore rests upon a prior established precedent, that is, the apodictic law of the Ten Commandments. The case law is located primarily in two places in the writings of Moses: Exodus 20:22–23:33 (the Book of the Covenant; see Ex. 24:7) and the Book of Leviticus.

Arbitrary Division between Moral, Civil, and Ceremonial

It has been common to divide the case laws into categories; moral, civil, and ceremonial law being the most common categorization. This approach is somewhat artificial, however. The determination of the category to which a particular law belongs is often considerably subjective. For example, can a law be civil but not moral in character? While a ceremonial law might be the easiest to identify, dealing as it does with Israel's worship and sacrificial life, a ceremonial law also reflects the moral character of God; and a moral law, as part of Israel's public witness to the nations, bears civil overtones.

All of Life under God's Lordship

The case laws of Moses cover a wide range of practices and behaviors. They relate to eating and hygiene, dress, agriculture, sexual relations, finance, slavery, warfare, criminal justice, and property. Looking at a text like Deuteronomy 27:15–25, one cannot help but notice the all-embracive character of God's law:

> Cursed is the man who carves an image or casts an idol . . . and sets it up in secret . . . Cursed is the man who dishonors his father and mother . . . who moves his neighbor's boundary stone . . . who leads the blind astray on the road . . . who withholds justice from the alien, the fatherless or the widow . . . who sleeps with his father's wife, who has sexual relations with an animal, who sleeps with his sister . . . with his mother-in-law . . . who kills his neighbor secretly . . . who accepts a bribe to kill an innocent person . . . who does not uphold the words of this law.

Fairness, holiness, justice, and mercy are to characterize every endeavor of the people of God. As William Dyrness observed:

> A proper understanding of the law leads one to see that all of life lies under the controlling will of God, whether one is getting up in the morning, sitting down to eat, walking along the way or going to sleep. Whether one is concerned with life in the state or the cult, in business or in the home, nothing lies outside the purview of the law.[15]

Leviticus 17–26 is often referred to as the Holiness Code because of its repeated reference to and demand for holiness. Yet the holiness spoken of there is by no means a merely ritual holiness but rather the round-the-clock, day-in-and-day-out holiness that God demands of the people who represent his rule in every area of human existence. The case law was meant to express the holiness of God in all of Israel's life, not just in the sacrificial service of its priests or its reli-

---

15. William Dyrness, *Themes in Old Testament Theology* (Downers Grove, Ill.: Inter-Varsity Press, 1979), 138.

gious observances (only the priestly code of Leviticus 1–7 stipulates procedures for sacrifices and offerings).

The great variety and scope of the case law reminds us that there is no area of life, public or private, family or business, sexual relationship or political activity over which God's rule does not extend. God lays claim to the entire world, and the entire person who lives in his world. The law recognizes no sacred-secular distinction.

Internal as Well as External

Nor does the law recognize a private-public distinction. It is significant that all these prohibitions address the sin committed in secret. As Gerhard von Rad comments:

> There are many areas of life that the arm of earthly law and justice is too short to reach, or with which perhaps such law is incompetent to deal. But none of these areas escapes the watchful eyes of God, and the people are called to recognize that he exercises his righteous judgment even over that which is hidden from the eyes of men.[16]

Not Comprehensive but Paradigmatic

The great number and breadth of the laws might lead us to believe that the case law constitutes a comprehensive legal code. But this conclusion would be a mistake. Much of the case law application of the Ten Commandments was illustrative and paradigmatic in nature rather than providing a fully expressed law code. For example, the law prohibits work on the Sabbath, but it does not legally define what constitutes work. Principle rather than exhaustive detail always characterizes the law.

The Spirit over the Letter

This confirms that we keep the law not by rigidly following a detailed list of dos and don'ts. We are rather to demonstrate in our obedience an appreciation of the purpose and spirit of the law that requires application in the affairs of life. It must always be remem-

16. Gerhard von Rad, *Moses* (London: Lutterworth, 1960), 57–58.

bered that the individual laws stand upon the precedent of the Ten Commandments, which themselves are informed by the law of love. This is the law given by Israel's Redeemer God. It is his fatherly intention that his children walk in his holy ways that defines and situates biblical law.

DEUTERONOMY'S RESTATEMENT

Preparation for Entry

Forty years after the exodus and Sinai, after wandering in the desert for a generation, Israel camped in the plains of Moab, waiting to cross over the Jordan. Moses prepared the people to begin the conquest of the land by reminding them of God's word delivered at Sinai.

The Book of Deuteronomy, which consists of a series of sermons on the law (Deut. 1:5), is set out as a covenant renewal document (cf. Deut. 29:1). Moses recounts the historical experiences of the people (Deut. 1–3) in order to excite their gratitude for God's faithfulness and lead them to wholehearted obedience to his law (Deut. 4–11).

"Deuteronomy" means "second law" in Greek, but it's not really a second law. It is rather a restatement, and something of an expansion, of the law given at Sinai. Through repetition, exhortation, motivation, and warning, Moses seeks to inspire renewed commitment to God's revelation given at Sinai a generation before.

Vision Statement

Throughout the book, the message rings out that Yahweh gave the law not as a mere civil legislation but rather as a vision statement for the people of God. "They are not just idle words for you—they are your life" (Deut. 32:47). Thus Moses calls the people to "take to heart all the words solemnly declared" to it, and to instruct their children to keep the law.

167

Intended for Life and Well-Being

The law exists for Israel's benefit, to ensure Israel's well-being. Saved by God's grace, Israel would enjoy life to the full if she obeyed the law. Over and over again, the point of the law is "that it may go well with you" (Deut. 6:18; cf. 4:40; 5:33; 6:24; 12:28; 30:15–20). Moses tells them, "The LORD commanded us to obey all these decrees and to fear the LORD our God, so that we might always prosper and be kept alive, as is the case today." It will not do, therefore, to view the law as a set of arbitrary restrictions, intended to inhibit life, to make the people of God miserable, or to heap guilt upon man. Although regulatory, the law has a rich life as its object.[17]

A few summers back I built a deck on the back of my house. Our city building code stipulates that a deck must have a railing thirty-six inches high and that the railing is to have balusters every four inches. But the code says nothing about gates. My deck has a gate, a good strong gate, and a childproof latch. I put in that gate to keep my youngest son, who was then just a toddler, from straying off the deck. I did not build it because I am a curmudgeon, an enemy of joy who wanted to deprive my son of the adventure of the next-door neighbor's way too frisky Labrador retriever or cheat him of the joys and freedom of the traffic in the street. My goal was not deprivation. My restriction had his life and well-being in mind.

Yes, the law is regulatory. But its goal is life. It serves to remove the threats to life and loving relationship. Its discipline and regulation tell us that God loves his creation and his people. God calls Israel his son (Deut. 8:5; 14:1). Elements of emotional response are obviously present in such a relationship. Israel is to make the law a matter of its loving, thankful response to God (Deut. 15:7–16). The law is never merely outward as a legal requirement. Moses insists that it

17. That the law is for Israel's good is an often-heard incentive in the Book of Deuteronomy. "The assumption behind this kind of motivation is that God, as the creator of human beings, knows best what kind of social patterns will contribute to human well being. His laws were not meant to be negatively restricting, but to provide the conditions in which life can be most truly humane and beneficial." Wright, *Knowing Jesus Through the Old Testament*, 206.

is to be internalized, to become a matter of the heart (Deut. 6:5; 10:12; 26:16; 30:14).

A Privilege but Also a Duty

But Deuteronomy also includes an extended section enumerating covenant blessings and curses (Deut. 27:15–28:68). Their presence alerts us to the fact that the law is never a take-it-or-leave-it affair. While the law functions within relational, even familial parameters, it is law, not suggestion, request, or appeal. Breach of the law brings punishment. While the law is for our good and thus promises blessing to those who walk in its way, it also threatens those who spurn or ignore its instruction.

We should not forget that the family structure of the Old Testament was tightly authoritarian. Family life was carefully regulated by the family head, who disciplined his son as a sign of his ultimate concern (Deut. 8:5). The law is about love and duty. To love God and keep his law is a matter of full-bodied participation in the family of God and the duty a vassal owes to his lord.

The call to obey the law does not depend upon whether one wishes to obey. There is an absoluteness to its call, an absoluteness that is underlined by the presence of covenant curses. Duty has sometimes received short shrift in evangelical circles. We speak as if it is our attitude, our feelings about some activity, that make it worthy. But the law does not say honor your father and your mother if you love them or keep the Sabbath day holy when you are favorably disposed toward it.

God wants us to love him. He wants us to cherish his word. He wants us to obey his word out of gratitude for his gracious redemption and because we know that such obedience is an essential ingredient of a well-lived life. But God also demands our obedience because he is our Creator and rightful King.

10

LIFE IN THE LAND (I)
The King of Israel

I f you compare the Bible's story of the covenant relationship of Yahweh and his people to a story of a couple's marriage, we have so far considered the climactic and defining moment of the marriage (the resurrection), the story of how the couple first met and became involved (creation), how the hero saved the heroine (the flood, the exodus), and what they promised to each other in their wedding vows (the covenant words). What we look at next is how the couple got along in the marriage.

The Mosaic law, in the context of God's deliverance and sovereign, gracious choice, tells us what the marriage ought to look like. Much of the story of Scripture tells us what it did look like—how Israel sinned, and how God responded.

Israel's history offers ample testimony to justify a negative assessment of the relationship: This isn't working. There was nothing wrong with the covenant or the covenant Lord. The Lord loved unconditionally; the law was perfect. The problem was with the people's response. Something else was needed. That something would be the

Messiah, who alone would take away sin, extending forgiveness and changing the people's hearts.

What transpired in Israel's life in the land thus points both back and forward in time. Their continual idolatry, compromise, presumption, and disobedience point back to the covenant and law so graciously given and so ungraciously spurned. Yet their self-incurred plight and developing patterns in the relationship also point forward to a future hope, anticipating one who is yet to come who will be Prophet, Priest, and King.

In the Old Testament, these three offices of leadership emerge and give fuller definition to the covenant relationship. The priest, established by God in the law given at Sinai, represents the people in God's tabernacled presence and offers sacrifices in behalf of the people to atone for their sins. In this chapter, we chronicle the development of the office of king in Israel. In the next chapter, we consider the role of the prophet.

In the story of Israel's king, we witness grace indeed: a rebellious people rejects the Lord's direct rule, asking for a king like all the other nations have. Yahweh responds by giving them the king they demand, but one with an innovative job description that reserves sovereignty for God alone yet establishes Israel's king as covenant representative and premiere pointer to Messiah. In other words, God enfolds Israel's demand into his sovereign purpose and transforms it into something that someday will exceed their wildest dreams.

A THEOCRATIC CONFEDERATION

The Book of Joshua depicts a high point in the life of Israel as the covenant people of God. Despite setbacks as Israel enters the land promised to the patriarchs (Achan's sin, for example), the book presents a hopeful beginning, a time of glorious and public demonstrations of God's power and presence in Israel. Yahweh fulfills Joshua's promise to the people that "the LORD will do amazing things among you" (Josh. 3:5). The Jordan dries up just as the priests bearing the ark enter it. Jericho falls with the trumpet blast from Israel's parading army (Josh. 6). The southern confederation of Amorite

171

kings is defeated when God sends hailstones and halts the sun over Gibeon (Josh. 10). Israel defeats pagan kings and claims territory from Lebanon in the north to the Negev in the south.

With the book and the period of the Judges, however, the mood changes quite radically. Joshua's successes are replaced by frustrating inability to drive out alien peoples (Judg. 1:19, 28–36). Joshua's careful compliance with God's instruction to "be careful to obey all the law my servant Moses gave you" (Josh. 1:7) gives way to Israel's disobedience. Life in the land became a long struggle characterized by long periods of foreign occupation and short-lived Israelite victories.

Israel at this time is not what we would think of as a nation. Rather, it is a loose confederation of twelve tribes. It possesses no centralized government or capital city and none of the paraphernalia of an imperial court of the ancient Near East. Yet these confederated tribes share a single religious focus: the portable tent-shrine that houses the ark of the covenant, which itself contains the covenant documents of Sinai (Ex. 25:1–22; 37:1–9; Deut. 10:1–5). Traveling from tribe to tribe,[1] the ark visibly symbolizes the covenant relationship and God's ruling presence among Israel. Israel has no human king, for Yahweh, the Lord of the covenant, is the King of Israel.

The Judges: The Heroes of the Story?

This loose political organization under the theocratic rule of God survives only so long as the tribes are relatively small and cohesive. During the time of the judges, internal dissension and external threat sorely test this cohesiveness.

A judge is a person whom God called and anointed with his Spirit for the specific purpose of repelling the enemy. The judge succeeds, often without raising an army, because Yahweh is the Warrior-King of Israel. Albert Baylis rightly affirms that "the book of Judges is not a series of heroic tales. Its only hero is Yahweh, who works his vic-

---

1. The ark and the tent eventually found a permanent resting place at Shiloh (1 Sam. 1–4). There the people gathered for feast days, sought the presence of God, and renewed their covenant allegiance to him.

tories through the weaknesses of the judges."[2] The judge pushes back the enemy, but neither he nor anyone else follows up these victories with attempts to besiege and capture enemy cities. Instead, the judge's army disbands and the judge retires, returning to his land and his cattle.

The judge is not a king. He is no more than a surrogate for Yahweh, a rallying point in times of distress. Even though the judge enjoys wide powers of jurisdiction in Israel, he holds an episodic, nonpredictable, and nontransferable office under the sovereignty of the Spirit of God. Thus, Israel's judges do not fit the Near Eastern dynastic kingship pattern.

Why This Sad Cycle?

The Book of Judges depicts a continual pattern of Israel's failure to keep the first commandment. The framework of the book reflects a recurring cycle of sin (Judg. 2:13–18):

1. Israel forsakes Yahweh and serves the Baals.
2. Yahweh, incited to anger, gives Israel over to foreign plunderers.
3. The people cry to God because of their oppression and repent from their sins.
4. Yahweh, moved to pity, raises up a judge who saves Israel from the invader.

But almost as soon as the judge retires, this cycle of sin-servitude-supplication-and-salvation begins again.

Upon entering the land, Israel begins to worship other gods, especially the fertility deities of its neighbors. Israel had known many generations of slavery and then one as a nomadic people. Now Israel is becoming an agrarian people. And in this process it copies much of the indigenous Canaanite agrarian patterns. Since Canaanite

---

2. Albert Baylis, *From Creation to the Cross: Understanding the First Half of the Bible* (Grand Rapids: Zondervan, 1996), 38.

agrarian society included worship of the Baals, it was easy to copy the Canaanites here as well.

The Baals were deities of the earth, of the soil. But Israel knew Yahweh as a deity of events, a powerful doer of mighty deeds in history. The question is whether he also exercises power over the processes of nature. Is the God of the exodus also the Lord over the soil? Yes, Israel should have understood God's sovereignty over all the earth from the creation stories of Genesis. It should have understood his sovereignty over fertility from the seed drama of Genesis. It should have understood that the first commandment required exclusive allegiance to Yahweh. But it did not. In a polytheistic world that believed that deities exercise only territorial or domain power, it was easy—perhaps even reasonable—to associate Yahweh with history but not nature. The monotheism of the first commandment would not easily become part and parcel of Israel's ethos.

Ancient Near Eastern peoples commonly thought that the land belonged to the earth deities. In order to till the soil, a farmer needed divine permission and divine assistance. The Canaanites believed that the copulation of the god Baal with his female consort produced the ground's fertility. A farmer could enlist Baal's aid and blessing on his efforts by offering sacrifices and by participating in ritual prostitution. By having sex with a temple prostitute, the farmer paid homage to the god, participated in the divine mystery of the soil, and hence increased the fertility of the ground. By exercising his own sexual potencies, the farmer came into worshipful contact with Baal.

When Israel begins imitating these behaviors, the result is a syncretistic joining of the worship of Yahweh with the worship of Baal.[3] Israel splits allegiance between Yahweh and the Baals. The people thank Yahweh for military victories with one breath and Baal for good crops and healthy children with the next.

The difference between Yahweh and Baal is not merely a matter of perceived sovereignty, however. People understood the Baals in fairly impersonal and amoral terms. They do not summon people

---

3. Syncretism is the joining together of two opposing principles into a single reality in such a manner that the claims of neither are truly affirmed.

174

beyond their sexual nature, and they pose no moral standards and seek no real relationship with human beings. Worship is purely a matter of ritual. Thus, the syncretistic mind found it easy to reduce Yahweh and the worship of him to the level of Baal worship, to make the worship of Yahweh also a matter of mere cult participation. God's people find it easy to forget what we learn throughout the biblical story, that we can worship Yahweh only when we obey him.

As a result of this religious syncretism, during the period of the judges Yahweh becomes largely an occasional deity. Whenever an enemy threatens, Israel has only to tear down the altars of the Baals and convert to the worship of Yahweh. When peace returns to the land and the farmer can return to his crops, Israel returns to the Baals. Their vacillating religious allegiance is captured in Elijah's famous question atop Mount Carmel: "How long will you waver between two opinions? If the LORD is God, follow him; but if Baal is God, follow him" (1 Kings 18:21).

This sad cycle underscores Israel's failure to keep God's covenant. But it also underscores all that Israel should already have known about their God: his sovereign love, continually and graciously expressed in mighty deeds of deliverance, his lordship over and care for all creation, the goodness of God's law, and the fact that their relationship with him, while not effected by their obedience, is nevertheless nurtured by it. Something definitely needs fixing, and it isn't God or his covenant.

The Philistine Threat

The period of the judges lasted for about two hundred years after Israel's conquest of the land under Joshua. During that time Israel refrained from following the city-state model of the Canaanites and continually rejected the idea of a monarchy. For example, the judge, Gideon, when invited to be king over Israel, responds: "I will not rule over you, nor will my son rule over you. The LORD will rule over you" (Judg. 8:23).

The onslaught of the Philistines begins to change these sentiments, however. The confederation of tribes can survive only so long as its enemies are small and occasional. But unlike previous foes, the Philistines do not pose only a limited threat to neighboring tribes, a threat that a quickly rallied army could dispense with at a blow. The Philistines were western sea people who had been driven from their own lands by the Greeks. They pushed into Palestine in force. The Philistines possessed a disciplined army. What is more, the Philistine iron technology made their weapons vastly superior to those of the Israelites. Israel had never faced a strong, well-organized state like the Philistines. The ill-trained and poorly equipped Israelite tribal levies stand little chance against the disciplined army of the Philistines. Aiming at conquest and occupation, the Philistines threaten the existence of Israel in the land of promise.

In the decisive battle (1 Sam. 4), the Philistines defeat Israel and capture the ark of the covenant. Israel's war potential is destroyed, it is forbidden to work with metal (1 Sam. 13:19), and it becomes a vassal state of Philistia.

Under the leadership of Samuel, the last and the greatest of the judges (1 Sam. 7), Israel gathers enough strength to liberate itself from Philistine oppression. Unlike former judges, Samuel does not retire after the threat has been removed but judges Israel for the rest of his life. But as Samuel grows older, the people fear what may happen after he is gone.

ISRAEL ASKS FOR A KING

The pressures posed by the Philistine invasion eventually lead Israel to demand a monarchy (1 Sam. 8–12). Israel sees what power other nations have when they unify under the leadership of a king. They desire similar power and security. So they demand that Samuel "appoint a king to lead us, such as all the other nations have."

Israel had confessed Yahweh as its King at Mount Sinai (Ex. 15:18). How can a nation request a king if it already recognizes Yahweh as its exclusive King? The potential absolutism and dynastic succession of the ancient Near Eastern imperial model hardly conform to Yahweh's theocratic, covenantal leadership of Israel. Samuel interprets the request as a rejection of God's kingship. He perceives it as motivated by a desire to be like all the nations and reject their God-given vocation and mission to be a peculiar nation (Ex. 19:3–6), one that influences rather than conforms to surrounding nations.

Samuel warns the people of what they may lose by having a king. A king's army will require their sons, and his palace will need their daughters. And the king will require their taxes to pay for it all (1 Sam. 8:10–18). Whatever beneficial effects a monarchy might bring, when weighed against the debits, the demand for a king will cost Israel more than it will gain. From a strictly human standpoint the reality of Israel's kingship will prove to conform more to Samuel's warning than to the benefits they envision in their demand.[4]

At first Samuel will not hear of it. But God commands him to give in to the request. "It is not you they have rejected, but they have rejected me as their king" (1 Sam. 8:7).

Saul's Failure

Yahweh grants the request for a king even though it apparently rejects his own kingship. People in the ancient Near East viewed kings either as deities or as mediators between the people and the gods. This leads to an absolutization of the power and authority of the king. The law is the will—or even the whim—of the king. Furthermore, the fact that they also viewed kings primarily as political-military office bearers made ever present the temptation to reduce the life of the people to political terms.

God will not allow these endemic problems of monarchy to reign in Israel. He refuses to sanctify the political machinery of the ancient Near Eastern king. God and the king cannot be confused. The polit-

---

4. Christopher J. H. Wright notes that "it was kings who split the nations, who infringed the traditional pattern of the land tenure and accelerated the economic forces of oppression and inequality, whose pride cost the nations dear in the game of political alliances and wars, who introduced, or did little to prevent, recurring popular apostasy and idolatry. There were of course, notable exceptions. But in broad terms it can be said that the course of monarchy in Israel ran closer to the fear and warning of Samuel (1 Sam. 8:10–18) than to the hopes of the people." *Knowing Jesus Through the Old Testament* (Downers Grove, Ill.: InterVarsity Press, 1992), 117.

ical should serve the public, rather than the people serving the machinery of the king's court.

At God's instruction, Samuel anoints Saul as the king of Israel. But Yahweh places the obligation of covenant obedience upon Saul. He is not an absolute monarch. The law of God stands above the king. He is an instrument of the law rather than the reverse (see Deut. 17:18–20). The king is not above the covenant. Like any other man, he serves a covenant calling, and he reigns only at the behest of Yahweh (1 Sam. 12:14–15).[5] Nor is Saul, the anointed king, to serve as a covenant mediator. That role remains with Samuel, the judge and now the prophet-priest.

Saul fails to rule within these parameters. When Samuel arrives late to offer a sacrifice before a battle against the Philistines, Saul usurps Samuel's priestly office and offers the sacrifice himself. Saul later excuses his action by saying, "When I saw that the men were scattering, and that you did not come at the set time, and that the Philistines were assembling at Michmash, . . . I felt compelled to offer the burnt offering" (1 Sam. 13:11–12). Saul's excuse is baldly political. He has brought all under mere political expediency. Despite Yahweh's stipulations, the kingship continues to undercut his covenant lordship.

Samuel replies that Saul's days as king are numbered, that God will replace him with another. Samuel later accuses Saul of arrogance and rebellion against the Lord (1 Sam. 15:23): "Because you have rejected the word of the LORD, he has rejected you as king." Appointed as king for the purpose of leading Israel against the Philistines, Saul dies in battle against them. With this battle the Philistines achieve their deepest incursion into Palestine, virtually cutting Israel's territory in half (1 Sam. 31).

5. Wright comments: "Monarchy in Israel is not in itself sacred or divine. Kings in Israel could not trace their ancestry back to legendary gods or heroes of the prehistoric past. The historical, human origins of the institution and the all too human failings of its first holder, and indeed his illustrious successors, were of great significance; for they kept Israel free of that king of royal mythology which in neighbouring cultures gave unchangeable sacrosanctity to social stratification and 'pyramid' power-politics." Ibid., 117.

Three Mediatorial Offices

Through his prophet Samuel, God chooses and anoints David as king. But the threat to the covenant posed by kingship still exists. Monarchy meant a centralized, dynastic, and bureaucratic office that offered political solutions to internal issues and responded to external issues by constructing treaties that incur foreign entanglements.

How does God respond to this ongoing threat of political reductionism and the risk of loss of a covenant nation posed by the rise of the kingship? God's answer here is twofold. First, at this time we see a diversification of mediatorial offices. Israel had had prophets beginning with Moses. Up to this time, the prophetic function had, like the judge, been episodic and charismatic. Already during the reign of Saul, the role of prophet began to solidify into a permanent religious office. During David's reign the office comes into its own, distinguishable from the office of the king.

The prophet retains the right to censure the king on God's behalf should that be needed. Indeed, the message of censure will come to dominate the prophetic office during the era of the pre-exilic prophets. The prophetic office insists that its voice, and not that of the king, must prevail in issues that bear directly upon Israel's future as a covenant people.

The priestly office does trace back to the anointing of Aaron (Ex. 40:15).[6] Now, however, with the addition of kingship, the three begin to be established as the three primary offices in Israel. This separation of mediatorial offices ensures that Israel's king will rule under Yahweh's authority or be called to account.

God Makes Israel's King a Covenant Representative

In response to Israel's continuing temptation to political reductionism, God further amplifies his commitment to Israel's king. Here is the wonder: God will take up Israel's demand into his sovereign purposes. He will employ Israel's desire for a king within his covenan-

---

6. Cf. the covenant with Levi in Jer. 33:22–23.

tal program. God does not surrender his right to rule his covenant people but rather includes the office of the king as a structure within his theocratic rule. God will rule through the king. This God makes clear in the Davidic covenant of 2 Samuel 7.

Kingship and covenant will henceforth be linked under the kingship of Yahweh. In the typical ancient Near Eastern pattern, the king linked the people and the deity as the essential mediator between them. By contrast, in Israel, God will link the people and the king through covenant bonds and obligations. Israel's king is neither deified nor secularized. Rather, his office is established as part of the covenant between God and Israel.[7]

Kingship arises in Israel not from divine initiative but from questionable human motives.[8] Yet God in his mercy and sovereign foresight includes the king in his eternal plan. Through the king God will reveal some of the most glorious aspects of Israel's future. Christopher Wright concurs:

> The great paradox of the monarchy is that, though human in origin and infected from the very conception of the idea by tendencies to apostasy and corruption, God nevertheless took it up and wove it into the very heart of his redemptive purposes. The king became the focus of new dimensions of God's self-revelation. He represented God's rule among the people in the present and became the symbol of the future hope of God's ultimate perfect, Messianic rule among men.[9]

---

7. O. Palmer Robertson, *The Christ of the Covenants* (Grand Rapids: Baker, 1980), 250.

8. This is not to say that God did not intend a kingship in Israel from the beginning. When Jacob gave his final blessing to his sons (Gen. 49), he spoke of a kingship and a special single king who would come from the tribe of Judah and rule over Israel (Gen. 49:10; cf. Num. 24:17–19). Jacob's words seem to refer not only to David but also to the greater King yet to come, that is, to Jesus Christ. The problem of Saul's kingship is not that kingship is inherently evil in Israel but that Saul is the wrong king, for all the wrong reasons, at the wrong time, and from the wrong initiation.

9. Christopher J. H. Wright, *An Eye for an Eye: The Place of Old Testament Ethics Today* (Downers Grove, Ill.: InterVarsity Press, 1983), 118.

Although the sordid history of Israel will show that the monarchy will always be at best a mixed blessing, it will be through the monarchy that God works in Israel.

Thus, the king of Israel functions as covenant mediator. As the national head, the king represents the people. His obedience or disobedience will have enormous consequences for the national life. As a leader and a barometer of the national covenant life, the king embodies the cause of the people before God. Hence he is responsible to uphold and enforce the word of God in his personal life and the national existence of Israel. It was the king who set the pattern of life for good or ill. "As the kings went, so went the nation."[10]

Yet the kingly office supplants the calling of neither priest nor prophet. The king functions neither as cult leader nor as spokesman for Yahweh. Thus the mediatorship of the king is limited by the callings of the other two covenant offices.

The prophet's task is to declare God's covenant requirements and thus compel the political authority to acknowledge its inescapable accountability as a servant of God. In the next chapter we will see that it is the prophet who carries the covenant, for Yahweh calls him to speak the word of God to the people—and to the king.[11]

10. Dirk P. Bergsma, *Redemption: The Triumph of God's Great Plan* (Lansing, Ill.: Redeemer Books, 1989), 91.

11. While Robertson asserts the covenant mediatorial role of the king by connecting it to the Davidic blessing of the king as the son of Yahweh, and thus the king is an embodiment of God's rule in Israel, William J. Dumbrell approaches the king's role in the covenant through a comparison to the prophetic office. The king takes on the responsibilities of leadership in war (formerly the role of the judge), care over the political administration of the nation, and judicial oversight (1 Sam. 8, 20; 2 Sam. 15). Thus the king's responsibilities extend to the temporalities of life. It would be easy, however, to think of the prophet as a "spiritual" office and fall into a modern church-state distinction. Yet Dumbrell points out that the prophetic retains to itself the right to critique the king—even in political and military affairs—when the Spirit of the God so directs. Prophecy "acted under a system of final divine kingship and as a sort of first minister. Therefore, it constantly made the demand on kingship to submit in all areas and continually rebuked the naked and unbridled use of royal authority." William J. Dumbrell, *Covenant and Creation: A Theology of the Old Testament Covenants* (London: Paternoster: 1984), 138.

THE DAVIDIC COVENANT

It is in the Davidic covenant that we view Yahweh's full appropriation of the kingship for his own purposes, the new dimensions of revelation and the future hope of God's messianic rule.

David's kingly activities display his heart desire to bring his kingship under the greater throne of Yahweh. He wrests Jerusalem from the Jebusites and brings the ark to the city (2 Sam. 5–6), thus establishing Jerusalem as his capital. In response, through his prophet Nathan, Yahweh declares to David:

> This is what the LORD Almighty says: I took you from the pasture and from following the flock to be ruler over my people Israel. I have been with you wherever you have gone, and I have cut off all your enemies from before you. Now I will make your name great, like the names of the greatest men of the earth. And I will provide a place for my people Israel and will plant them so that they can have a home of their own and no longer be disturbed. Wicked people will not oppress them anymore, as they did at the beginning and have done ever since the time I appointed leaders over my people Israel. I will also give you rest from all your enemies.
>
> The LORD declares to you that the LORD himself will establish a house for you: When your days are over and you rest with your fathers, I will raise up your offspring to succeed you, who will come from your own body, and I will establish his kingdom. He is the one who will build a house for my Name, and I will establish the throne of his kingdom forever. I will be his father, and he will be my son. When he does wrong, I will punish him with the rod of men, with floggings inflicted by men. But my love will never be taken away from him, as I took it away from Saul, whom I removed from before you. Your house and your kingdom will endure forever before me; your throne will be established forever. (2 Sam. 7:8–16)

The word *covenant* does not appear in these promises. But Scripture confirms that David clearly regards it as a covenant. For he responds, "Is not my house right with God? Has he not made with me an everlasting covenant, arranged and secured in every part?" And Yahweh himself declares, "I have made a covenant with my chosen one, I have sworn to David my servant, 'I will establish your line forever and make your throne firm through all generations' " (Ps. 89:3–4; cf. 132:11–12).

Furthermore, Yahweh's message evidences a number of typical covenantal elements. It is divinely initiated. It contains promises. It is mutually binding. And, according to Psalm 132:1–12, it places upon the Davidic house the obligation of faithfulness to Yahweh and his law.

The Davidic Covenant Harks Back to God's Covenant with Abraham

Elements of the Davidic covenant refer most obviously to the Abrahamic covenant but also to the Mosaic covenant. In fulfillment of God's covenant promise to Abraham of a people and a land, Abraham's offspring have become a great nation under David.

David defeats Israel's enemies and fortifies its borders. His military victories have extended Israel's control over the entire territory promised to Abraham. God gives David rest from his enemies. David unifies the tribes of Israel into a single nation. He transforms it into a national entity.

Thus to no small extent, the kingship of David represents a marked fulfillment of the promises of the Abrahamic covenant. Israel is no longer a nomadic collection of tribes on their way to someplace but rather a nation, a people with a presence in the world, and hence positioned to fulfill their divine calling to be a kingdom of priests and a holy nation, living the word of God among the nations (Ex. 19:4–6). Under David's reign, Israel most fully fulfills this mission.

New Dimensions of the Davidic Covenant

This covenant also echoes further aspects of Yahweh's promises to Abraham. God's promises to David include a son and heir, a great name, and a special relationship (Gen. 12). But even as the Davidic covenant harks back to God's promises to Abraham, it also evidences astonishing new features. Something new is added to the unfolding story that will drive God's covenantal intentions forward.

183

First, this message reveals that it will be through the Davidic house that God will fulfill his patriarchal promise to protect his people and their land. Prior to this point, God had manifested himself as the Lord of the covenant. But now the king of Israel will serve as Yahweh's specific instrument to secure his people in the land of promise and give them peace.

Now God openly situates his throne in a single locality. Rather than ruling from a mobile sanctuary, God reigns from Mount Zion in Jerusalem. O. Palmer Robertson describes the significance of David's reign for the biblical theme of the kingdom:

> In the Davidic covenant God's purposes to redeem a people to himself reach their climactic stage of realization so far as the Old Testament is concerned. Under David the kingdom arrives. God formally establishes the manner by which he shall rule among his people.
>
> Not only has the kingdom come. The king has come. The ark is brought triumphantly to Jerusalem. God himself associates his kingship with the throne of David.[12]

In a climactic sense, it may be said that under David the kingdom has come.

Second, God promises to establish David's house forever (cf. Ps. 89:28–29). David has wanted to replace the portable tent-shrine with a stone temple in Jerusalem, a permanent dwelling place for the ark. He wishes to build a house for the Lord. God declares, however, that it will be the reverse: Yahweh will establish David's house. Robertson observes that when David says "house," he means "temple"; but when Yahweh says "house," it means "dynasty." Yet the two issues are linked together.

> [God] shall establish David's dynasty, and David's dynasty shall establish his permanent dwelling-place. But the order of grace must be maintained. First, the Lord sovereignly establishes David's dynasty; then the dynasty of David shall establish the Lord's dwelling-place.[13]

12. Robertson, *The Christ of the Covenants*, 229.
13. Ibid., 232–33.

Furthermore, the issue in both is perpetuity. "David wishes to establish for God a permanent dwelling-place in Israel. God declares that he shall establish the perpetual dynasty of David."[14]

The connection between houses has a further, more theologically significant, point to make. God now binds his presence, his dwelling with his people, to the Davidic kingship. Again Robertson comments: "The net effect of this close interchange on the basis of the 'house' figure is to bind David's rule to God's rule, and *vice versa*. God shall maintain his permanent dwelling-place as king in Israel through the kingship of the Davidic line."[15]

The wordplay on "house" takes on decidedly messianic overtones. In the Messiah, the one who will come from David's dynasty, God will be tangibly present with his people. God will dwell preeminently in the chosen son of David. In Jesus, the son of David (Matt. 1:1), God temples with his people (John 1:14). The temple of flesh eclipses the temple of stone (John 2:21). God abides, has his place of residence—his house—in Jesus Christ (John 14:1–10).

Third, God promises to be a father to David's royal descendants. On one level this is no more than a statement of adoption and protection. God promises to be with and protect the Davidic kingship and lineage. But more pointedly, David's reign symbolizes the reign of Israel's heavenly King. Finally, in linking the son of David and the son of God, the Davidic covenant bears immense messianic significance (see Ezek. 34:23–24). Not only will the Davidic king mediate and reflect the character of God. Robertson rightly claims that "at the heart of the Davidic covenant is the Immanuel principle."[16] Ultimately the two are a single kingship in Jesus Christ. It is in Christ that God establishes the throne of David's kingdom forever (cf. 1 Chron. 22:9–10; Heb. 1:2; 5:5–6).

14. Ibid., 232.
15. Ibid., 233.
16. Ibid., 232.

HOW IT GOES FOR ISRAEL'S KINGS

While some of Judah's kings seem to rise above the common expectations of their age (see e.g., 1 Kings 20:31ff.), many fail miserably in the Davidic calling to rule in Israel on God's behalf and reflect his glory. The history of the Davidic monarchy will record that no member until Jesus fully satisfies the kingly obligation of obedience and fulfills the promise of the covenant.

Solomon, David's son and successor to the throne, brings the people rest and joy as he builds the temple, giving a visible presence to the divine throne (1 Kings 8:66). But Solomon's reign is characterized more by political expediency, the corruption of power, and the introduction of foreign influences and ways into Israel, than it is by virtue and justice. Samuel's warning about monarchies (1 Sam. 8:10–18) comes to fruition more quickly than even he feared. The growing cost of the empire brought onerous taxation, military conscription, and forced labor upon the people.

Discontent grows during his reign and that of his son Rehoboam, especially among the northern tribes, who seem to suffer more than the royal tribe of Judah. The northern tribes are incited to rebellion. Rehoboam ignores the pleas of the people to end the oppression and exploitation. Instead he abuses his covenant office, exploiting it to accumulate personal wealth and prestige. The ten northern tribes, led by Jeroboam, secede from the Davidic kingdom (now known as Judah) and form a separate Hebrew nation (now designated Israel).

But we witness no reformation of the covenant life in the northern kingdom, despite its birth by resistance to covenant disobedience. Indeed, the pattern of following foreign styles and worship introduced under Solomon only worsens. And the subordination of the covenant to political ends—a kind of civil religion—characterizes the northern kingdom.

The Davidic king's disobedient actions thus unleash divine judgment. After Solomon's death much of the blessing of the Davidic covenant fades from sight. Yet God keeps his promise that the Davidic line will not fall. He refuses to let even disobedient kings or wayward people thwart his covenant. Scripture shows that sin brings punishment (2 Sam. 7:14) but not the removal of David's kingly line (2 Sam. 7:15; Ps. 89:30–33).

The Prophets Turn Royal Failure into Messianic Hope

One could argue that, as a mechanism for divine rule, the Davidic dynasty was a miserable failure. The Davidic dynasty was extremely long-lived in ancient Near Eastern terms—over four hundred years. However, about half of those years were lived either in exile or under foreign domination.

But the promises of the Davidic covenant take on a significant critical and eschatological import during the period of the prophets. Thus the prophets will anticipate an ideal King who will fulfill the Davidic promise (Isa. 9:2–7; 11:1–9; Jer. 23:1–8; Ezek. 34:1–31). God has appointed the Davidic house to be an instrument for establishing his kingdom among the nations. God will establish the presence of his kingship through the agency of the theocratic king. The prophets pick up this vision, and in their hands it will become a principle for the censure of a recalcitrant monarchy and a prayer for the coming of the Messiah.

LIFE IN THE LAND (2)
The Word of the Prophets

Prophets served Israel long before the eighth century B.C., the era of the writing prophets, men like Hosea, Amos, and Isaiah, through the time of Israel's exile in the fifth century B.C. Prophets minister in times of crisis, sounding the alarm, warning Israel of impending judgment whenever it has failed to seek the Lord, calling it back to its mission in the world. In all eras of Israel's history, the prophet's calling is to enforce the revelation God gave at Sinai—crises from Ahab's sponsorship of Baal worship, to the national and political crises posed by Assyrian and Babylonian threats, and the crisis with which the postexilic community struggles.

The prophets are complainers. They rant; they rave; they threaten. The prophets rail against Israel's worship, the monarchy, the cultic institutions, and the general lifestyle of the people. They aim their criticisms at the habits and presumptions, the complacency and waywardness of Israelite society.

A student once asked me why the vast majority of my criticism in lectures targeted the contemporary church and Christian culture rather than the sins of the secular world. I answered that I was merely following sound biblical precedent. The prophets do not expend their critical energies complaining about the militaristic cruelty of the Assyrians. Nor does Jesus deliver scathing rebukes of the easy syncretism of Roman culture. Rather, both level their criticism at Israel, the people whom God had called to be his light within a sin-darkened world.

But the fact that the prophets focus upon the covenant people of God shows that their complaints and threats have a positive purpose: to call the covenant community back to faithfully obeying the God who had redeemed them by his mighty deeds on their behalf.

THE PROPHETS CALL GOD'S PEOPLE BACK TO THE MOSAIC LAW

We rightly associate Moses with the writing of the Pentateuch, and we think of Scripture's story of him as beginning with his lowly birth to Hebrew slaves in Egypt, moving through his leading the Hebrews out of Egypt and receiving the law from God at Sinai, to his final addresses (the Book of Deuteronomy) about forty years after Sinai.

But this is not the end of Moses in the Old Testament. For in addition to holding this special place in redemptive history (Heb. 3:1–5), Moses is also the fountainhead of the prophets. Indeed, we may regard him as Israel's first prophet (Deut. 34:10–12).

We find the legacy of Moses and the Mosaic revelation written large on every page of the Old Testament prophets. Willem Van Gemeren's assessment is no overstatement: "The prophetic message was rooted in the Mosaic revelation, just as the apostolic teaching (*paradosis* or 'tradition') was rooted in Jesus' teaching."[1] Like Moses, all prophets are called by God and empowered by the Holy Spirit to speak God's word. And the words God give them to speak must be continuous with the word given through Moses (Deut. 13:1–5).

Innovators?

A surface reading of the Old Testament might suggest that the prophets are rejecting the Mosaic revelation. The festivals, sacrifices,

---

1. Willem A. Van Gemeren, *Interpreting the Prophetic Word* (Grand Rapids: Zondervan, 1990), 28.

and priesthood of Israel had been prescribed by Moses. Yet the prophets cast a decidedly jaundiced eye upon the formal elements of Israel's religious life. The prophets announce that Yahweh cares little, if at all, for the rituals and rites of religion. For example, God speaks through Amos:

> I cannot stand your assemblies.
> Even though you bring me burnt offerings and grain offerings,
>   I will not accept them.
> Though you bring choice fellowship offerings,
>   I will have no regard for them.
> Away with the noise of your songs!
>   I will not listen to the music of your harps. (Amos 5:21–23)[2]

Some commentators have interpreted the prophets' vehemence toward the cultic system of their day as indicating the rise of a new kind of religion in Israel, an internal and individualistic piety that rejected the formal and corporate religion of the Mosaic era. They argue that the prophets mean to replace temple and sacrifice with a thoroughly individualistic and informal religion of the heart.

As enticing as our contemporary culture finds this suggestion, it misses the point of the prophetic critique. What the prophets denounce is not the institutions of Hebrew religion but rather what the Israelites had come to make of these things. The people had come to presume that these gifts of God's grace assured them of God's favor, whatever their individual or corporate behavior might be—Yahweh is our God. Being an Israelite means automatic inclusion in the blessings of the covenant. And the covenant means automatic inclusion in God's elective love. The prophets' direct their most stinging vehemence at those who so presume upon the grace of God. The writing prophets write to counter just such presumption.

Thus their message does not entail a rejection or even a revision of the Mosaic revelation. Quite the contrary: the prophets, as reformers, seek to call Israel back to the covenant's original meaning and vitality.

---

2. Cf. Isa. 1:11–14; Jer. 7:21.

What they claim is the fundamental priority of obedience to God over ritual and sacrifice (Hos. 6:6; Isa. 1:11–12; 58:1–7; Jer. 7:1–11).

Covenant Enforcers

The prophets' message is in no way new. The Mosaic law specifies that essential covenant requirements of loyalty and obedience come before the sacrificial regulations. And almost three hundred years before the writing prophets, Samuel tersely captures this priority: "To obey is better than sacrifice" (1 Sam. 15:22).

The problem the prophets address is not some failure inherent in the promises or provisions of God but the failure of Israel to respond rightly to God's gracious initiations. Rather than being characterized by faithfulness and love, rather than being a light to the nations through its embodiment of covenant life, Israel engages in idolatry, gross social injustice, and religious syncretism. There is no shortage of religion and ritual, but the people have forgotten the covenant. They have forgotten why Yahweh had delivered them from Egypt and elected them, why he had given them the land, and why he had given them his law.

The rampant social injustice of the late eighth century B.C., for example, made a mockery of Israel's religious pretensions (Amos 4:4–5; 5:21–27; 8:5–6). All the prophets link righteousness inseparably with justice. Yahweh will not be worshiped and cannot be known apart from a commitment to justice (Jer. 9:23–24; 22:15–16).

The situation calls for a policing of Israel's response to the covenant. The prophets assume this role. Thus we might think of them as covenant enforcers. The prophets are not confessional, political, or social innovators. Rather, they serve as heirs and interpreters of a tradition that goes back to Moses and Abraham. They call Israel back to its true character and calling, back to the law, back to the covenant.

Curse and Blessing, Condemnation and Comfort

The message of the early writing prophets typically contained four elements:

1. A recitation of the history of redemption. In repeating the great things that God had done for Israel the prophets reminded the king and the people of the kingly, fatherly, and holy character of God.
2. A proclamation of Israel's covenant obligations. The prophets cast this declaration of God's requirements in terms from the Mosaic revelation. If the first element reminded Israel who the Lord is, the second reminded them who they were in covenant relationship with him.
3. A statement of covenant indictment. The prophets enumerated to Israel its sins.
4. A declaration of Yahweh's covenant curse upon Israel, the inevitable result if Israel refused to do God's will.
5. The prophets of the exile and the postexilic period tended to add a further element: a statement of the blessed consequences that would come upon the faithful who repented from sin and returned to God's covenant ways.

In all of this is implied the if-then structure of the Mosaic revelation. From the beginning the law was given with covenant curses. The prophet's job is to warn Israel of those curses when its manner of life runs counter to God's revealed expectations for his people. The prophets proclaim that the promised blessings will cease and Israel will incur God's wrath if it breaks the covenant.

As covenant enforcers, the prophets draw heavily upon the lists of blessings and curses in the Mosaic legislation. The message of the preexilic prophets consists almost entirely of indictment of covenant breach and declaration of the curses that attend disobedience. The curses include disease, destitution, drought, death, disgrace, defeat, danger, and deportation.[3]

Amos, the first of the writing prophets, addresses the northern kingdom in about 760 B.C., a generation before its fall to the Assyrians. Typical of the prophetic pattern, Amos recounts Israel's history:

---

3. Lev. 26:14–39 and Deut. 4:15–28; 28:15–32, the curse texts accompanying the Mosaic covenant, provided the well from which the prophets drew for their indictments against Israel.

beginning with the exodus, he recalls the wilderness and Israel's victorious entrance into the land, and his recitation follows though to the rise of the prophets (Amos 2:10–16). But he is not congratulating Israel for past glories or blessings. He appeals to the past out of prophetic concern about the present. The past stands in stark contrast to Israel's present condition. Israel's corruption of worship and rampant social injustice violates all that Israel's history was designed to make of them. Yahweh had intended Israel to exemplify his character in witness to the nations. If Israel kept the law, its walk in the world would be such that others would take notice and inquire about Yahweh (Deut. 4:6–8). But if they failed to obey, God would fulfill his threat of judgment upon his people. This too would elicit questions from the nations. But the nations would conclude the same thing either way: God faithfully keeps his covenant promises (Deut. 29:22–28).

The northern kingdom fell under Assyrian domination in 722 B.C. The southern kingdom of Judah remained independent—although often paying vassalage tribute—until the Babylonian invasion of that territory in 587 B.C. After 587, the prophets often offered comfort rather than warning. Thus covenant blessing rather than curse became prominent in the exilic and postexilic prophets. Typical blessings included life, health, prosperity, agricultural abundance, respect, and safety from external threat.

This historical sequence of curse and then blessing conforms to the pattern of divine judgment that we saw in the Noahic flood narrative. God is more interested in mercy than judgment. His judgment takes place for the sake of his grace. He means his discipline to restore his people to covenant relationship with him.

Corporate Oracles

Two further comments regarding prophetic curse: First, the prophets' declaration of curse and blessing is corporate—they were delivered to the nation of Israel as a whole. The modern reader should not individualize either the warnings or the blessings. It is always true that the relationship between the individual person and the covenant community is dynamic. The community is made up of persons. A disobedient nation is made up of disobedient people. But the interconnectedness of the individual and the nation is just what prevents our interpreting the prophets' words entirely individualistically.

Second, the prophets deliver their warnings in oracles, "thus says the Lord" sayings or sermons. The prophet does not speak for or from himself. He is little more than a mouthpiece for God. The language of the prophet is often so strong that, if it were not from God, it would be rejected as the ravings of a madman. Imagine, for example, a visiting preacher speaking this message from the pulpit of your church:

> Hear this word, you cows of Bashan on Mount Samaria,
>   you women who oppress the poor and crush the needy
>   and say to your husbands, "Bring us some drinks!"
> The Sovereign LORD has sworn by his holiness:
>   "The time will surely come
> when you will be taken away with hooks,
>   the last of you with fishhooks.
> You will each go straight out
>   through breaks in the wall,
>   and you will be cast out toward Harmon. (Amos 4:1–3)

You might well feel compelled to show the door to the preacher of these words.

Even though they spoke with divine authority, the prophets' condemnation of Israel's corruption, apostasy, and complacency was not well received. Their rejection of Israel's optimistic confidence in its manifest and glorious destiny appeared seditious to political authorities and dangerously heretical to the religious establishment.

Interpreters of Historical Events

Through the historic tradition and their experience with Yahweh, the prophets recognize his awesome presence and ceaseless activity in the world. They see him at work in the world-shaking events of

194

their times. The God who made himself known in the former times is also intensely active in current events.

> Ah, the thunder of many peoples,
> they thunder like the thunder of the sea!
> Ah, the roar of nations;
> they roar like the roaring of mighty waters! (Isa. 17:12 ESV)

God is speaking through events. And the prophet is sent to translate those actions into speech. The prophetic message is event plus interpretation: "This is happening because . . ." or "This is what will happen if you continue in your present behaviors."

ISRAEL FORSAKES THE COVENANT

Thus the *if* of the prophetic message is important. It is a misunderstanding of the prophets to think of them as delivering revelations of predetermined futures. Christopher Wright explains:

There is a conditional element in the promise, inasmuch as its fulfillment requires the response of faith and obedience from the recipients of the promise. The prophets ruthlessly demolished Israel's confidence in the very things that were replete with attached promises of God, whenever that confidence was not linked to moral response. Amos, faced with a people who were living in blatant disobedience to God's social demands, turned the fundamental promises upside down. Neither election itself (3:2), nor the exodus itself (9:7), nor the land itself (2:10–16, 5:2), were any guarantee of immunity from God's judgment.[4]

The Sin of God's People

Of the sins of Israel, the one that stands out as the wellspring from which all others flow is this: it presumes upon the covenant goodness of God. The prophets view the people's transgressions not merely as the common lot of fallen humankind, a breach of God's covenant

---

4. Christopher J. H. Wright, *Knowing Jesus Through the Old Testament* (Downers Grove, Ill.: InterVarsity Press, 1992), 69.

of creation. Its sin is much more reprehensible in light of God's gracious acts of deliverance on Israel's behalf. It is rejecting God's demonstrated love for Israel.

Amos hints that Israel's sinful lifestyle results, at least in part, from seeking to be like the other nations. They mimic the Canaanites by divorcing religion from personal relationship and moral response, reducing the worship of God to the bare formalities of religion. They also adopt the Canaanites' pagan religious practices. Its imitation of Canaanite styles of worship issues in a lifestyle precisely opposite of what God intended for his people.[5]

Idolatry

Idolatry takes one of two forms, and both appear to occur during the period of the prophets. First, one can worship a false god, Baal, for example. The prophets vehemently insist that only Yahweh is God. The prophetic assessment of the pagan deities is dismissive and sarcastic. They ridicule idols as the work of human hands (Isa. 2:8), manufactured things falsely invested with deity (Hos. 14:3). An idol is nothing but a "stick of wood" (Hos. 4:12). Although represented as having hands, eyes, and feet, the pagan gods cannot touch, see, hear or move (Ps. 115:3–8).[6]

The second form of idolatry is to misrepresent Yahweh. R. C. Sproul comments that "the very essence of idolatry involves the distortion of God's character."[7] To portray God other than he truly is, as less than he has revealed himself, is to worship a false god. "If you do not worship and serve the *right* God, you worship a *false* one."[8]

5. Amos 2:7–8 might indicate that the temple of Yahweh was even used for the purposes of ritual prostitution, as was the habit at the temple of the Baals.

6. Compare Elijah's contest with the priests of Baal atop Mount Carmel (1 Kings 18), where the same point is made. Baal does not hear and cannot answer the prayers of his devotees. Yahweh mocks the idols and the idol maker in Isaiah 41:21–29. He taunts them to speak, to "do something, whether good or bad, so that we will be dismayed and filled with fear" (Isa. 41:23). Over against the lifeless idol, Yahweh speaks and acts mightily in history.

7. R. C. Sproul, "Foreword,"in *Whatever Happened to the Reformation?* ed. Gary L. W. Johnson and F. Fowler White (Phillipsburg, N.J.: P&R, 2001), xiii.

8. Ibid, xii.

Israel misrepresents Yahweh by shutting him up in the temple, divorcing religion from life. This is to worship a false god under the name of Yahweh. Thus the prophets relay that God abhors their worship as a mockery and an abomination.

Israel comes to think of the covenant in purely biological and hereditary terms. They imagine that Yahweh is bound to them, that their visible traditions—temple, priesthood, possessing the promised land, the sacrificial system, the Davidic monarchy, and even the office of the prophet—guarantee divine favor. The temple becomes something of a fetish, a magical guarantee of their God Yahweh's protection and blessing (Jer. 5:12; 7:14).

Greed

The total and exclusive loyalty to Yahweh that the law requires is not just a matter of the worship of Yahweh alone, to the exclusion of all other gods. It involves also a moral commitment to the character and values of Yahweh. While Israel enjoys the benefits of covenant relationship with God—and indeed counts them its due—it does not care for the responsibilities that attend such a high calling in the world. What Israel wants is not a theocracy, a kingdom where Yahweh is the true King, but a kingdom like any other. They do not want to be peculiar but rather just like their neighbors. Israel prefers being a player in world politics and power to being a moral example to the world. Rather than following a law that encourages love, compassion, and justice, Israel seeks riches, power, and importance in the eyes of others.

The great economic expansion of the northern and the southern kingdoms in the eighth century B.C. produces an increasingly corrupt society as it divorced its religious life from its social and economic existence. From the time of David on, Israel begins to misuse its strategic location for profit, growing rich on the tolls levied on the trade caravan passing through Palestine. A wealthy, luxury-loving upper class arises which, in an ever-increasing lust for profit, exploits and abuses the less advantaged through corrupt business practices.

The sad irony of this is that the people who travel through Israel were meant to see and hear of the love and rule of Yahweh. But instead Israel becomes a covetous audience to the wealth of the world passing before it. Instead of Israel being a light to the nations, it is tempted to distraction by the wealth of the caravans.

Injustice

As Yahweh and his law are forgotten, basic justice for Israel's weaker citizens is increasingly circumvented. The richer upper classes retain few scruples in their lust to acquire land and possessions, and the disparity between the upper and the lower classes grows as the rich and powerful defraud and dispossess small land owners. These, we must not forget, are not the acts of godless pagans but rather those of extremely religious people, indeed the people that God had chosen to represent him in the world.

The prophets denounce the separation of religious observance and social morality (Amos 5:7; Isa. 1:27–28; 30:18). There is no righteousness without justice. Indeed, God calls Israel to walk justly in the world in order to model benevolence, kindness, and generosity of God's own gracious righteousness (Deut. 32:4; Isa. 5:16; 61:8).[9]

The prophets warn that if Israel does not change its ways, return to the covenant of Sinai and re-embrace its God-given calling, then it will lose its God-given blessings. The God who controls the movements of nations will use the very nations he intended Israel to serve

---

9. As the prophets understood and employed the ideas, righteousness is conformity to a standard or norm, while justice is bringing historical realities into conformity with the norm. While never questioning the grounding of righteousness in God's gracious action, the prophets maintained that showing mercy to the alien, the orphan, and the widow (a recurrent trinity in the prophets), releasing the oppressed, and seeking justice in the courts cannot be separated from righteousness. Failure to do justice will reap judgment, a judgment that could include expulsion from the land or even being cut off from the people of God. Isa. 1:18–20 promises redemption but only if Israel walks in the way of God. Isaiah 58 declares the way of the righteous God of Israel to be one of seeking justice. When one has acted justly, which Isaiah there defines as actively removing oppression, one will then find true personal healing. The *then* is repeated three times in Isa. 1:8–11. Seek justice, and then you will be righteous, and the glory of the Lord will be your protection. Seek justice, and then the Lord will hear your prayers. Seek justice, and then you will be a light to the nations.

as a rod of discipline against it. If Israel refuses to live according to the covenant, its people will know curses rather than blessings. If Israel fails to use the land for the mission of Yahweh, others will take it. Foreign powers will defeat Israel and take it captive into exile in distant lands (Amos 5–8). As Israel denies justice, Israel will have justice denied. Wanting to become rich and powerful, it will become destitute and enslaved. Worshiping foreign gods, Israel will serve foreign peoples who will force its worship until it gags on the stench of sacrifice and the immorality of the Baals.

THE PROPHET AND THE FUTURE

Many people think that the prophets were concerned only with the future, that their messages contained cryptic but exact information about future events, often very distant future events. Thus they understand "prophesy" to mean "to predict the future." Many evangelical Christians believe that the prophets foretell the course of world events, particularly the events immediately prior to or adjacent to the return of the Lord.

To counteract this imbalanced conception of the nature of biblical prophecy, some theologians have claimed that the prophets were not foretellers but forthtellers. They were primarily concerned to declare the word of God to their generation, a generation that desperately needed to hear a word of warning and encouragement.[10] While I appreciate the distinction, and I believe that its emphasis is in the right place, I think it runs the risk of lopping off the future from prophetic concern. In fact, the prophets have much to say about the future.

Divine Promise, Not Prophetic Prediction

What we need are some controls or guidelines for understanding the relationship between the biblical prophets and the future. I would

10. For example see Stephen Winward, *A Guide to the Prophets* (Atlanta: John Knox, 1969), 31–32.

like to suggest that rather than regarding prophecy as prediction, it is more helpful to think of it as divine promise.

The prophets emphasize neither a predetermined plan of occurrence, to which history conforms like an actor performing a script, nor God's precognition of future events. While God certainly knows the future exhaustively, precognition in itself is not very significant. Knowing the future is not the same as having the power to effect the future. And that is precisely what the prophetic word about the future concerns. The message of biblical prophecy is that God is faithful to his promises and able to see to it that his promises come to fulfillment.

Again, I want to affirm God's ability to know the future. In classical theological language, God possesses future omniscience. But no one would care about God's foreknowledge—say, whether you or I will enjoy good health next year—unless God's knowing the future was related to his power to make the future certain.

We see this same reality in our relationship to the future. When a judge passes sentence upon a criminal, he is not predicting what will happen or passively reporting a predetermined future. Rather, the judge is decreeing the future of the person before him: he has the power and authority to see that the sentence is carried out. Similarly, when I prepare a syllabus for a course in covenant theology in early August, I set down that on a given day in November I will lecture on the prophets and the future. I am not peering into a crystal ball and recording into my course syllabus history written beforehand. The significance of the syllabus is that as the instructor I am in a position to effect my intention. Neither the judge nor I possess an omniscient foresight as God does, but the point remains the same: the speaker possesses the power and authority to fulfill the promise. The biblical prophets testify to this: God will fulfill his promises. God shapes the future to fit his faithfulness.

The Prophets Speak of the Future to Encourage the People in the Present

Whatever the prophets say about the future they make understandable to and relevant for their generation. In fact, the future that

200

the prophets have in mind is usually the immediate future, the future from the standpoint of the prophets' contemporaries. Thus, the vast majority of the prophetic future is actually our past. Less than 5 percent of the oracles of the prophets deal with what is for us still future. To be sure, the prophets proclaim the coming of the Messiah, the dawning of a new age in the history of the covenant, and God's future consummation of history. But these elements of the prophetic vision are meant to warn and encourage the prophets' generation.

Seeing what God promises to do in and with history strongly transmits the message that God is sovereign: he is not taken by surprise, he is not thwarted, and he will be victorious in his redemptive purpose. This message comforts Israel the way Christ's resurrection from the dead comforts Christians today.

The Book of Isaiah provides a perfect example of how the prophetic declaration of the future for the purpose of warning, comfort, and encouragement comes to us. With the Assyrian incursions into Palestine and then with the rise of the power of Babylon, the people of Israel wonder whether Yahweh still controls history. Perhaps the gods of the conquering nations are more powerful than Yahweh. Through the prophet, Yahweh speaks to the issue in order to comfort his people. Yahweh challenges Israel to compare him to any of the deities of Babylon:

> To whom will you compare me or count me equal?
> > To whom will you liken me that we may be compared?
> Some pour out gold from their bags
> > and weigh out silver on the scales;
> they hire a goldsmith to make it into a god,
> > and they bow down and worship it.
> They lift it to their shoulders and carry it;
> > they set it up in its place, and there it stands.
> > From that spot it cannot move.
> Though one cries out to it, it does not answer;
> > it cannot save him from his troubles.
>
> Remember this, fix it in mind,
> > take it to heart, you rebels.

Remember the former things, those of long ago;
    I am God, and there is no other;
    I am God, and there is none like me.
I make known the end from the beginning,
    from ancient times, what is still to come.
I say: My purpose will stand,
    and I will do all that I please.
From the east I summon a bird of prey;
    from a far-off land, a man to fulfill my purpose.
What I have said, that will I bring about;
    what I have planned, that will I do. (Isa. 46:5–11)

Yahweh alone is the God who effects the future. And only such a God may be trusted utterly to redeem the people he loves.

The Prophets Warn of the Future Consequences of Israel's Moral and Covenantal Condition

The prophets were concerned with the future as the outcome of the present. The events that the prophets promised were the consequence of the moral-covenantal condition of the present generation. The if-then structure of the prophetic oracle is important, as Stephen Winward comments:

The crop to be harvested was already growing in the field of the world. There was a nexus of cause and effect between the state of the nation and the impending events announced by the prophet. The "not yet" was related to the "now"; the coming event would be the response of God at work in history to the situation which already confronted the prophet. That is why the future, even that predicted by the prophet, was not predetermined. For if the people would respond to the message in repentance and faith (and why deliver it, otherwise?) God might also modify or change what he had planned to do.[11]

For example, in Deuteronomy Moses lays out the coming history of Israel (Deut. 4:21–31). Long before the events transpire, Moses

11. Ibid., 31–32.

sets down the recurrent pattern that will typify Israel's covenant failure (sin, judgment, restoration). He explicitly refers to Israel's entering the land and possessing it, its apostasy and corruption, its exile to foreign lands, the survival of a remnant, Israel's repentance for its sin, and Yahweh's restoration of his people.

This prophetic oracle does not require that Moses possess some secret knowledge of an ironclad future. Indeed, the oracle is delivered as a warning, a possible future. Three times in the oracle Moses uses the conditional *if*: "if you then become corrupt and make any kind of idol, doing evil in the eyes of the LORD your God" (Deut. 4:25), "if from there you seek the LORD your God" (Deut. 4:29), "if you look for him with all your heart and with all your soul" (Deut. 4:29). Moses warns Israel not to abuse the blessings of God. Yet she follows the way that Moses lays out here, virtually to the letter.

What Moses possessed was a Spirit-informed insight into the character of Israel. That insight, though it exactly conformed to how Israel would transgress God's law and warp the covenant, does not take anything away from Israel's responsibility or its ability to have behaved otherwise. Israel was not following a script. Israel followed its own depraved heart.

The Prophets Proclaim the Coming of God in Judgment

That which the prophets promise as a consequence of the present moral condition of the nation is the advent of God in judgment. The prophets herald a coming catastrophe. It may be inflicted through invaders, locusts or earthquake, drought or famine. Yet whatever the instrument, it will be an act of God, punishing the sinner and the oppressor and righting wrongs. The prophets shock their contemporaries with the unacceptable news that the victim will be Israel.

The Prophets Promise the Coming of God in Salvation

In the prophetic message, comfort and hope often break through even in the midst of covenant discipline. In the early work of Amos and Zephaniah, Israel scarcely hears the announcement of Yahweh's coming salvation after judgment, preoccupied as these prophets are almost entirely with the impending judgment. Amos's word contains no more than a hint that a small minority will survive the coming disaster: "Then the LORD said to me, 'The time is ripe for my people Israel; I will spare them no longer'" (Amos 8:2).

Yet just a few years after Amos prophesied, the prophets begin to offer more than Amos's simple indictment-judgment oracle. Hosea too speaks of covenant divorce, but he cannot sustain a message of judgment throughout his entire prophecy.

> I will plant her for myself in the land;
>> I will show my love to the one I called "Not my loved one."
> I will say to those called "Not my people," "You are my people";
>> and they will say, "You are my God." (Hos. 2:23)

This note of hope develops into the remnant theme of the Book of Isaiah. Even as eight people were delivered through the cataclysm of the flood, so some of Israel will be saved from the coming catastrophe.

The prophets often depict salvation of the remnant as a return to life, a return to the land where they will live in peace and security. Jerusalem will be rebuilt, and the land will become astonishingly fertile. Yahweh will change the people in the core of their hearts, the root problem after all. All will know Yahweh, and all will live in obedience to his commandments.

Still, judgment and deliverance always accompany the prophetic preaching. The promised deliverance will follow the judgment. Israel will go down to death and only then be raised up to life. Salvation comes in the aftermath of judgment.

The Prophets Promise the Final Reign of God on Earth and in History

The prophets envision the establishment of the kingdom of God on earth, although upon an earth transformed by the power of God. There will be continuity between the new thing and the former things.

As we previously noted, the bulk of the prophetic oracles deal not with the distant future but rather with the present and immediate future of the prophet's contemporary audience. Yet the prophetic vision holds a distant future or eschatological aspect. Isaiah 61 and other texts envision a yet future day of the Lord, a day in which the messianic King will come. He will finally and decisively address the problem of sin, bring final judgment upon the unrighteous, establish the people of God in the land, and restore and transform the earth.

The Mosaic law, in the context of God's deliverance and sovereign, gracious choice, tells us what the marriage ought to look like. Much of the story of Scripture tells us what it did look like—how Israel sinned, and how God responded.

The Prophets Link Backward and Forward in History

Thus, Israel's prophets interpret its misbehavior in a way that points backward and forward in history. In the period of the prophets Israel is ungraciously forsaking the covenant to which their redeeming Lord had graciously bound them. The consequence of this will be divine judgment as promised.

But Israel's incorrigible rebellion and self-incurred plight underscores its need for something that the prophets cannot give but which Yahweh through them promises: a further and final coming of God in salvation. The prophets comfort the people with this future hope. And their office anticipates one who is yet to come who will be not only Prophet but also Priest and King.

JESUS
A New and More Glorious Covenant

E ven though God has been faithful to the covenant and has been wondrously gracious to Israel, something is amiss. Israel's history has been one of continuous failure of God's covenant people to live according to the terms of the covenant. Each and every promise and provision of the covenant—although kept by Yahweh—has been misunderstood, misapplied, laid aside, ignored, or presumed upon by Israel. Now its inability to keep the covenant has brought ruinous consequences.

SEEING JUDGMENT AND BEYOND

From Curse . . .

The cruel and militaristic Assyrians reign over a vast empire that stretches from Asia Minor all the way to Egypt at the time that Amos and Hosea prophesy. In 722 B.C. the Assyrian juggernaut overruns the northern kingdom of Israel, taking portions of its population into exile. The capture of the Assyrian capital of Nineveh in 612 B.C. by the Babylonians signals the rise of a new master for the northern kingdom. Soon Judah also serves Babylon, for in 587 Babylonian armies conquer the southern kingdom, destroying the temple in Jerusalem.

In 627 B.C., king Asherbanipal, the last great ruler of the Assyrian empire, dies. At about the same time, Josiah, the king of Judah, begins to purge Judah of pagan worship and foreign influences (2 Kings 23). But Josiah's restoration of the covenant fails to produce the thoroughgoing repentance that is needed. Most of his reforms address only the externals of Judah's worship.

Also in 627 B.C. God calls Jeremiah to the prophetic ministry. As the scepter of the Babylonians looms ever larger, Jeremiah complains that the deeply rooted idolatry and social corruption of Judah have not been addressed (Jer. 2, 5). All Josiah's reforms have produced is a more elaborate cult (Jer. 6:16–21; 7:9–11). Something much more radical than Josiah's reform is called for. Jeremiah sees nothing but judgment in Judah's immediate future, for Judah's failure to live according to the covenant will reap only the curses of Sinai.

But Jeremiah also sees beyond the judgment. Because he knows that God intends the judgment of his people for the sake of discipline and that the goal of discipline is restoration, Jeremiah anticipates the dawning of a different future for Israel. The covenant story has not been fully told. A new chapter is coming.

. . . To Blessing

Thus, the prophets begin to speak of a future work of the Lord. They envision this future work in a number of ways. Most significantly, they anticipate a restoration of Israel's relationship to God under a new covenant, they relate God's promise of a coming day of the Lord, and they chronicle their growing realization of God's promise of a special coming King.

The Davidic line had failed to actualize the kingdom of God. Yet the prophets know that God promised that a single member of David's house will sit upon the throne of David forever (2 Sam. 7). This coming King will rule not only Israel but also the whole world, and righteousness will characterize his kingship. Under this ideal Servant-

King, a chastened Israel will return to the land. It will receive rest from oppression, and it will enjoy full communion with Yahweh. This Messiah will be anointed to fulfill not only the kingly office but the prophetic and priestly offices as well. What is more, the coming Messiah "shall merge God's throne with his own, for he shall be Immanuel, Mighty God, God himself."[1] He will be more than merely a descendant of David. He will be divine.[2] The prophets begin to hold out this hope for Israel.

The prophets describe the impending day of the Lord as both a covenant threat and a promise of ultimate salvation. Amos, the first to use the notion, turns the presumptions of Israel upon their ear when he speaks of the day of the Lord as Yahweh's coming to judge his people (Amos 5:18–20). The coming visitation of God will bring disaster upon sinful Israel.[3] For their contemporaries, the coming day promises defeat and exile. Yet there are hints of a more hopeful ultimate day.

> In that day I will restore
> David's fallen tent.
> I will repair its broken places,
> restore its ruins,
> and build it as it used to be . . .
> I will plant Israel in their own land,
> never again to be uprooted. (Amos 9:11, 15; cf. Zeph. 3:9–20)

The day of the Lord will be a day of judgment and salvation. It will bring great upheaval and great blessing.

The prophet Isaiah calls it "the year of the LORD's favor" and "the day of vengeance of our God" (Isa. 61:2). Typical of the prophetic vision, Isaiah conflates the immediate future with a more distant future. In that day God will bestow a crown of beauty upon his people instead of the ashes of destruction, and gladness will replace

---

1. O. Palmer Robertson, *The Christ of the Covenants* (Grand Rapids: Baker, 1980), 251.
2. See Amos 9:11–12; Hos. 1:11; 3:4–5; Mic. 4:1–3; Isa. 7:14; 9:6; 11:1–10; Jer. 23:5–6; 33:15–26; Ezek. 34; 37:24.
3. Cf. Joel 1:15; Zeph. 1:7–17; 2:5–15.

mourning (Isa. 61:3). When God rebuilds Israel, he will return it to its mission in the world as priests of Yahweh (Isa. 61:6, 9) so that the righteousness and praise of God will "spring up before all nations" (Isa. 61:11). God's final and complete salvation will reach to the ends of the earth.[4] The prophetic hope is that God will finally and for all time lift the curse from the earth and himself come to dwell with humanity in the earth.[5]

THE PROPHETS ANTICIPATE THE NEW COVENANT

But Isaiah, in this portrait of the coming day of the Lord, also mentions an everlasting covenant that God will make with his people (Isa. 61:8). Jeremiah depicts this new covenant more fully:

> "The time is coming," declares the LORD,
> "when I will make a new covenant
> with the house of Israel
> and with the house of Judah.
> It will not be like the covenant
> I made with their forefathers
> when I took them by the hand
> to lead them out of Egypt,
> because they broke my covenant,
> though I was a husband to them,"
> declares the LORD.
> "This is the covenant that I will make with the house of Israel
> after that time," declares the LORD.
> "I will put my law in their minds
> and write it on their hearts.
> I will be their God,
> and they will be my people.
> No longer will a man teach his neighbor,
> or a man his brother, saying, 'Know the LORD,'
> because they will all know me,

4. Cf. Isa. 42:5–6; 49:6–8.
5. Jer. 31:11–14; Ezek. 34:26–29; 36:8–12.

> from the least of them to the greatest,"
>   declares the LORD.
> "For I will forgive their wickedness
>   and I will remember their sins no more." (Jer. 31:31–34)

The hope for a yet future work of God, a new episode in the covenant story, surfaces repeatedly in the prophets.[6] Yet because it is quoted twice in the Epistle to the Hebrews (Heb. 8:9–13; 10:15–18), it is Jeremiah's portrayal that is most associated with the new covenant.[7]

Continuity: What's Not New about the New Covenant

Jeremiah distinguishes between the new covenant and the Mosaic covenant: "It will not be like the covenant I made with their forefathers." The apostle Paul also distinguishes between them, or between law and grace (2 Cor. 3; Gal. 3–4). Throughout the history of the church, theologians have debated the relationship between these two covenants. Opinions have ranged from one extreme to the other. Some interpreters have thought that the new covenant represents little more than an adjustment to the Mosaic covenant. Others have thought that the prophets foresee an eschatological rejection of the law and all that Sinai represented. In truth, we find continuity and discontinuity, and it is important to mark the nature of each.

The first thing we should notice in Jeremiah's prophecy is that although Jeremiah sets the new covenant in tension with the old, he refuses to lay any fault upon the Mosaic covenant. Failure is indeed implicit in the passage, but it is not the failure of Sinai. Despite God's gracious salvation and commissioning, the people proved unable to keep the covenant.

The Hebrew text confirms this, for it explicitly and vividly distinguishes the relevant pronouns in this passage. In the Hebrew language, typically the verb is inflected in such a way that it also com-

---

6. Hos. 2:18; Isa. 24:5; 42:6; 49:8; 54:10; 55:3; 59:21; 61:8; Jer. 43:37–41; 50:5; Ezek. 16:60–63.

7. The quotation in Heb. 8:8–12 of Jer. 31:31–34 is the longest direct quotation of the Old Testament in the New.

municates the subject of the verb, both person and number. Thus, "he went" is a single word in Hebrew. Yet sometimes the pronoun "he" is also stated explicitly, yielding the literalistic translation "he he went." This construction serves to emphasize the subject in some way. This is what Jeremiah uses throughout this prophecy. They broke the covenant. Hence, they, yes they, broke the covenant. I, indeed I, was a husband to them. The point is that God's provision was sound, yet Israel did not keep the covenant. His people had proven faithless, even though God had always been faithful. The fault belongs to Israel,[8] not the covenant.

A second item we note in this passage is that Jeremiah affirms the place of the law in the life of the people of God. Jeremiah anticipates neither the abrogation of law nor the writing of a new law. God speaks simply of "my law." Indeed, God will write his law upon the heart.

The covenant goal Jeremiah describes, of intimate relationship between God and his people, is not new. The covenant formula—you will be my people and I shall be your God—formed the essence of the covenant relationship from the beginning (Ex. 6:7).[9]

Jeremiah's idea of the law written upon the heart of God's people is not a new element either. The popular conception that the Old Testament religion was one of legalistic externals is far from the truth. The internalization of the law—a religion that came from the heart— had always been the goal of the covenant. The Book of Deuteronomy repeatedly insists that the law of God never be understood as some external or mechanical reality. God's people should internalize, personally appropriate, the law, lodging it in their heart, nationally and individually (Deut. 6:4–6; 11:18).

And even though such texts as Deuteronomy 10:16 call Israel to circumcise their hearts, it is understood throughout the Old Testament that God will circumcise Israel's heart (Deut. 30:6). Israel's faithful response to God is always the product of his grace.

---

8. Jer. 2:5, 13, 20, 32.
9. Cf. Isa. 54:5–10; Jer. 32:38–40; Ezek. 37:23–27.

A heart right with God has always been a precondition for fruitful covenant experience (Ps. 37:31; 40:8; Isa. 51:7).[10] While the covenant most certainly includes legal and obligatory aspects, the obligatory always serves the relational. We have seen clearly that the law was first given to Moses in the context of God's gracious initiative, emphasizing the priority of grace and relationship over obligation. All of God's covenantal relationships are based upon his gracious initiative. In writing the law upon the heart, in giving Israel a believing and obedient heart, God is fulfilling the original intent of the Sinai covenant. That the law will become "the wellspring of all they think, say and do"[11] is not a new covenantal element.

Jeremiah labors to proclaim that the covenant has gone awry due to the hardness of the hearts of the people. Elsewhere he describes Israel's apostasy from covenant intimacy with God during the prophetic era:

> These people have stubborn and rebellious hearts; they have turned aside and gone away. (Jer. 5:23)

> Judah's sin is engraved with an iron tool,
>   inscribed with a flint point,
> on the tablets of their hearts
>   and on the horns of their altars. (Jer. 17:1)

Jeremiah is not saying that the Mosaic covenant represents a religion of ritual externals over against the new covenant's promise of internalized religion. The issue is that Israel has divorced the internal from the external. It has forgotten that the rites and observances of its religion are meant to picture its covenant loyalty to Yahweh. The prophets indict not religious form but rather religion reduced to mere formalism.

Jeremiah couches the covenant in the familial—and thoroughly personal—language of marriage and parent-child relationships. Such

10. See Deut. 4:29; 10:12; 13:3; 26:16; Josh. 12:20; 22:5.
11. Walter Roehrs, "Divine Covenants: Their Structure and Function," *Concordia Journal* 14 (January 1988), 17.

relational intimacy cannot be reduced to formal obligation.[12] Jeremiah thus underscores the true character of apostasy as spiritual adultery and rebellion. Yahweh rebukes his covenant people:

I myself said,

"How gladly would I treat you like sons
    and give you a desirable land,
    the most beautiful inheritance of any nation.
I thought you would call me 'Father'
    and not turn away from following me.
But like a woman unfaithful to her husband,
    so you have been unfaithful to me,
        O house of Israel." (Jer. 3:19–20)

The description of Yahweh as husband does not, however, originate with Jeremiah's prophecy. Rather, it belongs to the nature of the covenant as a relationship of sworn, intimate relationship. Because the covenant that God laid upon it made it more than a vassal, Israel was never to view its allegiance to Yahweh as a merely formal, ritual, or even legal obligation.

Thus, Scripture displays a substantial element of continuity between Sinai and the promise of the new covenant. These elements of continuity between the promise of the new covenant and the old covenant that it will eclipse are so substantial that Walter Kaiser has referred to Jeremiah's prophecy as the *locus classicus* on the subject of covenant continuity.[13]

Discontinuity: What Is New about the New Covenant?

Yet the fact that Jeremiah calls the covenant new requires that there be some discontinuity between the covenants. What then is new here? What sets the new covenant apart from God's previous

---

12. See Jer. 2:20; 3:1–14, 20; 23:14. Cf. Ezek. 6:9; 15:8; 18:24; 16:8; 23:1–29.

13. Walter Kaiser, "The Old Promise and the New Covenant: Jeremiah 31:31–34," in *The Bible in Its Literary Milieu*, ed. John Maier and Vincent Tolliers (Grand Rapids: Eerdmans, 1979), 109.

covenantal dealings with his people? How does the new covenant represent an advance in the covenant story?

What is new is that God is going to address the issue of Israel's inability to keep the covenant. He will cure the disease of sin.

Sinful hearts have been the problem from the beginning. Remember that when the ark came to rest upon the mountain, God started over again with eight regenerated people. But they were still sinners, as Noah's sin in the vineyard displays.

The failure of the Davidic kings, the massive apostasy and corruption of the people, and the inevitable covenant curse in the expulsion of Israel from the land dramatizes the covenant breach of Israel under the old covenant. This sad history also highlights the need for a greater work of God. Clearly the covenant as it was envisioned and administered under Abraham, Moses, and David was insufficient in effecting either the promised covenant intimacy or the creation of Israel as a model of the kingdom of God. "Because of the radical incapacity of man to keep God's covenant, no lasting purpose will be served through a future reestablishment of the same covenantal relationship."[14]

The new covenant, however, will know such a full forgiveness of sins that Yahweh will remember sin no more. The sin problem will be finally and definitively dealt with. Sin will no longer be a problem. Covenant breach will come to an end. While the new covenant shares much of the substance of the Mosaic covenant, it differs radically in its ability to effect the goal of covenant intimacy and obedience. The obedience of God's law that did not come about under the Mosaic covenant will be realized under the new covenant.

Ezekiel describes God's future work as a cleansing of the people of God (Ezek. 36:25–37:33). Isaiah invites the sinner to a divine grace and pardon that surpasses all human understanding (Isa. 55:6–9).

Jeremiah depicts the new covenant as unilaterally or monergistically imposed. In this he shows that in the new covenant the emphasis falls upon God's sovereign intention to effect the goal of his redemptive plan. There is no talk here of Israel's covenant obliga-

---

14. Robertson, *The Christ of the Covenants*, 261.

tion, no mutuality. It is all a sovereign work: "*I* will make . . . *I* will put . . . *I* will write . . . *I* will be their God"; and finally and climactically, "*I* will forgive . . . *I* will remember sin no more."

When Will It Come?

The coming of the new covenant will create a revolutionary new age. Human nature's inrooted tendencies will be reversed or uprooted. A fresh and utterly new demonstration of divine grace will occur.

But when will the new covenant come? Jeremiah introduces this prophecy with the eschatological formula "the days are coming." He uses this phrase six times in the book, in apparently the same way other prophets use the "day of the Lord." But while Amos applies this phrase to describe the judgment of the exile and Ezekiel to speak of Israel's restoration to the land, Jeremiah seems to refer to something beyond the restoration of Israel to the land. In this prophecy he pictures the final or definitive act of God. Ezekiel and Isaiah do so as well, if, as appears to be the case, their references to a "covenant of peace" and an "everlasting covenant" are synonyms of the new covenant of Jeremiah.[15]

To be sure, the immediate reference of this prophetic vision is the regathering of Israel and the restoration to the land after the exile.[16] Yet the foreshortening of future events that typifies these prophets suggests that the new covenant does not refer merely to the postexilic period of Old Testament Israel.

Indeed, the prophetic vision includes elements that lie in the distant future, even our future. The scope of the new covenant transcends national and international boundaries. It will extend to the ends of the earth and ultimately encompass all nations and a rejuvenated universe (e.g., Isa. 56:4–8; 66:18–24). Thus P. R. Williamson comments that "while the restoration of the Jews in the Promised Land marks the beginning of the fulfillment of new covenant prom-

---

15. Isa. 54:8–10; 61:8; Ezek. 34:25; 37:24–28; cf. Jer. 32:37–41; 50:5.
16. Barry D. Smith, "New Covenant," in *Evangelical Dictionary of Biblical Theology*, ed. Walter A. Elwell (Grand Rapids: Baker, 1996), 560.

ises, it was only a beginning. The best was yet to come, when the 'rest' foreshadowed in Joshua would finds its ultimate consummation in the new heavens and new earth."[17]

Further and most significantly, the prophets associate the new covenant with the coming of the Messiah. Not only will the new covenant age bring about a consummation of creation (Isa. 11:6–9), but also the covenant will be fulfilled and consummated by the promised descendant of Judah, the shoot and branch of David (Isa. 11:1), the divinely provided shepherd who is Yahweh's servant and Son (Ezek. 34:24). The new covenant then, in its fullness, belongs to the messianic age.

The New Testament Perspective on the New Covenant: It's All about Jesus

The Epistle to the Hebrews offers further insight on the relationship between the old and new covenants. Jesus and his blood inaugurate the new covenant. Jesus is God's new mediator and he unleashes a new power for forgiveness.

Hebrews 7–10 describe how Jesus and his blood are essential elements of the new covenant. Quoting Jeremiah 31:31–34, the author declares that the new covenant was fulfilled by the death of Jesus, for he was both the great High Priest and the sacrifice.

Two inherent shortcomings plagued the Old Testament sacrificial system. First, the priests were sinners who had to offer sacrifice for their sins as well as for the people (Heb. 5:3; 7:24–27). Second, the sacrifices were but tokens lacking inherent power to cleanse or forgive (Heb. 10:4). Animal sacrifice was a substitution for the death of the sinner, through which God was promising to redeem the sinner.

We can liken this to writing a check. A check is a promise of payment, but there must be money in the bank to cover the check in order for it to be good. The entire Old Testament rite of sacrifice was about promise. God promised to fulfill the token of forgiveness—to cover the substitutionary deaths of animals with a future effective sacrifice.

17. P. R. Williamson, "Covenant," in *New Dictionary of Biblical Theology*, ed. T. Desmond Alexander et al. (Downers Grove, Ill.: InterVarsity Press, 2000), 426.

The author of Hebrews thus describes the old covenant sacrifices as "weak and useless" (Heb. 7:18) and able to accomplish only a ceremonial purity (Heb. 9:13). The sacrifice did not take away sin, which it was impotent to do (Heb. 10:11), but only passed by it, promising that someday God would cover the token.[18]

This passage in Hebrews also notes that the structure of the Old Testament tabernacle served to keep sinners away from God rather than provide a way into his holy presence (Heb. 9:8). And the constant repetition of sacrifice served only as a reminder of sin (Heb. 10:2–3). These inadequacies further confirm that what the Old Testament lacked was fulfilled completely in Christ.

The prophetic vision of the new covenant is that the promise of forgiveness will become an actual reality. O. Palmer Robertson comments:

> Jeremiah anticipates a day in which the actual shall replace the typical. Instead of having animal sacrifices merely represent the possibility of a substitutionary death in the place of the sinner, Jeremiah sees the day in which sins actually will be forgiven, never to be remembered again. The continual offering of sacrifice to remove sin not only provided a symbolical representation of the possibility of substitution . . . By saying that sins would be remembered no more, Jeremiah anticipates the end of the sacrificial system of the Old Testament . . . The new factor of forgiveness anticipated in the new covenant is the once-for-all accomplishment of that forgiveness.[19]

Jesus embodies the longed-for actual reality. The once-for-all sacrifice comes in the death of Christ (Heb. 9:12; 10:14), the fulfillment

---

18. The question is often asked how people were saved under the old covenant. If the realization of forgiveness comes only with Christ, does that mean that there was no true salvation in the Old Testament? By no means. The Old Testament sacrificial tokens were promises. While nothing under the old covenant had the inherent power to reconcile the sinner to God, the sacrifices anticipated the work of Christ. They were, if you will, promissory notes of future payment. In short, people under the old covenant were saved by the same blood, the same sacrifice, the same Savior as people under the new covenant. They were saved in the promise of God's coming messiah. We are saved in the finished work of Christ.

19. Robertson, *The Christ of the Covenants*, 283–84.

of all that the old order promised. Christ is the better high priest[20] since he, being sinless (Heb. 4:15; 9:14), did not have to offer sacrifice for himself (Heb. 7:27), and he holds his priesthood permanently (Heb. 7:23). As the better high priest, Christ provides a better hope "by which we draw near to God" (Heb. 7:19), a better covenant (Heb. 7:22; 9:15) based on better promises (Heb. 8:6), and a better sacrifice (Heb. 9:23).[21]

Old Testament Faith?

All this talk of "better" and "new" may incline us to think the faith of people under the old covenant was decidedly inferior to that of those under the new covenant. But there is no reason to demean Old

---

20. Gerard Van Groningen comments regarding the significance of the new covenant: "The greatest change will be in regard to the administrator of the covenant. No longer will this one be a Moses, a David, a high priest, or a great prophet like Isaiah. Jesus Christ, who had been typified by these Old Testament mediators, will be the Mediator of the covenant. He will inaugurate, fulfill, and permanently establish the renewed covenant. He did this by becoming the High Priest who offered himself as the Passover Lamb." "Covenant" in *The Evangelical Dictionary of Biblical Theology*, 131.

21. C. C. Newman cogently summarizes the contrast between the old covenant and the new in the Book of Hebrews: "The old covenant was earthly; the new covenant is heavenly (Heb. 8:1; 9:1). The old covenant ministry was a copy and shadow (Heb. 8:5; 9:23; 10:1); the new covenant is real (Heb. 9:24) and true (Heb. 8:2; 10:1). The old covenant featured human priests who were destined to die; the new covenant possesses a high priest who lives forever (Heb. 9:28). The administration of a priest under the old covenant occurred according to the dictates of the law (Heb. 8:4); the new covenant is directly and divinely administered (Heb. 8:1–2). A priest under the old covenant had to offer sacrifice for his own sins (Heb. 9:7); Jesus' sinlessness means that he did not offer sacrifice for himself (Heb. 9:7). Under the old covenant multiple priests had to enter repeatedly the sanctuary to offer numerous sacrifices (Heb. 9:6–7, 25; 10:11); under the new covenant a single high priest, Jesus, enters the heavenly sanctuary once (through his death and resurrection) and offers a singular sacrifice once for all time (Heb. 9:12, 26; 10:10, 12). The old covenant contained the sacrificial blood of animals (Heb. 9:18–22); under the new covenant Jesus offers his own blood (Heb. 9:12, 26). The efficacy of the old covenant offerings was limited (Heb. 10:1–2); the efficacy of the new covenant sacrifice was definitive—there are no more offerings for sins. Under the old covenant the worshiper could not be perfected (Heb. 9:9); under the new covenant a process of moral transformation has been enacted that will completely purify (Heb. 9:14; 10:14)." C. C. Newman, "Covenant, New Covenant," in *Dictionary of the Later New Testament and Its Development*, ed. Ralph P. Martin and Peter H. Davids (Downers Grove, Ill.: InterVarsity Press, 1997), 248.

Testament religion. A careful understanding of the relationship of the new covenant to the old enhances our appreciation of the faith of the Old Testament believers.

The new covenant is not, after all, categorically new. The difference is redemptive-historical. That is to say, it is not a difference between two categorically different religions, or two different sorts of covenant relationship between God and humankind. It is rather a single unfolding covenant story that moves toward greater levels of fulfillment of divine promise.

All that was promised under the terms of the new covenant, at least as far as Jeremiah envisioned it, was also sought under the old covenant. Abraham or Moses would have recognized the terms of the new covenant as being part of God's covenant goal. The old covenant believer understood that a heart turned toward the law of God, intimate knowledge of God and his ways, and God's gracious forgiveness of sins constitute the very heart of the covenant.

The old covenant believer experienced the same union and communion with God that the new covenant saint does. For example, David writes concerning the forgiveness of sins:

> The LORD is compassionate and gracious,
>   slow to anger, abounding in love.
> He will not always accuse,
>   nor will he harbor his anger forever;
> he does not treat us as our sins deserve
>   or repay us according to our iniquities.
> For as high as the heavens are above the earth,
>   so great is his love for those who fear him;
> as far as the east is from the west,
>   so far has he removed our transgressions from us.
> As a father has compassion on his children,
>   so the LORD has compassion on those who fear him;
> for he knows how we are formed,
>   he remembers that we are dust. (Ps. 103:8–14)

This forgiveness is not merely a hoped-for eschatological state of affairs but present and real in the life of the old covenant saint. David praises Yahweh as the one who "forgives all your sins and heals all your diseases" (Ps. 103:3).[22]

A new covenant believer—one who knows Jesus by name, knows what he did for us, knows what it cost him, and knows that a tomb stands forever robbed of its victory—may struggle to appreciate the faith of the old covenant believer. Yet there was real union and communion with God before the coming of Christ. There was true forgiveness of sin before the appearance of the one through whom all sin—for the old covenant believer as well as the new—is forgiven. And there was real faith in God in the Old Testament. It is not accidental that the New Testament repeatedly uses Abraham as the example of faith (e.g., Rom. 4; Gal. 3).

Old Testament believers also shared with us the well-known already–not yet tension of New Testament eschatology. For them, the coming of Christ was not yet, although the promise of his coming was already. Indeed, we for whom Christ's coming is already still share with them the tension of that which for us is still not yet—the resurrection of the dead, the judgment of the world, the coming of the Son of man in power and glory, and the restoration of creation.

Hebrews 11 tells us that, like all other Old Testament saints, Abraham did not receive the things promised but only "saw them and welcomed them from a distance" (Heb. 11:13). He did not know precisely how God would fulfill his promises, but when the time came for him to be tested, Abraham offered his son as a sacrifice, believing that, if need be, God would raise Isaac from the dead (Heb. 11:17–18). I doubt that any greater eschatological tension between the already and the not yet of divine promise can be imagined than that which Abraham experienced in that moment (Gen. 22).[23]

---

22. Cf. Ps. 32:1–2: "Blessed is he whose transgressions are forgiven, whose sins are covered. Blessed is the man whose sin the LORD does not count against him and in whose spirit is no deceit."

23. Anthony Hoekema suggests that this eschatological tension "specifically characterizes New Testament eschatology." While he admits that "one could say that the Old Testament believer already experienced this tension," he holds that the tension is "heightened for the New Testament believer since he has both a richer experience of the present blessings and a clearer understanding of future hopes than his Old Testament counterpart. I believe that Hoekema fails to appreciate properly the eschatological tension of the

Faith after Jesus

While Abraham is "the man of faith" and "the father of all who believe," the content of his faith is not interchangeable with that of the New Testament believer. Once Jesus comes, he becomes the central and essential focus of the biblical faith. This means that a person who affirms the faith of the Old Testament, even though he heartily affirms its messianic hope, if he denies that Jesus is the promised Messiah, he denies the entire biblical faith.

Jesus is the goal of the Old Testament faith. Failure to confess Christ, the New Testament insists, is a failure to confess Yahweh. Jesus criticizes a group of Jews who claim their solidarity with Abraham:

> If God were your father, you would love me, for I came from God and now am here. (John 8:42)

> If you do not believe that I am the one who I claim to be, you will indeed die in your sins. (John 8:24)

Once Jesus comes, the person of the Messiah is declared and must be acknowledged. Jesus both links and separates the old covenant and the new.

In themselves, the Old Testament prophecies of the new covenant do not demand Jesus of Nazareth. But once Jesus of Nazareth fulfills and certifies those prophecies, we must now read them in light of him. From the incarnation of Jesus on, the particular historical realities of Jesus' life and work become the normative interpretive grid for the Old Testament promise of the new covenant.

What is new about the new covenant is that the entire covenant story must now be seen in Christ. The union with God foreseen in Jeremiah 31:31–34 is union with Christ. The people of God are the community of which Christ is the head. The law written upon the heart is the law of Christ. The knowledge of God is communion with

---

Old Testament faith. Anthony Hoekema, *The Bible and the Future* (Grand Rapids: Eerdmans, 1979), 14–15.

Christ. The forgiveness of sins is the costly forgiveness won by Christ. Once Jesus takes the cup and says to his disciples, "This cup is the new covenant in my blood, which is poured out for you" (Luke 22:21), it is impossible to imagine God's covenant relationship with his people without Jesus Christ at its center.

JESUS IS THE NEW IN NEW COVENANT

When we look at Jeremiah 31:31–34, it is not hard to see that the fullness of its promise lies still before us. Every human being will know God. The law of God will be written on every heart. No longer will we require teachers who will instruct us in the knowledge of God. Sin will be finally and utterly put away. The rule of God will finally and fully come to earth, and God will be all in all. Yet in the coming of Christ, the end times have begun. The cosmic drama in which God has promised to end Adam's rebellion has begun the episode of fulfillment.

"This Is the New Covenant in My Blood"

C. S. Lewis famously observed that the claims Jesus made for himself were so extravagant and absolute that it is impossible to think of him as a harmless moral teacher:

> A man who was merely a man and said the sort of things Jesus said would not be a great moral teacher. He would be either a lunatic—on a level with the man who says he is a poached egg—or else he would be the Devil of Hell. You must make your choice. Either this man was, and is, the Son of God: or else a madman or something worse.[24]

Jesus makes just such an outrageous claim at his last Passover meal. He blesses the cup of the Passover and tells his disciples: "This is my blood of the covenant, which is poured out for many for the forgiveness of sins" (Matt. 26:28).[25] In saying this Jesus makes two claims, one about his own identity and one a historical proclamation.

24. C. S. Lewis, *Mere Christianity* (New York: Macmillan, 1943), 41.
25. Cf. Mark 14:24; Luke 22:20.

The identity claim is that he is divine. Only God can forgive sins, yet here is Jesus saying that he has that same authority and power. As we have seen, the prophets associated forgiveness of sin with the age of the new covenant. Now Jesus also associates forgiveness of sins with the new covenant. On the eve of his crucifixion Jesus proclaims himself to be the Passover sacrifice who will accomplish salvation. John the Baptist's confession, upon first seeing Jesus, captures the significance of Christ's coming into the world: "Look, the Lamb of God, who takes away the sin of the world!" (John 1:29).

The historical claim is that the new covenant era is inaugurated in Christ. All that the prophets have looked for, Jesus implies, the end of history, is here in me. Jesus is Yahweh's answer to the sin problem of his people, the new chapter in the covenant story.

Jesus Fulfills Old Testament Promise

The good news of the gospel story is that the God who has promised his covenant love and presence to his people, who acted on their behalf time and again in the events of their history, who constantly held before them the vision of his future coming when he would make all things new, has now come in Jesus of Nazareth to fulfill his promises. Jesus is the essential link between the Old and New Testaments: the salvation of God promised, the salvation of God fulfilled.

Fulfillment of Old Testament promise is a theme that runs deep and strong in the Gospels, especially in Matthew. While Matthew uses the word *covenant* only in reference to the cup of sacrifice that Jesus offers at the last Passover, covenantal themes abound in the book.

At the outset of his Gospel, Matthew presents Jesus as the son of Abraham and the son of David, the one who has come to fulfill all the divine promises that those two names recall for the Old Testament reader. The promises God made to Abraham find their ultimate fulfillment in Christ (Matt. 1:1, 17; 3:9; 8:11–12).[26] He is the one anticipated by Moses, the one who would fulfill all the obligations of the Mosaic covenant (Matt. 3:15; 5:17–48; 9:16–17;

---

26. Cf. Luke 1:55, 72–73; John 8:31–39.

11:28–30). He is the royal son of David (Matt. 1:1; 3:17; 4:15–16; 15:22; 16:16; 21:5; 22:41–45), the true heir to and goal of the Davidic dynasty. All that has gone before has anticipated, promised, and prepared for Jesus. All that for which Yahweh established Israel in the world is fulfilled in Christ. The goal and climax of Israel's history has come.

Jesus Alone Fulfills the Covenant through Perfect Obedience

Important to Christ's fulfilling the covenant is his life obedience (sometimes called Christ's active obedience in Reformed dogmatics). While Abraham obeyed God's voice—keeping his requirements, commands, decrees, and law—he was a sinner. The Book of Genesis records some quite unflattering facts about Abraham's life. Moses too was a sinner like any other son of Adam. And none of the Davidic dynasty, not even David, fully complied with the covenant stipulation of obedience to the Word of God. Only Jesus displays irreproachable behavior relative to the divine law (Matt. 5:17). The call to obedience that God placed upon Abraham (Gen. 17:1), the law God delivered to Moses (Ex. 20), and the obedience of sonship that God demanded of the Davidic king (2 Sam. 7:14–15) were fulfilled by Christ, and only by Christ.

Jesus is the one man of God who meets the obligation of creaturely trust and obedience. He is man as man was meant to be (1 Tim. 2:5), obeying God perfectly in all things. Jesus submits to baptism to "fulfill all righteousness" (Matt. 3:15). He knows that man cannot live by bread alone but by every word that comes from God's mouth (Matt. 4:4). He shows that integral to being truly human is obeying God's will, for that good will defines the very essence of creatureliness. Therefore, his food is to do the will of the Father and to finish his work (John 4:34). The Father is with Jesus and does not abandon him because he always does that which the Father wills (John 8:29). "Here at last, is a Son with whom God is truly pleased (Matt. 3:17)."[27] It is the combination of Christ's heavenly status, anointing

---

27. S. Motyer, "Israel (Nation)," *New Dictionary of Biblical Theology*, ed. T. Desmond Alexander et al. (Downers Grove, Ill.: InterVarsity Press, 2000), 585.

to mission, and real-life lifelong obedience that allows him to say, "It is finished" (John 19:30).

Jesus Is the True Israel

Matthew includes in his presentation the theme of Jesus as true Israel (e.g., Matt. 2:15ff.). As the Son of God, Jesus is called to be a true son, to reflect the character and ways of his Father. In doing so, he also proves himself to be the true Israelite, succeeding where Israel failed in its mission, obeying the law where they disobeyed, and submitting to his Father's will where they rebelled.

Matthew draws the correspondence vividly. The prophet Hosea had described Israel's exodus out of bondage as the election of God: "Out of Egypt I called my son" (Hos. 11:1). Matthew openly applies this statement to Jesus (Matt. 2:15). Matthew then tells the story of Jesus in such a way that we see it as a re-enactment of significant events in Israel's history: the exodus from Egypt (Matt. 2:19–20), the crossing of the Red Sea (Matt. 3:13–17), the temptations in the desert (Matt. 4:1–11), and the coming of Israel to Mount Sinai to receive the law (Matt. 5:1–2). The Spirit descends upon Jesus in fulfillment of the prophetic promise that the outpouring of the Spirit would come upon Israel (Matt. 3:16; cf. Isa. 44:2–3; Ezek. 36:25–27). Jesus is not just the savior of Israel; he is also the embodiment of what Israel was meant to be.

The True Covenant Partner

From the beginning the intention of the covenant has been the union and communion of God and man, man in intimate relation with God. As the true Israelite, Jesus is the man who is on God's side, flying his flag, championing his cause, embodying his character. As such he becomes—not just by virtue of his divine nature but also in his fully human and full-bodied trust and obedience—the true covenant partner of God. He fills this role, however, not for himself, for he had nothing to gain, but for us, the faithless covenant partner. And in his representative work, his standing in for us, he achieves righteousness and obedience for the people of God. As the true son

225

of Abraham, the true Davidic king, and the true Israelite, Jesus is also the true shepherd, the one who will lead the people of God (Matt. 2:6; 9:36; 15:29–39).[28] In the giving of the Sermon on the Mount (Matt. 5–7), he is the new and greater Moses as he gives his people the law of the new covenant. Jesus, the remnant of true Israel, will finally bring salvation to the nations.[29]

Christ the True Adam

Though rarely using the word *covenant*, the apostle Paul speaks of the work of Christ in explicitly covenantal terms. We can find no greater example of this than in Paul's trenchant declaration of the effect of the cross: "God made him who had no sin to be sin for us, so that in him we might become the righteousness of God" (2 Cor. 5:21).[30] This is the language of covenant representation and substitution. Christ stands in, representing us before God. And his merits—the merits of a sinless sacrifice—come to us.

Paul expands this thought in Romans 5 and 1 Corinthians 15, where he reflects on the historical-redemptive distinction between Adam and Christ. Adam is the first man, the representative head of the human race in the covenant of creation. Through his disobedience, sin and death come to reign over all men (Rom. 5:12; 1 Cor. 15:21), indeed over all creation (Rom. 8:22). Paul calls Adam a "pattern for," a type of the "one who is to come," Christ (Rom. 5:14–15). He calls Christ the second man (Rom. 5) or last man (1 Cor. 15).

Both men, Adam and Christ, function as representative persons within the history of the covenant. Their responses to God, either in obedience or disobedience, will greatly affect those whom they represent. Adam sinned, and thus sin and death came to all people. Through his obedience, Christ brought grace, righteousness, and justification unto life.

---

28. Cf. Ezek. 34:11–16; John 10:1–16.
29. Matt. 2:15; 4:1–11; 5:13–16; 8:11; 12:18–21; 13:47; 21:42–44; 24:14; 25:31–33; 28:19.
30. Cf. Rom. 5:8: "God demonstrates his own love for us in this: while we were yet sinners, Christ died for us."

Sometimes Scripture draws a historical connection between persons or events in redemptive history in order to create an analogy, a comparison that draws attention to God's faithfulness to his redemptive purpose. Here, however, Paul's intent is to underline the great difference between Adam and Christ, their respective responses to God as covenant mediators, and the effect each has upon those they represent and the covenant story as a whole. Thus the comparison that Paul sketches between Adam and Christ is not truly an analogy but a dis-analogy. Christ comes into the world for the express purpose of undoing the condemnation of Eden. According to John Murray:

> It would not be correct to say . . . that Christ's obedience was the same in content or demand. Christ was called on to obey in radically different conditions, and required to fulfill radically different demands. Christ was a sin-bearer and the climactic demand was to die. This was not true of Adam. Christ came to redeem, not so Adam. So Christ rendered the whole-souled totality of obedience in which Adam failed, but under totally different conditions and with incomparably greater demands.[31]

Christ comes as our covenant head to effect the forgiveness of sins and put death to death. Christ's righteousness defeats Adam's sin. God's rightful condemnation over sin is replaced by justification. And death gives way to life.

Jesus did more than just win back a lost righteousness and a lost relationship to God. Paul ends his discussion of Adam and Christ by proclaiming the surpassing excellence of Christ's work:

> But where sin increased, grace increased all the more, so that just as sin reigned in death, so also grace might reign through righteousness to bring eternal life through Jesus Christ our Lord. (Rom. 5:20b–21)

31. John Murray, "The Adamic Administration," in *Collected Writings of John Murray*, 4 vols. (Edinburgh: Banner of Truth, 1977), 2:58.

The result of Christ's obedience, Paul is saying here, is dispropor-
tionately gracious in reference to Adam's disobedience.[32] Through
his victory over death, the one true man—who is also the one true
Son of God—brings the heavenly life of the resurrection to earth,
and we who are in Christ "shall also bear the image of the man from
heaven" (1 Cor. 15:49).

Luke draws upon the same Adam-Christ typology to draw attention to Christ's active life obedience in contrast to Paul's focus upon
his passive obedience (passive being a reference to Christ's passion,
his sacrificial death on the cross). Immediately prior to his account
of Christ's temptation in the desert, Luke provides us with a genealog-
ical table that traces Jesus' lineage back to Adam (Luke 3:23–38).
Sinclair Ferguson notes:

> Here the *inclusio* of the whole of human history between Adam and
> Jesus suggests that the temptation and victory of the latter are to be
> interpreted in the light of the testing and defeat of the former with all
> its baneful entail. The second man-Son thus undid what was done by
> the first man-son; he obeyed and overcame as the last Adam, and now
> no further representative figure is needed.[33]

32. Leon Morris comments: "Paul learnt from his Jewish faith the close tie-up between
events at the beginning of the world and a setting right of earth's wrongs at the end of the
age. This principle (known as *restitutio in integrum*) permitted him to teach that as the
old creation had been ruined by Adam's fall and paradise lost, so Christ's obedience and
vindication by God would lead to a new order of harmony and reconciliation, with paradise regained. But he does not say simply, 'The second Adam restores what the first Adam
lost,' although that is included. By his use of the 'much more' contrast (vv. 17, 20) he goes
on to demonstrate that the ultimate Adam gains for His people far more than ever their
connection with the old order could have meant." Leon Morris, "1 John," in *The New Bible
Commentary: Revised*, ed. D. Guthrie et al. (Grand Rapids: Eerdmans, 1970), 1025–26.

33. Sinclair Ferguson, *The Holy Spirit* (Downers Grove, Ill.: InterVarsity Press, 1996),
49. Ferguson uses the temptation of Christ to make the point that we should be careful
not to reduce redemptive-historical events to illustrations of our own spiritual journey:
"It has been commonplace to interpret Jesus' temptations as analogous to, almost a model
for, the tempting of the Christian: Christ was tempted as we are, but resisted; therefore
we should resist in similar ways. But this leads to a partial and negative interpretation of
his experiences. His temptations constitute an epochal event. They are not merely personal, but cosmic. They constitute the tempting of the last Adam. True, there is a common bond between his temptation and ours: he is really and personally confronted by
dark powers. But the significance of the event does not lie in the ways in which our temp-

Thus the temptation of the second Adam is a "re-run of Eden." Like Adam before him, Jesus is tempted to reject the word of God. Unlike Adam, however, he chooses the path of obedience.

Jesus the Perfect Sacrifice

Jesus Christ rendered the old covenant obsolete. The Book of Hebrews uses the words "weak," "ineffectual," a "shadow," "abolished," and "annulled," to describe the old covenant. Tied to this "present age" (Heb. 9:9), the old covenant is "growing old" and "passing away" (Heb. 8:13).

Paul proclaims the fulfillment of Old Testament promises in the arrival of Jesus the Messiah (Rom. 1:2–3). Thus, he uses Old Testament sacrificial language to describe Christ's work on the cross. Christ's blood is a sacrifice that effects atonement for sin (Rom. 3:25; 5:9; 1 Cor. 11:25; Eph. 1:7; 2:13; Col. 1:20). Christ is "our Passover" (1 Cor. 5:7). As a sin offering (Rom. 8:3), Christ's death fully replaces the Old Testament sacrificial system.

The Descent of the Holy Spirit

Moses looked forward to a day when God would circumcise the heart of his people and there would be a new obedience to the law (Deut. 30). This, along with Jeremiah's prophecy of the writing of the law upon the heart, takes a giant step toward fulfillment at Pentecost. Ferguson rightly draws the connection:

> The revelation of God to Moses at Sinai had been accompanied by fire, wind and a divine tongue (Heb. 12:18–21). Moses had ascended the mountain. When he descended he had in his possession the Ten Commandments, the law of God. Christ too had recently ascended. At Pen-

tations are like his, but in the particularity and uniqueness of his experiences. He was driven into the wilderness as an assault force. His testing was set in the context of a holy war in which he entered the enemy's domain, absorbed his attacks and sent him into retreat (Matt. 4:11, and especially Luke 4:13). In the power of the Spirit, Jesus advanced as the divine warrior, the God of battles who fights on behalf of his people and their salvation (cf. Ex. 15:3; Ps. 98:1). His triumph demonstrated that 'the kingdom of God is near' and that the messianic conflict had begun," 48–49.

tecost he comes down, not with the law written on tablets of clay, but with the gift of his own Spirit to write the law in the hearts of believers and by his power to enable them to fulfill the law's commands. Thus the new covenant promise begins to be fulfilled (cf. Jer. 31:31–34; Rom. 8:3–4; 2 Cor. 3:7–11).[34]

The outpouring of the Spirit at Pentecost also moves the covenant story toward the fulfillment of Jeremiah's promise that the Old Testament system of the mediation of the knowledge of God would come to an end. The Spirit of God is poured out by Christ in unrestricted measure on all people. In his Pentecost sermon, Peter quotes Joel's prophecy of the day of the Lord (Joel 2:28–32) to announce that God's people now enjoy a new immediacy and access to the knowledge of God (Acts 2:14ff.). Again Ferguson comments:

> In the old covenant, the typical effect of the Spirit's coming was prophecy, with its various modes of production (cf. Num. 11:24–29; 1 Sam. 10:10–11). It was, generally speaking, limited to only a few, almost exclusively men. Now, in the new covenant, the boundaries of the Mosaic economy within which the Spirit had, by and large, previously manifested himself are rendered obsolete. Both sons and daughters prophesy; young men have visions, old men have dreams. These were, of course, modes of communicating the knowledge of God under the old covenant. Now all of the Lord's people possess the knowledge of God formerly experienced only by the prophets. This was exactly what Moses himself had longed for, although it could never have been experienced under the Mosaic economy: "I wish that all the Lord's people were prophets and that the Lord would put his Spirit on them" (Num. 11:29). Now it was a reality.[35]

In Christ, all God's people have a personal knowledge of God. No longer is intimate knowledge of God limited to the prophet, for "now all have received the messianic anointing"[36] (see 1 John 2:20, 27). The central issue and essence of the covenant, oneness between God

34. Ibid., 61.
35. Ibid., 62–63.
36. Ibid., 63.

and his people, union and communion with God ("I shall be your God and you shall be my people"), is upheld, emphasized, and heightened.[37]

New covenant realities—the incarnate flesh of Jesus, his sacrifice for the forgiveness of sins and the coming of the Holy Spirit at Pentecost—replace the symbols and tokens that represented God's presence in the Old Testament. The dawn of the new covenant brings better—and closer—access to God.

The Final Covenant

We may appropriately describe the new covenant as the last covenant, the covenant of eschatological realization. It is not that all of God's promises are now fulfilled. They are not. But they have begun to be. The kingdom is coming in its fullness, for the King has come.

It is not insignificant that the prophets speak of the new covenant as an everlasting covenant (Isa. 61:8; Jer. 50:5; Ezek. 37:26). To be sure, former covenant episodes were also characterized as eternal,[38] and each is as it is fulfilled in Christ. What distinguishes the new covenant as the final covenant is its character of consummation in the work of Christ. P. R. Williamson appropriately writes that

> the new covenant is the climactic fulfillment of the covenants that God established with the patriarchs, the nation of Israel, and the dynasty of David. The promises of these earlier covenants find their fulfillment in the new covenant, and in it such promises become "eternal" in the truest sense.[39]

The association of Christ, God's son, with the last Adam, and the mediator of the covenant, marks the new covenant as the "covenant

37. The Gospel of John develops these themes in John 14–16 in Jesus' promise to abide with his people and lead them into all truth through the ministry of the indwelling Spirit.

38. The Abrahamic covenant (Gen. 17:7; Ps. 105:10), the Mosaic covenant (Ex. 40:15; Lev. 16:34; 24:8; Isa. 24:5) and the Davidic covenant (2 Sam. 7:13, 16; Ps. 89:3–4; 132:11–12) are all described as eternal or everlasting.

39. Williamson, "Covenant," 426.

of consummation."[40] Robertson begins his treatment of the new covenant on this very note:

> The heart of this consummative realization consists in a single person. As fulfiller of all the messianic promises he achieves in himself the essence of the covenantal principle: "I shall be your God and you shall be my people." He therefore may be seen as the Christ who consummates the covenant.[41]

All of God's previous covenant promises and works culminate in the new covenant. After all, it is here that God definitively effects his resolution to the folly of Eden. Sin is forgiven in the death of Christ and will be utterly purged from his creation when Jesus returns. The blessings of the promised future have begun to be realized in Christ. The final chapter has begun to be written.

THE NEW COVENANT AND THE LAW

A key feature of the new covenant, Jeremiah promised, was that the law of God would be written on the hearts of God's people. Indeed, we have seen that the descent of the Holy Spirit, given by Christ to his church, advances the fulfillment of this promise. Yet many Christians contend that whereas law typified the Mosaic covenant, when the coming of Christ eclipsed the Mosaic epoch of covenant history, the law was rendered obsolete and was abolished.

The apostle Paul writes as if law and grace belong to two different eras of redemptive history and stand in opposition to one another. The believer is not under law but grace (Rom. 6:14–15). The new covenant people of God have died to the law (Rom. 7:4; 8:2; Gal. 2:19; 1 Cor. 9:20). Christ has abolished the law (Rom. 10:4; Eph. 2:15) so that the believer serves God not through the law but "in the new way of the Spirit" (Rom. 7:6).

However, Paul seems to affirm the place of the law in the life of the believer. Christians are to fulfill the law (Rom. 3:31; 8:3–4, 8–10;

---

40. Robertson, *The Christ of the Covenants*, 271ff.
41. Ibid., 272–73.

1 Cor. 7:19; Gal. 5:14). This implies that the Mosaic law continues as a standard of conduct for the people of God. Joe Sprinkle summarizes the positive New Testament attitude toward the law:

> It is "holy" and "spiritual," making sin known to us by defining it; therefore, Paul delights in it (Rom. 7:7–14, 22). The law is good if used properly (1 Tim. 1:8) and is not opposed to the promises of God (Gal. 3:21). Faith does not make the law void but the Christian establishes the law (Rom. 3:31), fulfilling its requirement by walking according to the Spirit (8:4) through love (13:10). When Paul states that women are to be in submission "as the Law says" (1 Cor. 14:34) or quotes parts of the Decalogue (Rom. 13:9), and when James quotes the law of love (2:8 from Lev. 19:18) or condemns partiality, adultery, murder, and slander as contrary to the law (2:9, 11; 4:11), and when Peter quotes Leviticus, "Be holy, because I am holy" (1 Peter 1:16 from Lev. 19:2), the implication is that the law, or at least part of it, remains authoritative.[42]

So which is it? Does the new covenant outdate or update law? How may we reconcile these apparently contradictory claims?

The New Testament Acknowledges the Law of God Written in Creation and on All Human Hearts

First, it is important to recognize that God had revealed norms for human life and obligated people to them long before Sinai. From the beginning, holiness has meant living one's life in accordance with God's revealed will, whether that will is built into the order of creation or is a spoken command. Paul suggests man's knowledge of his obligation to worship God and to live in accordance with the order of creation does not depend upon a written law, for God has written the law upon the human heart (Rom. 2:15). God created human beings in his image, endowing them with moral conscience and an innate knowledge of his moral requirements, calling them to reflect his character and live in harmony with him, other human beings, and the world about them. God holds all people responsible to live

---

42. Joe M. Sprinkle, "Law," in *Evangelical Dictionary of Biblical Theology*, 469.

within his moral order, an order that God has impressed upon the structure of his good creation. Though sin corrupts man's ability to see God's moral order with all the clarity that it possesses, God never withdraws the order, and sin never fully eradicates man's ability to perceive it.

Well before Sinai, Scripture tells us, men like Enoch and Noah walked with God in holiness. Abraham, the father of faith, also walked with God (Gen. 15:16; 17:1). Willem Van Gemeren notes that "even though [Abraham] did not receive the Decalogue, he kept the law of God. He was 'blameless' in that he adhered to God's unwritten law ([Gen.] 17:1; 18:19)." Although Abraham was saved by a divine righteousness apart from the law of Moses, "it is important to note that the 'father of faith' was a lawkeeper!"[43]

As we saw in chapter 9, the Mosaic code expressed a written summary of the moral law of God. While there never was a time in the history of the world in which idolatry, murder, or disrespect of parents were acceptable behaviors, these and the rest were "written down in the Ten Commandments and incorporated in the Mosaic covenant. The Decalogue summarizes the moral law and is clearer, more fixed, and more effective than the natural law."[44] Because of human blindness due to sin, God's written moral law served as a reminder and a spur for the hard-hearted. This is precisely Paul's point when he says that the Mosaic law "was added because of transgressions" (Gal. 3:19).

The New Covenant Renders the Temporary Aspects of the Mosaic Law Obsolete

Further, the Mosaic law served to guide Israel's life in the land. In keeping the law Israel would enjoy a familial fellowship with God and fulfill its mission as Yahweh's light to the nations. Since the Mosaic code applied God's moral law to the conditions of Israel's Old

43. Willem Van Gemeren, "The Law Is the Perfection of Righteousness in Jesus Christ: A Reformed Perspective," in *Five Views on Law and Gospel*, ed. Greg L. Bahnsen et al. (Grand Rapids: Zondervan, 1993), 20.
44. Ibid., 47.

Testament experience, it addresses a specific but temporary context. Thus, we should not be surprised to find that the New Testament explicitly abrogates much of the Mosaic code. The New Testament deems the civil and cultic aspects of the law obsolete. The realization of the new covenant in the death of Christ and the coming of the Spirit at Pentecost abrogates food laws, circumcision, temple, sacrifices, and the Old Testament priesthood. Christ has abolished the commandments and regulations that separated Jew from Gentile (Eph. 2:15).

Paul Takes Issue with Pharisaical Legalism

The historical transition from the old covenant to the new was not an easy one. During the postexilic era, elements within Israel became very legalistic in their observance of the Mosaic law. For some groups such as the New Testament–era Pharisees, law keeping took on redemptive significance as conformity to the law became the mark of belonging to the people of God. One proved his election by carefully observing the Mosaic law, especially its Sabbath instructions and its regulations concerning ritual cleanliness. When Jews became believers in Jesus Christ, they often retained these notions about the centrality of the law. And when Gentiles became believers, in some cases Jewish Christians would seek to require them to observe Jewish traditions.

Paul writes the Epistle to the Galatians to oppose just such a problem. The Judaizing heresy threatened to undermine the work of the gospel in Galatia. The Judaizers held that if Gentile Christians wanted to share in the blessings of the covenant, they must be circumcised and submit to the Mosaic law. Paul argues that the old covenant was a temporary arrangement meant as a guide and tutor for the people of God until Christ. The law was to lead to Christ (Gal. 3:24).[45]

Paul carefully notes that the Mosaic law was given after God's gracious promises to Abraham and that the law could not revoke those promises. The law came in as the servant of God's grace, a grace that

---

45. Jesus said the same thing: "If you believed Moses, you would believe me, for he wrote about me" (John 5:46).

meets its acme in Jesus Christ and the coming of the Spirit (Gal. 3:15–25).

Through their exaltation of the law, the Judaizers have given priority to the Mosaic covenant rather than the Abrahamic, which the Mosaic served. This error has led them into the dangerous heresy of thinking that the observance of the law offers a way of salvation. But it is the new life of the Spirit, not the regulations of the old covenant, that enables the Christian to fulfill the will of God (Gal. 5:14).[46] It is not true, as the Judaizers allege, that one must become a Jew (i.e., observe old covenant cultic regulations) in order to be or become a Christian.

The New Covenant Climactically Fulfills the Old

The coming of Christ is the climactic fulfillment toward which the whole history of Israel has been leading. Once Christ comes, one can no longer live in the old covenant. All of God's work with and in Israel, if viewed apart from its proper perspective of the promise of salvation in Christ, is nothing more than a curse and a slavery.

Above all things—and grounding all—is the reality that the covenant is fundamentally a relationship, a personal and committed relationship with God. Worship serves and nurtures covenant relationship, and moral behavior is the natural expression of the covenant in our lives. While true religion can never be separated from morality or religious observance, neither morality nor religious observance is the essence of religion. Neither rite nor morality can make one right with God. Outside of Christ, the law kills.

Paul links his claim that the Mosaic covenant is no longer in force for new covenant believers to the idea that the new covenant is superior to the old (Gal. 3–4; 2 Cor. 3). As a parable for the passing away of the old covenant, Paul describes the fading glory of Moses. He does not disparage the Mosaic covenant but says that it came in glory and was a glorious covenant. Thomas Schreiner explains that in 2 Corinthians 3, as in Galatians 3–4,

46. Cf. Rom. 8:3–4; 13:10.

The defect in the law was due to human inability to perform it. The law provides no power to obey so that "the letter kills" (v. 6), and it results in "death" (v. 7) and "condemnation" (v. 9). The new covenant ministry of the Spirit is superior because the Spirit writes the law on the heart (v. 3) and "gives life" (v. 6). Moreover, the new covenant is superior because its glory lasts forever (vv. 8, 11) and it provides righteousness (v. 9).[47]

Paul's argument here is comparative. The old covenant was glorious, but its glory fades. As such, it does not compare to the abiding glory of the new covenant. Since the Mosaic law demanded obedience to the revealed will of God but in itself was powerless to effect that obedience, we may consider it a ministration of death and condemnation. The new covenant, however, is a ministry of the Spirit and a ministry of righteousness, for it effects the forgiveness of sin and the power to live out the righteousness of God.

Moses was good, but Christ is greater. The old covenant had its glory, but the glory of the new covenant exceeds it. Paul's argument, then, is much like that of the author of the Epistle to the Hebrews. It is an argument from the lesser to the greater, from the glorious to something even more glorious. And just as is the case in Hebrews, Paul writes to proclaim the preeminence of Christ. "If the old covenant is good, then how much better will the new be?"[48]

Outside of the Pauline corpus, John 1:17 is a verse that, read in isolation, may seem to pit Moses against Jesus and law against grace: "For the law was given through Moses; grace and truth came through Jesus Christ." Many Christians read this as a statement of sharp contrast. The Old Testament was a revelation of law; the New Testament is one of grace; and the two stand in opposition to one another.

John's point, however, is the same historical-redemptive comparison that Paul and the author of Hebrews put forth, that the greatness of God's grace in Jesus Christ claims preeminence. It is not that

47. Thomas R. Schreiner, *The Law and Its Fulfillment: A Pauline Theology of Law* (Grand Rapids: Baker, 1993), 130.
48. Newman, "Covenant, New Covenant," 248.

there was no grace or truth in Moses,[49] for there was. But when compared with Jesus and the new covenant, the era of Moses is law. "Grace and truth in complete manifestation and embodiment came by Jesus Christ," comments John Murray.[50]

The Believer and the Law

Despite the fact that the realization of the new covenant renders obsolete the Mosaic covenant and its articulation of the law, this does not suggest for a second that the believer lives without law. God's moral law abides, and Paul exhorts believers to fulfill its demands in love (Gal. 5:14; Rom. 13:8–10).[51]

The power of the indwelling Spirit makes it possible that the requirements of the law may be met by people who live by the Spirit (Rom. 8:14). The principle fruit of the Spirit is love, "for he who loves his fellow man has fulfilled the law" (Rom. 13:8).

Although the New Testament stresses the new mode by which God's law is administered under the new covenant, it harkens back constantly to the Decalogue of Exodus 20. Thus O. Palmer Robertson is able to say that "since the 'ten words' of the Mosaic covenant provide a basic summation of the will of God, their abiding significance in the life of the believer is assured."[52] The great underlying continuity between the Old Testament and the New is that "we recognize *the moral will of the same God* behind the specific, culture-related Israelite injunction and principle applied to relationships within the Christian church."[53]

This means that the Old Testament law is still of great value to the church. Christians today are as prone to the evils of idolatry and selfishness, secularism and injustice that Israel was. By applying the

---

49. On the Old Testament background of "grace and truth" in John 1:17 see Lester J. Kuyper, "Grace and Truth: An Old Testament Description of God and Its Use in the Johannine Gospel" *Interpretation* 18 (1964), 3–19.

50. John Murray, *Principles of Conduct* (Grand Rapids: Eerdmans, 1957), 150.

51. Cf. Rom. 12:1–15:13; Gal. 5:13–6:10; Col. 3:1–4:6; 1 Thess. 4:1–5:22.

52. Robertson, *The Christ of the Covenants*, 185.

53. Christopher J. H. Wright, *An Eye for An Eye: The Place of Old Testament Ethics Today* (Downers Grove, Ill.: InterVarsity Press, 1983), 161.

moral law of God to concrete situations within Israel's life, the Mosaic law gives us a paradigm for living out the law under the new covenant. God called Israel continually to fight against the idolatrous, the perverted, the destructive, and the callous. "Here at least is a framework," writes Christopher Wright. "Israel was called to fight these things. There is a battle for the church as well."[54]

Jesus Radicalizes the Personalism of the Law

But the heart and soul of the law is not the call to confront the idols and false ideals of the world. Nor does it engender the piety of negation, the creation of sin lists. The law exists to remind us of our true allegiance and to challenge us to walk in the way of the Lord. This is the personalist core of the biblical faith. *You* must worship *me*.

The new covenant picks up this covenant personalism and radicalizes it in two ways. First, Jesus emphasizes the fact that the law is about personal allegiance in his great summary of the law:

> Love the Lord your God with all your heart and with all your soul and with all your mind and with all your strength . . . Love your neighbor as yourself. (Mark 12:30–31)

The law demands our whole-souled commitment to the worship of God alone and to his service in our love of our neighbor. Jesus calls us to personal relationship with God.

Second, by declaring himself to be the Son of the Father, the one through whom the Father is known, Jesus associates himself with the God of the Decalogue's first commandment and the God of the new covenant's great commandment. Under the terms of the new covenant, personal relationship with God is personal relationship with Jesus.

The messianic promises of the new covenant have begun in Christ. It is now unthinkable to live as though Christ has not been born, died for our sins, and risen to resurrection life. The old covenant pales in comparison with the power of the end of the ages that has dawned

---

54. Ibid., 188.

in Christ. God's one covenant story holds together in his Son; and the entire drama must be understood in his light. Thus the covenant is newly shaped by the death and resurrection of Jesus. And Jesus is the true glory of the old covenant as well as the new. God's covenant revelation in Moses looked toward Christ; and now that Christ has come, the entire covenant story is redefined in terms of him. Jesus Christ is the *new* in new covenant.

13

THE CHURCH

The Messianic Community of the New Covenant

The obvious result of Jesus' coming and his giving the Holy Spirit is the New Testament church. In the context of the overarching covenant story of Scripture, the church is the messianic community of the new covenant. In this chapter we consider how the church relates to Israel, the people of God in the Old Testament.

We must also relate the church to the kingdom of God. Jesus in his earthly ministry announces that the kingdom of God is at hand. How does this fresh phrase relate to the idea of covenant? And how does it relate to the New Testament church?

THE KINGDOM IS AT HAND

In this book we have followed the leading of Scripture's covenant theme. But there are other ways to tell the story. One such way utilizes the biblical notion of the kingdom of God. While the phrase

241

kingdom of God does not appear in the Old Testament, the concept lies at the heart of the Old Testament.

The King of Creation

The Old Testament centrally conveys that Yahweh is the great King who rules over creation, all creatures, the kingdoms of the world, and in a special way over his chosen people. The rule of the sovereign Lord is to be realized throughout the length and breadth of creation. A number of psalms celebrate God's kingship over the world (Ps. 93:1; 96:4–10; 104; 136; cf. Isa. 6:5; Jer. 46:18). S. G. De Graaf begins his four-volume work *Promise and Deliverance* with Yahweh's kingship: In the beginning God created the kingdom of God. In Genesis 1 "we are not just told that God created all things. What is revealed first and foremost is the Kingdom of God."[1]

The King of Israel

Through Adam's rebellion, a rival regime establishes a beachhead in God's world. While God is the rightful King, the fallen sons of Adam refuse to swear allegiance to his rule or follow his commands. Yet in his grace, God commits himself to reclaim lost allegiance and to deliver man from the awful regime of sin and death.

God's strategy showcases his kingship. When he calls Abraham, it becomes apparent that God will focus his redemptive work upon one people, a people who will receive his word, embody his kingly rule, and be his testimony in the world. At Sinai God constitutes the descendants of Abraham as a theocratic nation to model the kingdom of God in the world and thereby to bless all nations. When David becomes king over Israel, God adopts him as the representative of God's own kingship. Thus the Davidic rule over Israel becomes an emblem of God's rule over all nations. The Old Testament writers frequently refer to God as the King over his people Israel (Deut. 33:5; Ps. 84:3; 145:1; Isa. 43:15).

1. S. G. De Graaf, *Promise and Deliverance* (St. Catharines, Ont.: Paideia, 1977), 1.29.

But the kingdom of sin and death still reigns. And the kingdom of God on earth has not been fully realized. Consequently, the prophets begin to look for a future realization of the kingdom under an ideal Davidic king, the Messiah (e.g., Dan. 2:44–45; 7:13–14; Obad. 21). While the covenant theme looks back to beginnings, the kingdom theme has a decidedly future trajectory in Scripture. The kingdom is the ideal future reign of God in which the forces of sin and death will be defeated and the people of God will live in intimate and eternal relationship with God.

The King Has Come

The kingdom theme comes into its own in the New Testament. Covenant language and imagery predominate in the Old Testament, while the kingdom of God takes center stage in the New, especially in the Gospels of Matthew, Mark, and Luke (the Synoptics). Covenantal elements do appear within the New Testament, but they often serve the kingdom theme. The kingdom comes to the fore in the Gospels for a singular and eminently simple reason: the King has come.

All three Synoptic Gospels present Jesus' public ministry as beginning with a proclamation of the kingdom:

> After John was put in prison, Jesus went into Galilee, proclaiming the good news of God. "The time has come," he said. "The kingdom of God is near. Repent and believe the good news!" (Mark 1:14–15; cf. Matt. 4:17)

The kingdom is not simply near—contrast John the Baptist's proclamation of the nearness of the kingdom (Matt. 3:1–2). The time has come. The kingdom is here.

Luke's account makes this even more obvious. Standing to read the Word of God in the synagogue, Jesus reads aloud from Isaiah:

> The Spirit of the Lord is on me,
>> because he has anointed me
>> to preach good news to the poor.

He has sent me to proclaim freedom for the prisoners
    and recovery of sight for the blind,
to release the oppressed,
    to proclaim the year of the Lord's favor. (Luke 4:18–19)

Luke relates that Jesus makes the further declaration: "Today this scripture is fulfilled in your hearing." In this Jesus does nothing less than claim that he is the Messiah, the one who will come to usher in the kingdom of God. The God who came to Israel in Egypt to make them his people, who came to them again and again in their history, had promised that he would come again in the future to establish his kingdom. The time has come, and God has come in Jesus. The future tense of the Old Testament expectation of the kingdom (as in Jeremiah's "Behold the days are coming") has become an emphatic present ("the kingdom of God is at hand" [Mark 1:14]). The dominion of God over all things and all powers has begun.

We experience history in linear fashion from past to present, with the future still out before us as little more than a possibility. In the person and work of Jesus, however, the future is reality. The future collides with the present in Christ. "The powers of the coming age" (Heb. 6:5) are present. John's Gospel portrays Jesus as the man from heaven; the Synoptics call him the man from the future. For John, heaven has come to earth in Jesus; for the Synoptic Gospels, the future has come into the present in the person of Jesus Christ. The future has invaded and the *eschaton* (the end times) has poured into history.

Kingdom Blessing Precedes Kingdom Judgment

When Jesus finishes reading Isaiah 61:1–2, Luke adds, "he rolled up the scroll, gave it back to the attendant and sat down. The eyes of everyone in the synagogue were fastened on him." Luke seems to draw attention to Jesus' abrupt ending of his reading. Indeed, Jesus omitted the line "and the day of vengeance of our God" which finishes the parallelism of "to proclaim the year of the Lord's favor."

Isaiah's prophecy describes Messiah's coming at the outset of the eschatological day of the Lord. In this day of salvation and deliverance God will come to his people, consummate the promises of the new covenant, and bring the kingdom of God to realization. Jesus' hearers knew from prophecy that the coming day of the Lord would bring, inseparably, blessing and judgment. Salvation and judgment, redemption and vengeance, mercy and wrath, blessing and curse went hand in hand in the prophetic understanding of the coming kingdom of God. If God is going to save his people from their enemies, then he must judge their enemies.

John the Baptist, for example, expected this dual thrust of God's promised eschatological work. When John announces that the kingdom of God is near, he points to Jesus as the Messiah and indicates that he brings salvation and judgment. To the Sadducees who have come to him while he was baptizing John says, "You brood of vipers! Who warned you to flee from the coming wrath? . . . The axe is already at the root of the trees, and every tree that does not produce good fruit will be cut down and thrown into the fire" (Luke 3:7, 9). The Messiah has arrived. Therefore the salvation and judgment have begun.

But when Jesus reads from the Isaiah scroll, he omits the reference to judgment. This curious and pregnant omission says something important about the kingdom as proclaimed by Jesus and the writers of the New Testament. The Old Testament had expected a singular eschatological event, a day in which the Messiah would come, save, and judge, all at the same time. Here Jesus is saying that the kingdom is staged or progressive rather than a unitary, single divine event.

The coming of the kingdom will not transpire all at once. The day of judgment is yet to come. First comes "the year of the Lord's favor." A season of grace will precede the judgment.[2] Jesus has come not to judge the world but to save it. The judgment announced by the prophets and John the Baptist has been delayed so that the gospel of the kingdom can be preached. Jesus says exactly this in

---

2. Hoekema has called the New Testament understanding of the coming of the kingdom an "inaugurated eschatology" in that it allows for both a present and a future dimension to the fulfillment of God's eschatological promises. See Anthony Hoekema, *The Bible and the Future* (Grand Rapids: Eerdmans, 1979), 1–75.

Matthew 24:14: "And this gospel of the kingdom will be preached in the whole world as a testimony to all nations, and then the end will come."

This, writes George Ladd, is the central and distinctive element in Jesus' own message, namely, that before the final visitation of God to judge sin and transform creation into a new heaven and a new earth, the kingdom has come in the person, words, and deeds of Jesus, bringing the blessings of the future kingdom of God to man. Heaven has come to earth in Jesus Christ.[3]

This is not to say that the ministry of Jesus postpones to the future all kingdom judgment. Even as Jesus as Messiah brings the salvation long promised, he also begins to engage and conquer the powers of sin and the devil. Jesus cites his power over the demonic forces as an evidence of the arrival of the kingdom:

> If I drive out demons by the Spirit of God, then the kingdom of God has come upon you.
> Or again, how can anyone enter a strong man's house and carry off his possessions unless he first ties up the strong man? Then he can rob his house. (Matt. 12:28–29)

When the seventy-two evangelists Jesus has commissioned return and joyfully report the success of their mission, that "even the demons submit to us in your name," he replies that he has given them the authority to overcome the power of the enemy, for Satan has been vanquished: "I saw Satan fall like lightning from heaven" (Luke 10:17–18).

The Hidden Kingdom

But in what way has the kingdom already come? Our continuing experience of brokenness tells us that the powers of sin and death have not been routed. The creation still groans under the burden of sin. Men and nations still evidence the effects of the fall.

---

3. George Eldon Ladd, *The Pattern of New Testament Truth* (Grand Rapids: Eerdmans, 1968), 54–56.

The New Testament answers that the kingdom at present is hidden, advancing in secret. As the parables of the kingdom (Matt. 13) reveal, the kingdom has invaded history without disrupting the present order. It grows slowly within human affairs. The reign of sin and death will be destroyed and God's rule will know its full glory, but until that day the kingdom of God is hidden to all but those who have faith in Jesus Christ. The glorious manifestation of the rule of God that will effect the utter defeat of sin and death will be preceded by an indefinite period of hiddenness and ambiguity. In fact, sometimes the rule of God will be scarcely discernible in the world.

The kingdom at present advances not by revolution or overt power but by the spiritual transformation and the moral reformation of the people of God. As a small seed produces the mature tree, the kingdom works from the inside out, transforming and redirecting the life of the believer—and through him his society—toward obedient service to the will of God.

If Jesus does not come to effect the fullness of the kingdom in all its cosmic glory, what then is the purpose of his incarnation and his message? What is the significance of his separating "the year of the Lord's favor" from "the day of vengeance"? This time between the first and second comings of Christ, this time between the inauguration of the kingdom and its eschatological consummation, is typified by Christ's calling men and women into a new community, a new people of God, a people who will bear the name of Christ. It is in this community that we see kingdom transformation underway.

THE NEW COVENANT COMMUNITY OF FAITH

The most common New Testament designation for the people of God is the church. Many scholars have noted that the word *church* (*ekklēsia*) means "called-out ones," and it does. But let us not read too much theological significance into the bare word. *Ekklēsia* is not a uniquely biblical term but a nontechnical word meaning "gathering" or "assembly," and it is used in classical Greek to refer to political gatherings of people. The Romans used it to refer to guilds or clubs. Thus an *ekklēsia* was a group of people who came together for a distinct purpose.[4]

The Septuagint, a third century B.C. Greek translation of the Old Testament, used *ekklēsia* to refer to an army gathering to prepare for war (1 Sam. 17:47) and the coming together of an unruly crowd (Ps. 25:5). Most significantly, however, the Septuagint used *ekklēsia* to render the Hebrew word for the *assembly* of the people of Israel before God in worship. As the congregation of the people of God, the word *ekklēsia* appears about one hundred times in the Greek Old Testament.

As Paul uses the word *ekklēsia*, it denotes not just gatherings of believers but also a corporate entity. Thus Paul envisions particular churches—for example, "the church which is at Corinth" (1 Cor. 1:2; 2 Cor. 1:1)—and the church as a people, the elect of God (e.g., Eph. 1:22–23; Col. 1:18). As a corporate entity, the church is the body of Christ (Eph. 4:15), God's workmanship (Eph. 2:10), the people of God (Eph. 2:12), the household or family of God (Eph. 2:19; 3:15; 4:6), the temple of God (Eph. 2:19ff.), the bride of Christ (Eph. 5:25), and the church for which Christ died (Eph. 5:23–27).

Jesus mentions the church only twice in the Gospel record. John Murray claims that these references compliment Paul's notion of the church, for "in Jesus' own teaching we find the particular and inclusive uses of the term."[5] Matthew 18:17 addresses discipline in the church (particular), and in Matthew 16:18 Jesus says that he will build "my church" (inclusive).[6]

4. Robert Banks, *Paul's Idea of Community: The Early House Churches in Their Historical Setting* (Grand Rapids: Eerdmans, 1988), 34.

5. John Murray, "The Nature and Unity of the Church" in *Collected Writings of John Murray*, 4 vols. (Edinburgh: The Banner of Truth, 1977), 2:324.

6. Murray carefully avoids the phrase *universal church* when he speaks of the church as an inclusive or generic reality. Eager to head off any abstraction in our understanding of the church, Murray rightly insists that "the church may not be defined as an entity wholly invisible to human perception and observation. What needs to be observed is that, whether the church is viewed as the broader communion of the saints or as the unit or assembly of believers in a home or town or city, it is always a visible observable entity. The spiritual facts that constitute persons members of the church, though invisible, nevertheless find expression in what is observable." Ibid., 2:326.

Identifying the Church in Relationship to Israel

Jesus claims that he was sent "only to the lost sheep of Israel" (Matt. 15:24).[7] Yet an ever-increasing tension grows between Jesus and the Jews, a tension that will become an absolute distinction between Israel and the church in the apostolic and postapostolic times. It becomes essential to describe how these two relate.

The New Testament writers identify the church by relating it to what they already know—the Old Testament people of God. They recognize continuity and discontinuity, clear similarities but also significant differences between the Old Testament people of God and the church. Just as each unfolding epoch in covenant history picks up on and assumes what has gone before, so the church is in many ways continuous with Israel. But as the biblical fulfillment of promise always moves the people of God beyond what they were in former times, so the church is more than Israel and superior to it. What we find is that, even as Jesus is the new in new covenant, he is the new in the people of God also.

Old Testament Imagery Describes the Church

The New Testament uses language and imagery from the Old Testament to describe the new covenant community of faith in ways that suggest a real degree of continuity with the Old Testament people of God. The image of Jesus as the bridegroom (Mark 2:18–20) and the church as the bride of Christ (2 Cor. 11:2) develop the Old Testament image of Israel as the wife of God (Isa. 54:5–8; 62:5; Jer. 2:2). Other Old Testament imagery for the people of God that is carried over into the New and applied to the church includes the church as the branches of a vine (John 15), a flock led by a shepherd (Luke 12:32; John 10:1–8), the elect (Rom. 11:28; Eph. 1:4), a priesthood (1 Peter 2:9; Rev. 1:6), the remnant (Rom. 9:27; 11:5–7), the true circumcision (Rom. 2:28–29; Phil. 3:3; Col. 2:11), and Abraham's seed (Rom. 4:16; Gal. 3:29).

7. Cf. Luke 1:6, 68, 80; 2:25, 32–34; 24:21; John 1:31.

New Testament writers even apply the name *Israel* to the church (Gal. 6:15–16; Eph. 2:12; Heb. 8:8–10). The apostle Peter addresses the church utilizing the same depiction of the covenant community that Moses laid upon Israel as its charge:

> But you are a chosen people, a royal priesthood, a holy nation, a people belonging to God, that you may declare the praises of him who called you out of darkness into his wonderful light. Once you were not a people, but now you are the people of God; once you had not received mercy, but now you have received mercy. (1 Peter 2:9–10)

Just as Israel had been called to be a chosen race, a royal priesthood, a holy nation, and God's own people, so too is the church. While the calling to be a holy people appears frequently in the Old Testament,[8] this particular depiction of Israel is repeated nowhere else in the Old Testament. Yet here it is applied to the church by Peter.

The New Israel

Why do the New Testament writers call the church Israel? Is it that the church receives the same charge to bear the name of God before the world? Or is it that the calling laid upon Israel by Moses has now passed to the church of Christ?

There appears to be more than some truth in both propositions. Ladd, for example, says that the fact that Jesus calls twelve disciples and that they will have the eschatological role of judging the tribes of Israel (Matt. 19:28; Luke 22:30) is "a symbolic act setting forth the continuity between his disciples and Israel." But Ladd almost immediately says that "by the acted parable of choosing the twelve, Jesus taught that he was raising up a new congregation to displace the nation that was rejecting his message."[9] Writing in the same vein, Herman Ridderbos said, "the church springs from, is born out of

8. E.g., Deut. 7:6; 14:2, 21; 26:19; 28:9; Dan. 8:24.
9. George Eldon Ladd, *A Theology of the New Testament* (Grand Rapids: Eerdmans, 1974), 109.

Israel; on the other hand, the church takes the place of Israel as the historical people of God."[10]

We must recognize that "the Old Testament view of the people of God is more subtle than one which simply equates them with ethnic Israel."[11] The Old Testament prophets drew a distinction between Israel as an ethnic community or merely political state and Israel as a people faithful to God. Israel as a whole was rebellious and disobedient and thus destined for judgment. But still there remained, within the faithless nation, a remnant of believers who were the object of God's love. This remnant was the true Israel of God.[12] The remnant theme carries over into the New Testament. While Israel as a whole rejects Jesus and his message (Mark 6:16; Luke 4:16–30), many Jews respond in faith.

The believing remnant of the old Israel, along with believing Gentiles, constitutes a new Israel, the church. Paul refers to this new community, the old vine of the remnant of Israel and the new engrafted branches of believing Gentiles (Rom. 11) as the true circumcision (Phil. 2:2–3), the seed of Abraham (Rom. 4:16), and heirs according to the promise (Gal. 3:29). Their connection to the historic covenant community is not only of blood but faith. God's great covenantal promises to Israel will be fulfilled, but only in the genuine heirs of the covenant, Abraham's spiritual descendants (Rom. 9–11; cf. Eph. 2:11–22). C. Marvin Pate writes, "Thus, the people of God are those in both the Old and New Testament era who responded to God by faith, and whose spiritual origin rests exclusively in God's grace."[13]

Christ Is the Key

Thus the church does not replace Israel, nor is it simply identical to Israel. Some new historical and redemptive development

---

10. Herman Ridderbos, *Paul: An Outline of His Theology* (Grand Rapids: Eerdmans, 1975), 333–34.

11. J. G. Millar, "People of God," in *New Dictionary of Biblical Theology*, ed. T. Desmond Alexander et al. (Downers Grove, Ill.: InterVarsity Press, 2000), 685.

12. Isa. 10:20–22; 28:5; 37:31–32; Mic. 5:7–8; 7:18; Zeph. 3:12–13; Zech. 8:11–12.

13. C. Marvin Pate, "Church" in *Evangelical Dictionary of Biblical Theology*, ed. Walter A. Elwell (Grand Rapids: Baker, 1996), 95.

has forever transformed and redefined the people of God. That development is the incarnation and work of Christ the Messiah. Since Jesus becomes the new covenant representative, himself the true Israel, the people of God are constituted as such in relationship to him.

Jesus is the key to the distinction between Israel and the church. His calling the church "my church" (Matt. 16:18) is what makes it the true Israel of God. The new people of God are the people of the new covenant, the community of faith constituted in Christ. The ethnic, national, and ceremonial realities of the old Israel are gone. "What counts is to be of Christ."[14] The old concept of Israel will no longer do. Israel must be redefined in Christ; and the church is that redefinition.

The Church Inherits Israel's Privileges

The church inherits all the privileges of Israel. Ridderbos comments:

> To it, as the church of Christ, the pre-eminent divine word of the covenant applies: "I will be their God, and they shall be my people . . . I will receive you, and I will be to you a father, and you shall be to me sons and daughters" (2 Cor. 6:16ff). Out of this fulfillment in Christ the whole nomenclature of all the privileges Israel as God's people was permitted to possess recurs with renewed force and significance in the definition of the essence of the Christian church: being sons of God, . . . sharing in the inheritance promised to Abraham, . . . being heirs of the kingdom of God . . . All the richly variegated designations of Israel as the people of God are applied to the Christian church, but now in the new setting of the salvation that has appeared in Christ.[15]

As a new humanity, taking its origin not from the first Adam but the second (Rom. 5:12–17; Eph. 2:15), the church is the new temple of the living God (1 Cor. 3:16–17; 2 Cor. 6:16–18; Eph. 2:21).

14. Ridderbos, *Paul*, 334.
15. Ibid., 336–37.

The Church Fulfills Old Covenant Promises

The promises of the new covenant—promises looked for even under the old covenant—are fulfilled in the church. The promise that Abraham would be a father to many nations is fulfilled in the extension of the people of God beyond Israel. The Old Testament promise of a new covenant anticipates salvation for the nations. This is fulfilled in Christ, and in the community of the new covenant, the church, not in the Israel of old. Again, Ridderbos finds the nub of the issue to be Christ:

> For it is only in Christ, who by God has been made a stone of stumbling and a rock of offense, as well as a foundation by whom none shall be put to shame, that Jew and Greek, slave and free, male and female, have become a new unity, the one new man (Gal. 3:28; Eph. 2:15); in him the people of God, Israel, circumcision, promise, sonship, and heirship receive their new definition and content; therefore in him, too, is the only and utterly decisive criterion of what may be called by the name of Israel (cf. Rom. 9:33).[16]

The church is the redemptive-historical fulfillment of what Israel was called to be—a witness to the nations—and of what it could not yet be—an eschatological community incorporated in Jesus the Messiah. As such, the church is a redemptive-historical progression beyond Israel. As Ladd puts it, "Israel is no longer the witness to God's kingdom; the church has taken her place."[17]

In saying that ethnic Israel is no longer the historical bearer of the covenant community, we do not suggest that the church is a purely Gentile communion or that God has separated himself and his redemptive purposes from the Jewish nation. The biological descendant of Abraham is not disadvantaged under the new covenant. Biological Israel is not forgotten of God, but the covenant never existed in blood ties to Abraham.

The new covenant expands the old; it does not replace it. Paul offers the helpful image of Israel as a vine and believing Gentiles as a new graft to show that the new covenant community is more than

---

16. Ibid., 341.
17. Ladd, *A Theology of the New Testament*, 115.

Israel (Israel as the believing remnant). In the middle of Paul's discussion of the fate of Israel under the new covenant (Rom. 9–11), he puts his finger on the heart of the issue:

> If you confess with your mouth, "Jesus is Lord," and believe in your heart that God raised him from the dead, you will be saved. For it is with your heart that you believe and are justified, and it is with your mouth that you confess and are saved. As the Scripture says, "Anyone who trusts in him will never be put to shame." For there is no difference between Jew and Gentile—the same Lord is Lord of all and richly blesses all who call on him, for, "Everyone who calls on the name of the Lord will be saved." (Rom. 10:9–13)

New People

The church thus fulfills and continues believing Israel. Yet as a distinctly Christian community, the church differs from Israel in substantial ways. These relate to the mission of the people of God.

That mission remains substantially the same under the new covenant. God calls the church, as he did Israel, to be a royal priesthood and a holy nation, to mediate the blessings of the covenant to a world estranged from God, to proclaim and live out the word of God, to be a mission nation. The church, however, will embrace and employ far more than ethnic Jews.

The new covenant, in the age of messianic fulfillment, breaks down the old boundaries. Jesus includes Gentiles as well as Jews in the company of the community he came to found: "Many will come from the east and the west, and will take their places at the feast with Abraham, Isaac and Jacob in the kingdom of heaven" (Matt. 8:11). God is not only the God of the Jews but also of the Gentiles (Rom. 3:29). The gospel is the power of God for the salvation of everyone who believes, for the Jew first, but also for the Gentile (Rom. 1:16).

Israel had mistakenly presumed that the blessings of the covenant were its alone. Its ethnic particularism prevented it from fully obeying Yahweh's missional mandate. What Israel failed to do in its self-centeredness has come about in Christ. Those who were once strangers to the covenants of promise have been brought near through the blood of Christ, through his having broken down the wall of Jewish exclusivism (Eph. 2:12–14). Those who were once alienated from the commonwealth of Israel have become "fellow citizens with God's people and members of God's household," a temple in which God lives by his Spirit, built upon the revelation God gave to Israel "with Jesus Christ himself as the chief cornerstone" (Eph. 2:19–22). This description, first made of Israel, is now applied without distinction to those who belong to Christ. The church's membership knows no ethnic, national, or social boundaries (Gal. 3:28; Col. 3:11).[18] The international hope of the Old Testament Scriptures has become a reality in Christ.

New Scope, New Mission Strategy

In the evangelistic mandate Jesus gives his disciples (Matt. 28), he significantly widens the scope of the mission. To complement the expansion of the gospel to the Gentiles, the good news of Jesus Christ is to be preached throughout the whole world as a testimony to all nations (Matt. 24:14; Mark 13:10).

As we saw in chapter 7, God's missionary strategy in Old Testament times was largely centripetal.[19] Yahweh intended Israel to function like a spiritual magnet, attracting other nations to him through its witness to God. He did not call Israel to go to the ends of the earth with the message but to be a living testimony to his rule in Canaan. It was there as a mission station that Israel would witness to the kingdom. In his call, his deliverance, and his giving the law, Yahweh created a peculiar people, a people set apart even as they lived in the midst of the nations, to model his grace and rule in their worship lives, their personal lives and relationships, their commerce and political affairs. Since Canaan constituted a major trade route between Asia Minor, Africa, and Asia, all the other nations of the world would pass through. This one small people in one small but heavily trav-

18. Cf. Acts 10:1–11:18; 15:1–29.
19. Centripetal force is a force that moves toward the middle. Centrifugal force is a force that moves away from the middle.

eled place was to model in miniature God's kingdom intention for the world.

In contrast to the centripetal model of the Old Testament in which the land of Canaan was to be a mission station, Jesus charges his disciples with a centrifugal missionary mandate. Rather than the nations coming to Israel to hear the word of God, the disciples are to move out from the ancient land of the covenant to take the gospel to all nations. The church is called to cross all boundaries—national, cultural, racial, and linguistic—to take the gospel to all people.

> Go and make disciples of all nations, baptizing them in the name of the Father and of the Son and of the Holy Spirit, and teaching them to obey everything I have commanded you. (Matt. 28:19–20)

Yet a centripetal aspect remains a part of the church's mission. As God called Israel to shine as a light, to act as a magnet drawing the nations to it, so he calls the church to be the kind of community that attracts others to it. He intended Israel to live a life that made the nations long for the salvation they saw within it. He intends unbelievers to be drawn by the new life of love, peace, justice, zeal, and purpose that they see in the body of Christ.

In God's eternal plan unfolding in Christ we find "that now, through the church, the manifold wisdom of God should be made known" (Eph. 3:10). The church has been entrusted with the gospel not only to mature its own members but also to proclaim to those beyond its walls. God calls the church to the missionary task of proclaiming the significance of the gospel for all peoples. He calls the church to model the kingdom by displaying the righteousness, justice, and peace of the kingdom. The church will offer a living example of the power of the gospel to redeem men and heal the wounds of sin.

The goal of the church's mission is the realization of the kingdom, to bring the rule of God to man. Too often, especially in the twentieth century, we have truncated this mission by restricting it to verbal proclamation of the gospel and the salvation of souls. At the other extreme, some have restricted the purpose of the church to the realization of a just society. Still others have cast the church's proper task as the establishment of the institutional church. All were right. Preaching the gospel of salvation is mission. Seeking a society of justice is mission. Righteousness and justice go hand in hand in the prophetic vision of the coming kingdom of God.[20]

The new covenant calling to take the good news of the kingdom to all nations provides the essential clue to the disappearance of the land theme in the New Testament. How could something so important to the covenant and the mission of the people of God be virtually ignored by the New Testament Scriptures? We need to remember that Old Testament Israel in the land of Canaan was to model the kingdom for all nations and all locales. As Israel expands under the new covenant to include people from every tribe and nation, so the land also expands to embrace the entire earthly creation. Psalm 137:11 tells us that "the meek will inherit the land." In the Sermon on the Mount Jesus proclaims that the meek "will inherit the earth" (Matt. 5:5). We will have more to say about the creation-wide scope of God's redemptive intention in the next chapter.

New Resources: The Holy Spirit Comes

In his gift of the Holy Spirit at Pentecost, Jesus increases immeasurably his church's resources for the fulfillment of the new mission to which God has called them. After his resurrection Jesus instructs his disciples to wait for the Spirit whom the Father had promised (Luke 24:49; Acts 1:18). Fifty days later, in accord with Christ's word, the Spirit is poured out on them at the feast of Pentecost.

A sudden, violent wind fills the house where the disciples gathered. A tongue-shaped flame appears above each head. Every person is filled with the Holy Spirit, and they begin to speak languages

---

20. Modern missiology has emphasized not only the breadth of the church's mission, that its calling is as wide as creation, but also the centrality of mission to the church's very existence. David Bosch, for example, has written that "mission is not a fringe activity of a strongly established church, a pious cause that may be attended to when the home fires are first brightly burning . . . Missionary activity is not so much the work of the church as simply the church at work." David Bosch, *Transforming Mission* (Maryknoll, N.Y.: Orbis, 1991), 372.

previously unknown to them, praising God and testifying to his mighty deeds.

Luke recounts that Jews and Gentiles from places as far away as Asia Minor, North Africa, and even Rome had gathered in the city of Jerusalem for Pentecost. Each person hears of the wonders of God in his own language. The commotion draws a crowd of onlookers, some of whom suspect the participants of excessive drinking (Acts 2:1–13).

In response, Peter proclaims that the crowd is witnessing something far more radical and wonderful than drunkenness. They are experiencing, he claims, the fulfillment of what the prophet Joel promised concerning the last days. Joel had said that the eschatological Spirit would be poured out without discrimination upon young and old, servant and master, male and female.

Peter seizes the moment to explain that the Spirit has come because Christ has been exalted to the right hand of God the Father. When Jesus accomplished his work of redemption in his death and resurrection, he ascended to the Father. He is thus exalted to the right hand of God, enthroned as King of kings and Lord of lords. And the Spirit whom God poured out on him without measure during his ministry is now Christ's to send to his disciples. Jesus Christ is victor; his rule has begun. And the Spirit who has come to us is the evidence of Christ's exaltation.

Pentecost Marks the Transition to the New Covenant

The Old Testament prophets looked for a coming new exodus in which God would lavishly pour out his Spirit upon his people (e.g., Isa. 32:15; 44:3; Ezek. 39:29) and work a new revelation of his glory and power (Hab. 2:14). That day has arrived in Pentecost.

Sinclair Ferguson notes three historical-redemptive elements relative to Pentecost. First, Pentecost as an eschatological event "publicly marks the transition from the old covenant to the new covenant" looked for by the Old Testament prophets.[21]

---

21. Sinclair Ferguson, *The Holy Spirit* (Downers Grove, Ill.: InterVarsity Press, 1996), 57.

The long-looked-for day of the Lord had arrived; the powers of the age to come were now released. The characteristic feature of this was a distinction in the distribution of the Spirit. He was now "poured out" by Christ in unrestrained measure, and distributed without geographical and ethnic limitation, "on all people."[22]

The coming of the Spirit brings the powers of the age to come into the present (Heb. 6:4). No wonder that Paul can speak of the Spirit as the "deposit" of God's promised future, "guaranteeing what is to come" (2 Cor. 5:5). A deposit is not simply a promise of a future reality but also a down payment or first installment of the future. Thus the Spirit coming now, bringing salvation to the ends of the earth, gives a real foretaste of the joy, freedom, righteousness, and holiness of the kingdom for all people.

Paul also describes the Spirit poured out at Pentecost as a "firstfruit." More precisely, he says that those who are in Christ possess "the firstfruits of the Spirit" as they eagerly await the fulfillment of the coming kingdom and its renewal of the entire created order (Rom. 8:23). Just like a deposit, a firstfruit promises a future reality and grants part of that reality ahead of time. The kingdom that has dawned in the work of Christ and the coming of the Holy Spirit at Pentecost will come fully in the future, for the Spirit is a deposit of that kingdom, and the people of God living under the reign of Christ in the power of the Spirit are a firstfruit of the kingdom.[23]

Pentecost Marks the Obsolescence of the Old Covenant

Second, with its breaking down of all the parochial distinctions of Judaism in the egalitarian promise of the outpouring of the Spirit on all those who are in Christ, Pentecost marks not only the transition to the new covenant but also the obsolescence of the old

---

22. Ibid., 62.

23. "Thus, from the New Testament's standpoint, the 'fulfillment [or 'end,' *ta telē*] of the ages had dawned' (lit.) on those who, through the gift of the Spirit, are 'in Christ' (1 Cor. 10:11) . . . The gift of the Spirit is a central element of the new covenant promise that God had given to his people (cf. Ezek. 36:27), and the inner essence of the promise given to Abraham (cf. Gal. 3:14)." Ibid., 57–58, 59.

covenant. "The divinely given, but temporary, distinguishing features of the Mosaic economy were now rendered obsolete. This is the thrust of Acts 2:17–18."[24] The boundaries have been broken down. Sons and daughters prophesy; young men have visions, and old men have dreams. The mediation of the covenant, formerly the calling of the priest and prophet, now comes upon all.

Now, in Christ, the old distinctions are nullified. Now all of the Lord's people possess the knowledge of God formerly experienced only by the prophets. This was exactly what Moses had longed for, although it could never have been experienced under the Mosaic economy: "I wish that all the LORD's people were prophets and that the LORD would put his Spirit on them!" (Num. 11:29). Now it was a reality.[25]

That Pentecost represents the redemptive-historical obsolescence of the old covenant is testified to by the fact that Pentecost typologically corresponds to two Old Testament events: the confusion of the languages at Babel and the revelation of the presence of God at Sinai. At Babel, God scattered mankind from the tower they had built for themselves (Gen. 11). Instead, he selected a single mission people to bear the revelation of God to the nations (Gen. 12). From that point forward, God dealt with the descendants of Abraham as the mediators of his covenant to the rest of the world.

Consider the correspondence between Babel and Pentecost. At Babel, man was confused to ignorance, for he no longer spoke a common language. But at Pentecost, mankind was amazed and confused to knowledge as they heard people from the far-flung corners of the empire communicate with one another. Rather than seeking to ascend a tower to the heavens and make a name for themselves as the people did at Babel, those gathered together at Pentecost praised God because the Spirit had descended from heaven. Ferguson notes that Luke includes in his account of Pentecost a table of nations (Acts 2:8–12), just as the Babel story follows a table of nations (Gen. 10:1–32). At Babel, God came to judge and scatter the nations into

24. Ibid., 62.
25. Ibid., 63.

many tribes and tongues. At Pentecost, God comes to bless and scatter a new tribe, the church, who will take the gospel of the kingdom to many nations. No longer kept apart by their sin, a reconciled people who possesses one Lord, one faith, and one baptism (Eph. 4:1ff.) is united by one Spirit. Thus Pentecost reverses Babel and hence abrogates any need for a singular nation as covenant mediator.

Pentecost also bears typological connection to Sinai. The coming of the Spirit corresponds to the Sinai theophany, the descent of Yahweh on the mountain (Ex. 19:20). As Moses experienced the glory and presence of the Lord (Ex. 24:16–18), now all the people of God experience that presence. Ferguson neatly summarizes the typological parallel:

> The revelation of God to Moses at Sinai had been accompanied by fire, wind and a divine tongue (Heb. 12:18–31). Moses had ascended the mountain. When he descended he had in his possession the Ten Commandments, the law of God. Christ too had recently ascended. At Pentecost he comes down, not with the law written on tablets of clay, but with the gift of his own Spirit to write the law on the hearts of believers and by his power to enable them to fulfill the law's requirements.[26]

Pentecost Brings New Empowerment for a New Mission

The third historical-redemptive feature Ferguson names is that the Spirit empowers all Christ's disciples—every believer—to take the gospel to the ends of the earth. The Great Commission is to be realized in the power of the Spirit. The Spirit comes for the express purpose of fulfilling the messianic promises: "So will he sprinkle many nations, and kings will shut their mouths because of him . . . I will give him a portion among the great, and he will divide the spoils with the strong, because he poured out his life unto death, and was numbered with the transgressors" (Isa. 52:15; 53:12).

The hidden reality revealed publicly by Pentecost is that the ascended Christ had now asked the Father to fulfill his promise, had received the Spirit for his people, and had now poured him out on

---

26. Ibid., 61.

the church so that the messianic age begun in the resurrection of Christ might catch up in its flow those who are united to him by participation in the one Spirit. Thus, in Abraham's seed all the nations of the earth would now be blessed (Gen. 12:3; Gal. 3:13–14).[27]

Now that the disciples have received the promised power of the Spirit to enable them to be Christ's witnesses to the world, the word of God will be preached to many nations and in many languages (Acts 1:4).

The Spirit of Christ

In all of this we see the essentially christological nature of the Spirit's ministry. Jesus was conceived by the Holy Spirit (Luke 1:35). At the time of Jesus' baptism the Spirit descended upon him to equip him for his ministry of inaugurating the kingdom of God (Mark 1:10). The Spirit filled Jesus without measure (John 3:34), and Jesus carried out his work in the power of the Spirit (Luke 4:14).

But Jesus not only bears the Spirit; he sends the Spirit as well. The Holy Spirit comes in Christ's name (John 14:26), teaching and guiding the body of Christ, applying and fulfilling the work of Christ (John 16:13–15). The Spirit always draws attention to Christ. That is why Peter preached Christ at Pentecost! The Spirit has come to effect and realize the rule of Jesus Christ. The Spirit comes at Pentecost to complete the messianic mission and empower the body of Christ for its missionary task.

The Spirit in the Old and New Covenants

Jesus tells his disciples that the Spirit cannot come until he himself is glorified (John 7:39). This, along with the descent of the Spirit at Pentecost, raises the question of the Spirit's relationship to the people of God before Pentecost. How can the Spirit have been at work in the Old Testament if he is not sent until after Christ's ascension?

27. Ibid., 59–60.

Citing the limited Old Testament reference to the Spirit, many the ologians have suggested that the Holy Spirit had only an occasional ministry prior to Christ's coming. The Spirit empowered selected leaders of God's people, inspired the prophets, authenticated the legitimate king, and gave men wisdom for special tasks.[28] But the Old Testament offers no evidence of a regenerating, indwelling, or empowering ministry of the Spirit in the life of the common believer. Considering the vast scope of the Spirit's ministry in the life of the new covenant believer—the Spirit aids or accomplishes justification, regeneration, repentance, and sanctification—we might well wonder how people under the old covenant could be saved at all.[29]

Reformed theologians have sometimes suggested that this disparity has more to do with the greater revelation of the Spirit and his work in the New Testament, not that the Spirit had a limited ministry under the old covenant. If the work of the Spirit is as crucial to salvation and the life of faith as the New Testament data suggest, then the Spirit must have been engaging in those activities in Old Testament times.[30] After all, what is explicit in the New Testament is already latent in the Old. What is concealed in the Old Testament is revealed in the New. Just because something is not revealed until the New Testament, it does not follow that it is not so until the New Testament.

A good example here is the doctrine of the Trinity. The Old Testament materials are suggestive and evocative regarding a multiplicity within God, but never explicit. How could it be otherwise until the incarnation of the Son and the revelation of the Spirit at Pentecost? Yet the Son and the Spirit have always existed as persons of the Godhead next to the Father. Thus, it is both reasonable and a

---

28. See, for example, Isa. 63:7–14 and 1 Peter 1:10–11.

29. According to the New Testament materials, the Spirit is active in justification (1 Cor. 6:11) and sanctification (2 Thess. 2:13; 1 Peter 1:2). He effects regeneration (John 3:5–8; Titus 3:5), and he unites us to Christ through baptism (1 Cor. 12:13). The Spirit indwells and empowers the believer (John 14:12, 16–17). In that ministry he witnesses to Christ (John 15:26), intercedes for believers (Rom. 8:26–27), leads us to repentance (Acts 11:15–18), reveals divine wisdom (1 Cor. 2:8–12), grants faith (1 Cor. 12:3), and assures us of our adoption (Rom. 8:16–17; Gal. 4:4–6).

30. See n. 29.

matter of systematic consistency to conclude that the Spirit worked—although in nonexplicit ways—in the life of Old Testament believers.

While attractive, this approach remains problematic, for it elevates continuity between the Testaments at the possible expense of the progressive nature of the story of redemption. The Spirit is not just more fully revealed in the New Testament; he comes and empowers at Pentecost. Something new has taken place. Not only is the Spirit fully revealed to us only in and through Jesus Christ[31] such that his work under the old covenant remains somewhat enigmatic to us, but it must also be said that the Spirit comes in greater fullness, distribution, and power in the messianic age. By and through the Spirit Christ promises to be with his disciples (Matt. 28:19; John 16:7). And the coming of the Spirit at Pentecost promises God's abiding presence within his people and his power to undertake the mission of the kingdom, both of which appear to be distinctly new covenant ministries of the Spirit.

THE CHURCH AND THE KINGDOM

We have considered two fundamental new covenant entities: the kingdom of God and the church. Are the church and the kingdom the same? If not, how should we relate them? And what is at stake in this matter?

The Importance of Distinguishing Church and Kingdom

The New Testament theologian George Eldon Ladd has cogently argued that "church" and "kingdom" are not simply different terms for the same thing.

[The kingdom of God] is never to be identified with the church. The Kingdom is primarily the dynamic reign or kingly rule of God, and

---

31. Ferguson appropriately writes: "It is not only *because of Christ* that we come to know the Spirit more fully, but actually *in Christ*. It is apparently a principle of the divine Spirit's working that declines to disclose himself in any other way (John 16:13–15). He will not be known as he is in himself apart from Christ. Before the Spirit rests permanently on all the faithful children of God, he first must rest on the uniquely faithful Son of God (cf. John1:33)." *The Holy Spirit*, 30.

derivatively, the sphere in which the rule is experienced. In biblical idiom, the Kingdom is not identified with its subjects. They are the people of God's rule who enter it, live under it, and are governed by it. The church is the community of the Kingdom but never the Kingdom itself. Jesus' disciples belong to the Kingdom as the Kingdom belongs to them; but they are not the Kingdom. The Kingdom is the rule of God; the church is a society of men.[32]

The kingdom is nothing less than the rule of God. The church is the people of God called to live out and proclaim the kingdom.

A proper understanding of the church places it within the context of the kingdom because God's reign extends over more than simply the church. The kingdom of God has the whole creation in view and ultimately will lay claim to all things. God possesses the inherent right to rule the universe, because he is its creator, not because of any one earthly manifestation of divine reign, even his church. In contrast to this cosmos-wide scope of the kingdom, the church arises because God calls out a people to belong to him through Christ. The church is the citizenry of the kingdom, but the kingdom is broader than its citizens.

Should we confuse church and kingdom, we risk narrowing the scope of God's redemptive and covenantal concern. Wherever God's norms for human existence are realized, the kingdom is present. Whenever human beings sense that things are not as they ought to be, that something is amiss in their lives or in their societies, the kingdom of God is what they are hoping for. Wherever justice and mercy are sought, the kingdom of God pushes back the kingdom of evil. It may—by God's common grace—take place completely outside of the body of Christ. Indeed, the behaviors and attitudes of our unbelieving neighbors may sometimes come closer to the kingdom in some areas of life than those of believers. Conversely, wherever evil is done or pursued, whether by unbeliever or believer, the kingdom of the devil extends its grasp.

The rule of God is realized through the righteous action of God's people in spheres of life lying beyond the institutional church. Chris-

32. Ladd, *A Theology of the New Testament*, 111.

tian political action, for example—seeking a just society based upon biblical insights and commitments—belongs to the kingdom. But such action is not the church. Passing political legislation that coheres with the moral norms of God, whether it arises from Christian concern or is done by unbelievers, is an expression of God's rule in the world. But to call such the church stretches the word *church* beyond all possible recognition or reason.

The Church Is the Locus of the Kingdom, Christ in the World

While the kingdom of God is not limited to the church, the church is the locus, God's focusing point for the kingdom. The church is Christ in the world. Paul calls the church the body of Christ, using this image to portray the diversity within unity of the new covenant people of God. The Holy Spirit sovereignly bestows diverse gifts on the members of the body by means of which he renews individual people and the body as a token of the restoration to come (Rom. 12:3–8; 1 Cor. 12:14–31). While the Spirit gives gifts to individuals, he gives them in the context of the body. A believer outside of the body of Christ is like an amputated ear, utterly purposeless. Conversely, the body of Christ does not exist outside of the persons who comprise it.

Paul also uses the image of the body of Christ to emphasize the church's relationship to Christ. He is the head of the body. He is the unity of the body (Rom. 12:5; 1 Cor. 10:16; 12:27) and its source of life (Eph. 1:22; 5:23; Col. 2:17–19). The church aligns with him as a building takes its alignment from the cornerstone (Eph. 2:20–21). The church is maintained by its vital union with Christ and exists only in Christ (Eph. 2:21–22; 4:15–16).

The body image with Christ as its head suggests that in some way the church is the extension of Christ into the world. The church is to act on Christ's behalf, to be, as it were, Christ in the world. This notion accords fully with the reality of covenantal representation that we have seen throughout the covenant story. The church represents the rule and love of Christ. As Christ has brought the future kingdom into present history, he calls his church to embody the norms, values, and hope of the coming kingdom of God. As Christ was the man from heaven, the church should embody the life and power of heaven in this world. The life, fellowship, and ministry of the Christian community should offer a foretaste of life in the kingdom of God, to reflect something of what the coming kingdom will be.

The Church Serves the Kingdom

Ladd argues that the church serves the kingdom. He notes that Christ's disciples did not proclaim the church but the kingdom (Acts 8:12; 19:8; 20:25; 28:23, 31).[33] In fact, Ladd calls the church an "instrument of the kingdom." The church does not exist for its own sake apart from the kingdom. The power of the gospel of the kingdom has called the church into existence, and the church exists for the sake of the kingdom of God.

Thus, the kingdom must be the ultimate horizon of the church's existence and work. This does not demean the church but rather recognizes that God elects men to salvation for a purpose, that they will serve him.

It is in the church, the people of God, that God intends the power of the kingdom to be concentrated and visible. While the whole world will finally be the domain of Christ, the church is called to be an advertisement for Christ and his rule.

The Church Witnesses to the Kingdom

God alone can and will build his kingdom; it cannot be built by men. But God calls the church to witness to the kingdom. As redeemed sinners, the church is that people who have experienced the life of the kingdom and is thus poised to display that life to the world. Ladd comments, "If Jesus' disciples are those who have received the life and fellowship of the Kingdom, and if this life is in fact an anticipation of the eschatological Kingdom, then it follows that one of the main tasks of the church is to display in this present evil age the life and fellowship of the Age to come."[34]

33. Ibid.
34. Ibid., 115.

The church's role as witness to the kingdom of God calls up its responsibility to preach the gospel, to be apostolic (to use the language of the Nicene Creed).

Just as Christ ministered in word and deed, the church—as his body—must offer word-and-deed proclamation. Our words explain our deeds, and our deeds validate our lives. Unfortunately, sometimes we seem to be happy to limit our witness to verbal proclamation. Even though we preach that the redemptive power of the kingdom has come, our words will be empty if our lives do not evidence the kingdom's power. Thus, Lesslie Newbigin writes that the church is sent "not only to proclaim the kingdom, but to bear in its own life the presence of the kingdom."[35]

As Christ's body, the church is a community that demonstrates love and servanthood (John 13:1–7; 15:9–17) and obedience to Christ's commands (John 14:15–24). As people who have experienced the forgiveness of God, and broken relationships restored in Christ, the people of the new covenant value and practice forgiveness (Matt. 6:12–14). As the advance of the Spirit in this present age, the church evidences the fruit of the Spirit: "love, joy, peace, patience, kindness, goodness, faithfulness, gentleness and self-control" (Gal. 5:16–26). The church is people of the age to come living in this age. As an agent of the Holy Spirit, it models heaven within a fallen world.

The Church Points Toward the Kingdom's Future Restoration

By its nature, the kingdom of God is eschatological—oriented toward the future. The kingdom points us toward God's ultimate restoration of the cosmos, to that day when the reality of the kingdom and God's right to rule as Creator and Lord are again one. The kingdom thus constitutes the goal of God's work in history.

As God called Israel to model the kingdom, so he calls the church to fly the flag of the kingdom, to declare in its life and proclamation where God is going. The church's vision and purpose is constituted by its future hope. It pioneers in the present the principles that char-

---

35. Lesslie Newbigin, *The Open Secret* (Grand Rapids: Eerdmans, 1978), 54.

acterize the future reign of God. The church offers a foretaste of the eschatological reality, points toward the kingdom.[36]

The Church Is Custodian of the Kingdom

In addition to its role as instrument, agent, and sign of the kingdom in the world, the church also serves as the custodian of the kingdom. The church is the salt of the earth and the light of the world (Matt. 5:13–14). In this it must also preserve its saltiness (its kingdom critique of the powers of this world) and keep its light in working order. Part of its task in mediating the gospel of the kingdom to the world is to preserve the biblical message—to attend to it, study it, know it, and proclaim it.

In describing the church as apostolic, the Nicene Creed refers to the church's continuity with the apostolic teaching. This apostolic heritage obligates the church to "hold firmly to the trustworthy message as it has been taught" by the apostles, so that they "can encourage others by sound doctrine and refute those who oppose it" (Titus 1:9). In effect, apostolicity is about faithfulness to the Word of God. As Israel received and guarded the inscripturated Word of God, so does the church. Without a commitment to Scripture, the church cannot fulfill its kingdom mission.

Come, Lord Jesus

Although the kingdom is here in the finished work of Christ, the ministry of the Holy Spirit, and the witness of the church, this presence is partial and mysterious, for the kingdom is yet to be consummated. There remains a future eschatological aspect to the kingdom. Biblical theologians often say that the kingdom has been inaugurated but is yet to be consummated, or that the kingdom is both already and not yet.

---

36. The church's mission as a representative of Christ and his rule within the world provide the necessary insight for the church's relationship to culture. While the body of Christ must always be relevant to its culture in that it speaks in ways that it can be heard, the church is called to model heaven and represent the kingdom of God rather than live by the dictates of its host culture. Keeping in step with the Spirit means that we will always be out of step with Madison Avenue and Hollywood.

On the one hand, the divine reign has come in Christ's first advent. The kingdom of God is his powerful redemptive invasion into the world in the person of Jesus Christ. To enter the kingdom means to participate in the already inaugurated explosion of God's redemptive and transformative power in the world. In the kingdom as a present sphere of existence God calls his people to faith in Christ, obedience to his will, and witness to the kingdom (Matt. 6:10; 7:21–22; 21:31–32; Mark 9:47).

On the other hand, the consummation of the divine rule awaits the glory surrounding Christ's second advent. One day all people will acknowledge the lordship of Christ (Phil. 2:10–11). Likewise, one day the principles of God's kingdom will be universally realized in the new human society that God will establish in the fullness of the kingdom. Then what is God's by right will also be true in fact. The entire universe will be the realm of God's rule. Only then will the kingdoms of this world truly become the kingdom of God, and only then will God's will be done on earth as it is in heaven.

The more deeply we experience the end-time kingdom of God, the more we realize what a small beginning has been made in our lives and our world on God's behalf. Thus we long for the consummation of the kingdom. As we experience the future, we long all the more for its fullness. The more we experience the kingdom in our worship of God in the church, the more we seek the realization of his kingdom in all areas of life. In the light of what God has given us in the Spirit, we begin to discover how much our present situation clashes with God's good gifts in Christ and the Spirit. This causes us to look forward eagerly in hope of that time when Christ will return and complete the work that he has begun in us.

14

THE *ESCHATON*
The Renewal of All Things

Endings give closure; they wrap up a story. Imagine an engaging novel without a final chapter. Or, perhaps you have had to leave a really good movie ten minutes before the ending. You're left wondering what happened. Did the hero prevail? Were the stolen jewels recovered? You would feel that you missed the point of the story.

The final chapter of the drama of redemption not only tells us how the story ends, but also reveals the point of the whole story. It is not too much to say that in order to understand the biblical story, we must know how it ends. When we learn the goal toward which the biblical story moves, we understand the scope of God's redemptive and covenantal concern—what he values, what he holds dear, what he considers worthy of his love and his redemptive work in Christ.

What is more, humans are future-oriented beings. The middle-aged accountant lays plans for her retirement in Arizona. A young couple scrimps and saves, hoping that one day they will be able to buy a house. A college student studies toward a career in architectural design. We live our lives in light of our projected futures.

The future to which we aspire shapes our attitudes and decisions in the present. It's important to know where we are headed, for it tells us how to live in the present. That is as true of what we see to be our ultimate future—the issue of human destiny—as it is of our proximate futures. To live responsibly in the present requires that we be acquainted with our future end. When Jesus taught his disciples to pray, "Your kingdom come, your will be done on earth as it is heaven," he showed that he understood this. Thus we attend to the final chapter of Scripture's drama of redemption and orient our lives in view of it.

The issue of human destiny is taken up by eschatology, the study of last things. Unfortunately, it is one of the least appreciated aspects of Christian doctrine. We know that when we die we go to heaven to be with Jesus, for to be absent from the body is to be present with the Lord (Phil. 2:23–24). And we usually leave it at that. But the world does not end upon our individual deaths. History is not over; God has not finished his redemptive plan. The end of the story does not come until Jesus returns, judges all people, and consummates the kingdom.

But what will that be like? Will judgment bring destruction to the earth, or cleansing? Will the people of God know the bliss of the kingdom on this earth, or in a world so different that it cannot be thought of as earthly or physical in any way?

These have been some of the future scenarios common throughout the history of the church. We may call the belief that upon the Lord's return the world will be destroyed and the redeemed will spend eternity in heaven an escapist view of human destiny. It casts redemption as man's ultimate separation from the earthly creation. Life in the body is temporary. God's redemption will free us from bodiliness, earthliness, and physicality.

Another popular conception is that upon the judgment of Christ the present universe will be destroyed, annihilated. A new universe, one completely other than this present one, will be created, according to this annihilationist view. In support, this view cites Scripture texts that speak of a new earth (Isa. 65:17; Rev. 21:1).

A third scenario is restorational. The people of God will not escape physicality, nor will God create an utterly different world or alternative world for them. Rather, God will renew, purify, and cleanse this world of sin. As there is real continuity between Mike Williams before Christ and Mike Williams after Christ even though I have become a new creature in Christ, so there is a similar continuity between the present world and the world to come.

I believe that Scripture supports the third option above.[1] The Bible witnesses to a restored creation, one swept clean of sin. As we shall see, much depends upon how we view the *eschaton*: not simply the destiny of the redeemed, but also the nature and scope of redemption, the integrity of creation, and the character of God.

BIBLICAL SUPPORT FOR A RESTORATIONAL VIEW

Several aspects of the Bible's grand drama of redemption strongly suggest that Jesus' return will restore his people to renewed bodies and to this world renewed. In considering these indicators we also recapitulate the covenant story. This last chapter amplifies its message and confirms its significance.

The Overarching Story Is Historical and Earthly

The fact that the biblical drama of redemption treats man's historical existence within creation with utmost seriousness testifies to a restorational view of human destiny. The Bible is essentially narrative in form. All other forms of address in Scripture—prayer, poetry, moral imperatives, and so on—receive their fullest sense when seen in light of the overarching universal story that is the heart of Scripture. And it is only within the context of this universal story that our lives make sense as we embody the story and seek its promises.

Many of us have been taught to think of the Bible as a theological textbook, a loose collection of doctrinal statements, a collection of

1. This chapter is a condensation of two formerly published articles: "Rapture or Resurrection," *Presbyterion* 24.2 (Spring 1998), 9–37; and "On Eschatological Discontinuity: The Confession of an Eschatological Reactionary," *Presbyterion* 25.1 (Spring 1999), 13–20.

rational propositions. This leads us to take doctrine, so defined, as the skeleton of Scripture and the content of the Christian faith. But this obscures the primacy that history and story take in the Bible.

The Bible keys on historical events. Biblical doctrine is not a matter of decontextualized ideas but the proclamation of events, the mighty deeds of God for our redemption. Ideas are not sufficient to create or sustain Christian confession. The idea of Christ pales next to the historical man who walked the dusty roads of Palestine twenty centuries ago on his way to Golgotha. Each of his footprints was that of the this-worldly embodiment of the God who promised that he himself would correct the folly of Adam.

No one cares whether Hamlet and Socrates were historical persons. The portrait is sufficient without the subject. Not so with Jesus. The gospel story is tied to historical, particular events. Indeed, without the actual historical life of Jesus of Nazareth—his birth, career, death, and resurrection—all understood as thoroughly historical, the significance of the Word became flesh is lost, the gospel story is only of passing interest, and its declaration of cosmic significance is absurd. According to George Ladd, "existential impact results only from historical event."[2]

The Covers of the Book

As we all know, the Bible begins with a creation story. Interestingly, the Bible ends with a creation story. John the Evangelist uses the imagery of the Garden story of Genesis to describe the eschatological consummation. One cannot read Revelation 20–22 without noticing its similarities to Genesis 1–2. Its river of life (Gen. 1:9; 2:10) reappears (Rev. 22:1–2), and the Tree of Life (Gen. 1:11–12) is restored (Rev. 22:14, 19). The heavenly city descends, and the Lord again walks in the cool of the day with his covenant partner.

The structure of the biblical drama has matching book covers, we might say. It moves from a creation story through a drama of sin and redemption to a consummation in a new and restored creation. This

---

2. George Eldon Ladd, *The Pattern of New Testament Truth* (Grand Rapids: Eerdmans, 1968), 63.

balanced structure argues for a restorational vision of the future. For the covers to match and the story to be complete, it must be a garden restored in this world and history.

Humankind as God's Representative within Creation

God placed man in the Garden and commanded him to rule over and cultivate it. In doing this, God decreed that the earth is man's proper habitation and inheritance (Gen. 1:26–28; Ps. 115:16).

A crucial aspect of Adam's vice regency within the created order was his role as its covenant head and representative. This means that Adam's moral decisions and behaviors would affect creation. When he sins, the entire creation suffers. When he fails to fulfill his mandate as the covenant head of creation, the entirety of the earthly creation fails to work as intended. Genesis 3 shows not only that Adam's sin brought man under the curse of sin and death but also that his fall caught up and affected the entire world. Nothing escapes the infection of sin and its enslaving grip. We might state the principle this way: as man goes, so goes the world.

Creation was subjected to corruption by the fall of Adam. The curse comes because of the man. The created order was guiltless; it was victimized by the sin of the one who was created to image God within the world, to stand for God's rule and exercise authority over the world on God's behalf. The blame for this world's evil falls squarely upon ourselves. Thus, the problem of sin is not a problem of temporality or physicality—no culpability can be put on the doorstep of the nonhuman creation—but one of the fallen human heart.

Enter the second Adam, the one who sets things straight. Just as the fall of the first Adam was the ruin of the whole earthly creation, so the atoning death of the second Adam brings the blessings of redemption to the entirety of creation. As man goes, so goes the world. As the second Adam goes, so goes the world.

Man is not saved in abstraction from creation, but in the midst of a creation that looks forward to redemption. Indeed, our renewal is tied to the eschatological renewal of the creation. We cannot separate our present spiritual regeneration from cosmic regeneration because our present restoration to life is the first stage in the eschatological restoration of all creation to its proper vitality and relationship to God. We are the firstfruits. James 1:18 proclaims: "He chose to give us birth through the word of truth, that we might be a kind of firstfruits of all he created." Thus the resurrection of Christ from the dead is the firstfruits of a future harvest in which all reality will benefit from his saving work.

The goal of redemption is nothing less than the restoration of the entire cosmos. The scope of redemption is truly cosmic. Through Christ, God determined "to reconcile to himself all things" (Col. 1:20). Matthew 19:28 speaks of the renewal (the word is "regeneration") of all things. Acts 3:21 also indicates a cosmic regeneration when it says that Jesus must remain in heaven "until the time comes for God to restore everything."

Why must God regenerate, give new life and direction to, all things? Because the entire creation has been drawn into the mutiny of the human race (Rom. 8:19–24). Because man's fall affected not only himself but also the rest of creation, redemption must involve God's entire creation. Scripture tells us that creation groans, awaiting in eager expectation the renewal of the sons of God. Creation will be "liberated from its bondage to decay and brought into the glorious freedom of the children of God" (Rom. 8:21). All of this confirms a restorational understanding of the *eschaton*.

The Unnaturalness of Death

What happens at death? The vital functions of the bodily organism cease. The heart and lungs no longer move blood and oxygen; the nervous system ceases to transmit impulses to and from the brain; and the body begins to decompose.

But these bodily events often do not enter into believers' description of death. People often think of death as the separation of the soul from the body, usually with the further idea that the soul is the real person. Thus death is no more than the shedding of the nonessential physical shell of the body. The real person now lives on as a soul.

Since the body is not really the person, its loss means that the person merely undergoes a transformation from one form of life to another. Indeed, I've heard Christians speak of death as an aspect of life.

While I affirm the preresurrection survival of the soul with the Lord, I find this casual talk about death, as though it were akin to moving out of one's parents' house to go to college, most disconcerting and flatly unbiblical. The question of body and soul is a most vexing one from a biblical perspective, but one thing is clear: Scripture envisions human beings as psychosomatic unities, not merely souls stuck in bodies for a time. Genesis 2 affirms that "the LORD formed the man from the dust of the ground [*adamah*]" (Gen. 2:7). Hence God names him *Adam*. The very name the Lord gives him securely anchors mankind in God's creation.

John Murray rightly says:

> The bodily is not an appendage. The notion that the body is the prison-house of the soul and that the soul is incarcerated in the body is pagan in origin and antibiblical; it is Platonic, and has no resemblance to the biblical conception. The Bible throughout represents the dissolution of the body and separation of body and soul as an evil, as the retribution and wages of sin; and, therefore, as a disruption of the integrity which God established at creation.[3]

Listen to what Murray is saying here: Death is bad; it is evil. It does not fit into God's good creation. Death is not the release of the good soul from an evil body. Scripture refuses to put the onus of sin upon the body. It is out of the inner man that sinful corruption comes. The fall introduces a fracture, a breaking apart of that which is meant to function as a whole. Death, which is the wages of sin (Rom. 6:23), is the judgment upon that fracture. Death breaks the divinely designed unity of creaturely life and smashes man's relationship with his proper environs. Death does violence to God's creation, tearing asunder the human person as surely and violently as an eighteenth-

---

3. John Murray, "The Nature of Man," in *Collected Writings of John Murray*, 4 vols. (Edinburgh: The Banner of Truth, 1977), 2:14.

century execution by guillotine. Robert Morey describes it as "a terrible ripping apart of what was never intended to be separated . . . Death is an unnatural event and man's subsequent disembodied state is an unnatural existence which only the resurrection will remedy."[4]

Death is the enemy of life, David acknowledges in Psalm 16. He knows Yahweh as the Lord of life, yet he also knows that death faces every man. His only recourse is to place himself in God's hands and trust that somehow God will keep him secure. Looking into the pit of *Sheol*, David confesses that he has no one but the Lord (Ps. 16:2). Quoting David's confession in his sermon at Pentecost (Acts 2), Peter in effect calls back through time to comfort David—here is the answer to your query, David: the resurrection of Jesus Christ from the dead. He has conquered death! God's answer to death is resurrection, and in the resurrection God puts death to death.

While the pagan misconception of the body as a prison house of the soul supports an escapist scenario of human destiny, the biblical understanding of persons as embodied, bodies as good, death as a violent sundering, and Jesus' resurrection as the promise of restoration, roundly confirms a restorational view.

The Noahic Flood and the Promise of the Eschaton

The annihilationist thesis primarily cites 2 Peter 3:3–13 to support its view that the created order will be obliterated in a cosmic judgment upon the coming of the day of the Lord. Peter lists a string of vivid terms to indicate a violent conflagration that will bring this present world to an end and usher in the new heavens and new earth. This world will be destroyed; it will melt; it will be burned; and it will be laid bare. Thus some commentators have envisioned a cataclysmic undoing of creation, an annihilation of the material substance of creation.

Al Wolters suggests, however, that such interpretations are more Gnostic than Christian in origin. He argues that the verb translated as "laid bare"[5] does not denote destruction but rather smelting and

---

4. Robert Morey, *Death and the Afterlife* (Minneapolis: Bethany House, 1984), 94–95.
5. *Heurethēsetai.*

purification.[6] Gale Heide agrees, arguing that the verb should be rendered "purified through testing." Both commentators argue that the text is best understood as referring to a cataclysmic purification rather than an annihilation. Taking his cue from the resurrection, Heide comments:

> God will transform the existing creation. He will right all the wrongs that have taken place on the existing earth. The world on which we now live will continue to exist in a transformed state after God releases it from the bonds of corruption (Rom. 8:19–22). God will transform the earth in much the same fashion that he transformed the resurrected body of Jesus (Luke 24:36–43) and will transform . . . our bodies (Phil. 3:20–21).[7]

Peter's picture, then, is not one of eradication but purgation and purification through a process of smelting (cf. Mal. 3:2–4; 1 Cor. 3:12–15). To be sure, the judgment depicted in texts like 2 Peter 3 represents a radical overturning of our present world. But the coming consummation of the kingdom will not annihilate God's first creation, nor will it bring an utterly new cosmos. Rather, the consummation of the kingdom will be a fixing, a correction, a rehabilitation of God's first creation.

The context of the passage supports this interpretation as Peter refers to the Noahic flood. Peter describes three worlds: the world before the flood, the present world between the flood and the day of the Lord, and the future world after the coming of the day ("the new heavens and new earth" [2 Peter 3:13]). But these three worlds are not categorically different worlds—as Mars is different from Venus—but one and the same world in three different periods of history. Further, they are set off from one another by two cosmic crises: judgment by the deluge of the flood and the future judgment by fire on the day of the Lord.

---

6. Al Wolters, "Worldview and Textual Criticism in 2 Peter 3:10," *Westminster Theological Journal* 49 (1987), 405–13.

7. Gale Z. Heide, "What Is New About the New Heaven and New Earth? A Theology of Creation from Revelation 21 and 2 Peter 3," *Journal of the Evangelical Theological Society* 40.1 (March 1997), 37–56.

This structure sets up an explicit parallel between the judgment of the deluge and the eschatological judgment by fire. It suggests that the eschatological upheaval will be a judgment like the Noahic flood. The world will be destroyed as Noah's world "was deluged and destroyed."

God's judgment in the flood did not annihilate the creation, nor did God create an alternative universe. Noah's world was destroyed insofar as it was cleansed and purified of its corruption. God's creation survived the flood as a purified world, redeemed from the corruption that pervaded it. In like manner, we should envision the eschatological fire of 2 Peter 3 not as demolishing the current creation, but as the refiner's fire burning up the dross so that the purity of God's original creation can once again be revealed.

Jesus also cites the Noahic deluge as an analog to the future judgment as he talks about the signs of the end of the age:

> As it was in the days of Noah, so it will be at the coming of the Son of Man. For in the days before the flood, people were eating and drinking, marrying and giving in marriage, up to the day Noah entered the ark; and they knew nothing about what would happen until the flood came and took them all away. That is how it will be at the coming of the Son of Man. Two men will be in the field; one will be taken and the other left. Two women will be grinding with a hand mill; one will be taken and the other left. (Matt. 24:37–41)

This text is often cited as a proof text for what is called the rapture. Popularized by the Scofield Reference Bible (1909), the doctrine about the rapture is the idea that when the Lord returns, the redeemed will be caught up into the air and taken out of this world. In that event, the church is fitted for heavenly existence and takes up residence in heaven with Jesus. This position has Jesus saying that of the two men working in the field, one is taken to be with the Lord in heaven and the other is left to judgment. Likewise, one of the two women is raptured to be with the Lord but the other is left behind.

The problem here is that the text does not say that the ones taken are to experience God's grace. Interpreting this text as a rescue from earthly corruption imposes a reading upon it that is almost the complete reverse of its most natural meaning. The analogy to the flood strongly suggests that to be taken is to experience God's wrath; and to be left is to know God's grace. Jesus describes the general conditions immediately prior to the flood. People were carrying on their lives and conducting their affairs in disregard of the coming judgment right up until "the flood came and took them all away." The natural reading is that those who are taken are not Noah and his family but rather the ungodly, and they are taken not to redemption but to judgment.

We learned as we looked at the Old Testament story of the flood that Yahweh does not consider judgment an end in itself but rather a means to the restoration of his originally intended relationship with his people. These New Testament teachings, interpreted soundly, confirm this. Together they strengthen the case for a restorational understanding of the consummation.

The Descent of God

The idea of restoration receives further support when we step back and think about the general trajectory of relationship between God and his people. From heaven to earth, rather than from earth to heaven, is the flow of movement and energy, the direction of travel that we see in Scripture. The biblical hope is not one of man going to God. It is not the story of the ascent of man. Rather, it is the story of God coming to man, in man's createdness, redeeming both man and the creation. In short, the biblical hope is the descent of God.

We saw that John's Gospel presents the story as one of "come and see the Messiah. He is here!" In response to Nathanael's confession of Jesus as the King of Israel, Jesus replies that greater things are coming than a little special knowledge of Nathanael's proximity to a fig tree. "You shall see heaven open, and the angels of God ascending and descending on the Son of Man" (John 1:49–51). The point of John's famous heaven-earth distinction is not to pit one against the

281

other in some kind of dualism but rather to enlist heaven in Christ's cause, a redemptive program that includes the earth. When he comes, he brings the power and authority of heaven with him.

Ladd forcefully argues that "if Christ came from heaven to bring men eternal life, this life does not consist of flight from the world to escape to heaven; it is a life experienced on earth in history that will finally issue in the resurrection."[8] In his coming from heaven to earth, the preexistent Son brings light and life to man in the midst of the darkness and death of this present world. John does not conceive of Christ as a Gnostic heavenly Savior who comes from heaven to bring souls trapped in the world back to their home above. Rather, Jesus comes to bring his people eternal life on earth, a life that will mean the resurrection of the body at the last day (John 6:39–54).

The Incarnation of Christ

In the prologue to his Gospel, John declares that "the Word became flesh and made his dwelling among us. We have seen his glory" (John 1:14). Almost every word of this thunderous statement marries God to his creation, the creation to which he had bound himself by covenant promise (Gen. 9:8–16). The power that called the world into being took on the weakness of creatureliness. Contrary to the universality and changelessness sought by the philosophies of Greece, John declares that meaning and truth are to be found in historical particularity, a specific historical person: Jesus of Nazareth, the Word become flesh. The scandal of the Christian faith is that God became flesh in Jesus Christ.

By participating in our reality, the Man from heaven affirms the goodness of creaturely life, the redeemability of creation and creaturely existence. The gospel is not the fracture of heaven and earth but the wedding of the two, embodied as they both are in the incarnation of the one who is *vere Deus* ("fully divine") and *vere Homo* ("fully human"). In the incarnation God declared his intentions not only for humanity but also for all creation. The creation is as much

8. Ladd, *The Pattern of New Testament Truth*, 45; see also 56–57.

an object of the sovereign love and redemption of God as is the soul of man.

If the goal of redemption had been the extraction of the human soul from a corrupted physical creation, we might speculate that God could have chosen a redemptive strategy that did not include an incarnation, a literal embodiment of the Immanuel promise of Isaiah 7:14. It would have taken a soul to redeem souls. Indeed, early church heresies such as Gnosticism and Marcionism rejected the incarnation as a blasphemous confusion of the divine and the worldly. Affirming the reality and virtue of the soul over against a corrupt and corrupting material world, these people felt that incarnation was an irrelevant and messy addition to redemption. Consequently, they denied a true incarnation of God. They held instead that Christ only appeared to be human; or even worse, they separated the Christ (the divine principle) from Jesus (a human person who was the natural son of Joseph and Mary), saying that the Christ possessed the soul of Jesus of Nazareth.

In the Gnostic conception, salvation was nothing less than liberation from the body. Where early church heresies sought to eliminate any this-worldly part of man in the process or goal of salvation, the church fathers fully affirmed the integrity of the body and the earth. Following the logic of the incarnation, anti-Gnostic church fathers such as Irenaeus and Tertullian declared that as Christ was bodily incarnated, resurrected in the body, and bodily ascended to the Father, so salvation is for the whole man, including the body.[9] In the face of the Gnostic distortions that understood salvation as flight from creation and reduced in scope to the life of the soul, the church fathers came to speak not merely of the resurrection of the body but the resurrection of the flesh in order to gain as much clarity on the nature and scope of redemption as possible.[10]

The mutually supporting doctrines of bodily incarnation and bodily resurrection undercut a pessimistic worldview and escapist view

9. Lynn Boliek, *The Resurrection of the Flesh: A Study of a Confessional Phrase* (Amsterdam: Van Kampen, 1962), 31–33.

10. See J. N. D. Kelly, *Early Christian Creeds* (New York: Longmans, Green, and Co., 1959), 163–65.

of redemption. Both incarnation and resurrection affirm—even emphasize—the bodily and the creational. God utilizes fleshly creation to redeem fleshly creation. Neither the incarnation of Christ nor his resurrection runs counter to the purpose of creation. Rather, God's thoroughly this-worldly action in the historical and earthly events of the life of Jesus declares not only that he is sovereign over the material creation but also that the creation is the object of his covenantal love and redemptive intent. These commitments of Scripture lend strength to the idea that we hope for bodily restoration.

The Healing Ministry of Jesus

The Gospels report that "Jesus went throughout Galilee teaching in their synagogues, preaching the good news of the kingdom, and healing every disease and sickness among the people" (Matt. 4:23). Many people consider Jesus' healing miracles proofs of his messiahship. And so they are. But if we insist that he pursued his healing ministry solely to legitimate his kingship, we miss the intrinsic relationship between his miracles and the nature of the kingdom.

The kingdom of God is present in our Lord's proclamation of the kingdom and in his healing of the sick. The healing miracles were not separate or merely a benevolent addenda to his proclamation. Nor were his acts of healing merely products of his compassion. They were themselves embodied proclamations of the nature of the kingdom.

Jesus often healed without preaching. If on these occasions one were to ask, "Where is the word about the kingdom?" we may respond that the healing itself announces that the good tidings of God are addressed to all of his creation and to all aspects of human life. "The blind receive sight, the lame walk, those with leprosy are cured, the deaf hear, the dead are raised, and the good news is preached to the poor" (Matt. 11:5). Each clause proclaims the nature of the kingdom. The kingdom of God is about salvation, the return of health, removing the corruption of sin, and restoring man in the entirety of his existence, including his bodily existence.

Spiritualistic denials of bodily resurrection abstract one element of the living human being as the appropriate object of redemption.

This consequently devalues the healing ministry of Jesus by driving a spiritual-material wedge between his words and his deeds. But there is no room for spiritualization in Jesus' ministry, for much of it focuses on man in his bodily existence. G. C. Berkouwer puts it this way: "Not incorrectly, these miracles of healing have been seen as 'signs' of the kingdom to come. But they are not incidental or haphazard signs eventually to be replaced by other signs. They occur precisely where the bodily existence of man is threatened or disrupted."[11]

The Offense of an Escapist Eschatology

Our visions of the future say as much about our understanding of God as they do about our understanding of sin and redemption. Whether intentional or not, annihilationist and escapist understandings of the gospel portray a god who is either too weak to defeat the satanic powers of sin and death, or else one who refuses to commit himself to his creation. But we find neither of these false gods in the Bible.

The deity of ancient Gnosticism was powerless to do anything but rescue the occasional soul from the corruption of a damned and damning material creation, scrapping the world because it is so ravaged by sin that it is beyond rehabilitation. In the resurrection of Jesus Christ from the dead it was declared once for all, and for all to see, that Yahweh is the sovereign one. Sovereignty means just this: God wins! As Isaac Watts expressed it in his famous Christmas hymn "Joy to the World!" the grace of God in Jesus Christ extends "far as the curse is found."

To suggest that the sin of man so corrupted his creation that God cannot fix it but can only junk it in favor of some other world is to say that ultimately the kingdom of evil is more powerful than the kingdom of God. It makes sin more powerful than redemption, and Satan the victor over God. Reducing the gospel to a strictly spiritual dimension of human existence concedes everything outside of that dimension to the enemy.

11. G. C. Berkouwer, *The Return of the Lord* (Grand Rapids: Eerdmans, 1972), 21.

The Creator of heaven and earth remains ever committed to the work of his hands and refuses to surrender an inch to the enemy. What we see in the ministry of Jesus, in word and deed, is that grace is not only the divine counter to sin but also that grace is vastly more powerful than sin. Christ possesses the power and the mandate to fulfill the promise of Genesis 3:15. No matter how corrosive the powers of sin, the powers of grace are superior. No matter how apparent the finality of death, the resurrection puts death to death. The message of Romans 5 is that, though because of the sin of our first parents, sin and death abound upon the earth, God's grace in Christ superabounds in the resurrection life of Jesus Christ.

The God who repairs that which is broken and restores it to life and covenantal intimacy is the God of the Bible. And he is just the sort of God we fallen human beings need.

Grace Restores Nature

The goal of God's redemptive action in Jesus Christ is the destruction of the kingdom of Satan, sin and death, and the removal of the effects of sin upon man and creation. First John 3:8 declares: "He who does what is sinful is of the devil, because the devil has been sinning from the beginning. The reason the Son of God appeared was to destroy the devil's work." Herman Bavinck states, "Christianity did not come into the world to condemn and put under the ban everything which existed beforehand and everywhere, but quite the opposite, to purify from sin everything that was, and thus to cause it to answer again to its own nature and purpose."

When we speak of sin and redemption, fall and grace, we are actually speaking of healthy versus sick reality. Thus Bavinck claims: "Christianity does not introduce a single substantial foreign element into the creation. It creates no new cosmos but rather makes the cosmos new. It restores what was corrupted by sin. It atones the guilty and cures what is sick; the wounded it heals."[12] Bavinck's use of medicinal metaphors to speak of grace follows the example of Calvin,

---

12. Herman Bavinck, "Common Grace," trans. Raymond Van Leeuwen, *Calvin Theological Journal* 24.1 (April 1989), 61.

who spoke of sin as a disease and a contagion and spoke of redemption as a transfusion of Christ's righteousness.[13] God's gracious redemption in Christ is, then, a cure for the disease of sin, a cure that brings the patient to restoration and new health.

The purpose of grace is the removal of the cancer of sin, first from the heart of man, its root, but also, and finally, from the entirety of the created order. Rather than being anti-creational, grace is pro-creational. "Grace does not serve to take men up into a supernatural order, but to liberate him from sin. Grace is not opposed to nature, but only to sin."[14] The mother promise of Genesis 3:15 does not threaten the undoing of God's good creation but the undoing of sin and its effects within and upon creation, and thus it promises nothing less than the restoration of creation.

This thesis that grace restores nature derives support from the biblical vocabulary for redemption. As Wolters points out, "Virtually all of the basic words describing salvation in the Bible imply a return to an originally good state or situation."[15] To redeem is to buy back, in effect to liberate or return to a lost freedom. To renew is to make new again. Reconciliation is a restoration of a broken relationship and a return to a mended one. Regeneration is a return to life after being dead. Even the word *salvation* carries the idea of a return to health after a time of sickness. Wolters concludes that redemption is a re-creation in the sense that God salvages and restores his original creation and reinstates human beings as his image bearers on the earth.

The Meaning of "New"

The newness of the new heaven and new earth (Isa. 65:17; 2 Peter 3:13; Rev. 21:1) is thus best understood not as new in the sense of different, the creation of a replacement, but as a radical cleansing

---

13. "Christ came not for the destruction of the world, but for its deliverance." John Calvin, *Institutes of the Christian Religion*, ed. John T. McNeill, trans. Ford Lewis Battles, 2 vols. (Philadelphia: Westminster Press, 1960), 3.25.9.

14. Jan Veenhof, *Nature and Grace in Bavinck* (Toronto: ICS, n.d.), 4–24.

15. Albert M. Wolters, *Creation Regained: Biblical Basics for a Reformational Worldview* (Grand Rapids: Eerdmans, 1985), 57.

and purgation that makes creation like new. New means new in quality rather than new in time or origin.

This is no verbal trick; rather, it conforms to the nature of the
theme of eschatological newness in Scripture. The redeemed have
undergone a new birth; we are already new creatures in Christ, live
under the new covenant, and have new hearts. But we still remain
what we were before in the sense that we retain all of our substantial continuity with the world that God made before the fall. In the
act of regeneration, God does not perform open-heart surgery and
literally give us different hearts. Rather our hearts—a cipher for the
whole person or the seat of thought, emotion, and will—are rebuilt,
refurbished, renewed, restored, reconciled, redeemed, and regenerated. Same heart; new orientation, new direction, new power.

Further, if the promise of newness meant an annihilation of God's
first creation and the creation of a replacement, we could not participate in it, for we belong to the first creation. But we do participate in that newness, for we already live within its promise. Thus
Anthony Hoekema writes:

> It is we who shall be raised, and it is we who shall always be with the
> Lord. Those raised with Christ will not be a totally new set of human
> beings but the people of God who have lived on this earth. By way of
> analogy, we would expect that the new earth will not be totally dif-
> ferent from the present earth but will be the present earth wondrously
> renewed.[16]

Speaking of the newness of the age to come as a renewal of God's
original creation rather than a substantively different state of existence does not suggest that the destiny of the redeemed lies in a simple return to Eden, a cosmic "do over." In some ways, the world to
come will be breathtakingly different from the world that now is, or
even the world that Adam beheld on the sixth day of creation. In Revelation 21:1–4 we read the following description of the coming of the
heavenly Jerusalem to earth:

16. Anthony Hoekema, *The Bible and the Future* (Grand Rapids: Eerdmans, 1979),
280–81.

> Then I saw a new heaven and a new earth, for the first heaven and the
> first earth had passed away, and there was no longer any sea. I saw
> the Holy City, the new Jerusalem, coming down out of heaven from
> God, prepared as a bride beautifully dressed for her husband. And I
> heard a loud voice from the throne saying, "Now the dwelling of God
> is with men, and he will live with them. They will be his people, and
> God himself will be with them and be their God. He will wipe every
> tear from their eyes. There will be no more death or mourning or cry-
> ing or pain, for the old order of things has passed away."

Heaven will come to earth. God will dwell in the midst of his people. Death will be no more. Such a world is almost beyond compre-
hension. I, for one, cannot begin to imagine my own life radically
cleansed of corruption, weakness, sin, dishonor, death, tears, mourning, or pain (1 Cor. 15:42–44; 2 Tim. 1:10). The world to come will
be a startlingly new world, for the adamic curse of sin and death will
be forever put away (Rom. 5:21), but it will also be the very same
creation that God called into being in Genesis 1:1. The eschatological destiny of the people of God is more that the adamic garden; yet
it will be nothing less that creation glorified.

THE SHAPE OF THE BIBLICAL HOPE

We Shall Be Like Him

In order to grasp the shape of the world to come, we must look to
Easter morning. The tomb was empty on Easter morning. The same
body that went into the tomb rises to life.

The bodily resurrection of Christ from the dead touches the question of the character of the world to come in two simple but utterly
profound and connected ways. First, the resurrection provides us
with the pledge and model for our own ultimate redemption in Christ.
Paul claims that Jesus is both the firstborn from among the dead
(Col. 1:18) and the firstfruits of the resurrection (1 Cor. 15:20ff.).
What happened to Jesus that Easter morning two millennia ago is
the model for what will happen to each and every person who places
faith in him. As John puts the matter in his first epistle: "We shall be

like him, for we shall see him as he is" (1 John 3:2). That is to say, the future of the redeemed is in the body, not apart from it, for the resurrection was an event that included the body of Jesus.

Second, the corporeality of the resurrection body implicitly argues for a physically embodied future destiny for the redeemed. Bodies are not abstract, ethereal entities having nothing to do with physical space. Hence, the resurrection also argues for a corporeal and earthly destiny for the people of God.

Paul speaks of the resurrection of our Lord as being "of first importance" in the gospel message. It is the centerpiece not only of God's promised future for his people but of all Christian doctrine, for in it we see the goal of the biblical drama, both cosmically and personally.[17] In Christ's resurrection, God has begun to make good on the promise made in the Garden so long ago. Christ is the leading player, the protagonist of the drama of redemption. His work is the central theme of this drama, and his resurrection is the sign of the fulfillment of that work. The day of the Lord has been inaugurated in Jesus' rising from the dead. It is only in the context of the empty tomb that the biblical story holds together, makes sense, and declares the fundamental character of redemption.

The bodily resurrection of Christ not only signifies God's victory over sin and death but also declares the nature of that victory. As the first event of God's promised resolution of the rebellion of the Garden, it anticipates the goal of redemptive history. This is why Paul calls it the firstfruits of the age to come. In Christ's resurrection we have a picture of God's ultimate future for his people given before its arrival. It allows us a peek at the conclusion of the story within the midst of the historical struggle between sin and redemption. As we indicated in chapter 1, if we wish to know where God is going in his redemptive program, if we wish to know what the future has in store for us, we need look no further than the resurrection of Jesus Christ from the dead.

17. Lesslie Newbigin, *The Gospel in a Pluralist Society* (Grand Rapids: Eerdmans, 1989), 109–11.

The message of the empty tomb is that God's triumph over sin and death is total, that history is moving toward nothing less than a fully restored and glorified universe. All that went into the tomb under the curse came out raised to newness of life. The restoration of all things, signified and promised in the resurrection of Christ, is the direction in which redeemed creation is traveling. This is both the believer's hope and the horizon in which we must understand all reality.

A Spiritual Body?

In speaking of that first Easter morning, we readily admit that there are aspects of the resurrection of Jesus Christ that we do not understand. The body of Jesus is somehow changed from its pre-resurrection, premortem state. He suddenly and mysteriously appears in locked rooms. So there are discontinuities between pre-mortem and postresurrection life. Further, Paul's agricultural metaphor of the sown grain that grows into wheat (1 Cor. 15) is but the starting point of a list of striking contrasts that he draws between our present bodily life and the life of the resurrection. That which is sown in corruption will be harvested in incorruption. That which is sown in dishonor is harvested in glory. That which is sown in weakness is harvested in power. And that which is sown a natural body is transformed into a spiritual body.

The greatest difficulty here is the expression "a spiritual body." Under the impress of a faulty material/spiritual distinction, many interpreters have taken this phrase to suggest that the resurrection body (and by extension the nature of the world to come) will be non-material—a spiritual reality in distinction from a physical reality. In effect, the spiritual body is some kind of heavenly body, a body suited for a heavenly existence in distinction from earthly life.

Yet, as Berkouwer contends, "Nowhere in the gospel of Christ is salvation portrayed as the soul's liberation from the body. When Paul says, 'We wait for our adoption as sons' (Rom. 8:23), he adds, 'the redemption of our bodies,' not 'the redemption from our bodies.' "[18] The gospel is about the reclamation of the entirety of existence as the kingdom of God, an existence that includes our bodies.

By juxtaposing the natural body of this present age and the spiritual body of the age to come, Paul is not suggesting that in the *eschaton* we will exchange our this-worldly bodies for bodies made out of some sort of spiritual stuff. Paul's discussion of a spiritual body is not to be read in light of an extrabiblical material/spiritual dichotomy, but rather in light of the distinction that drives the passage—that between the first and second Adams. The context describes a historical antithesis between the kingdom of God and the kingdom of sin and Satan, not an anthropological dualism between body and soul. The tension is between that which is characterized and energized by the regenerative life of the Holy Spirit, over against that life which is characterized only by the sin of the Adamic creation. As Paul uses the word *spiritual*, that which is spiritual has been brought under the transformative power of the Holy Spirit and has been subjected to the kingship of Christ (see 1 Cor. 2:15; 14:37; Gal. 6:1). As the adjectival form of the noun *spirit*, the word *spiritual* refers to that which is guided by the Spirit of God and thus participates in the age to come. What is more, elsewhere Paul explicitly associates the spiritual with the material, thus dismissing any dichotomy between them (Rom. 12:1). Paul's use of the simile of the seed argues for a material continuity between our present bodies and our bodies in the age to come. While the seed is transformed in the process of growing into a mature plant, the full-grown plant is organically one with the seed.

Put most simply, the biblical use of the word *spiritual* does not designate what is nonmaterial or nonphysical. The spiritual body is not an incorporeal body but rather the redemption of the whole person—including the body—as it is brought under the domination of the Holy Spirit. The spiritual-material distinction is extrabiblical, and we should be careful not to read it into Scripture.[19] In fact, if you

18. Berkouwer, *The Return of Christ*, 9, 232.

19. See Robert H. Gundry, *Soma in Biblical Theology: With Emphasis on Pauline Anthropology* (Cambridge: Cambridge University, 1976), 164ff.; and Ronald J. Sider, "The Pauline Conception of the Resurrection of the Body in 1 Corinthians XV.35–54," *New Testament Studies* 21 (April 1975), 428–39.

think about it, the notion of a spiritual body as it is commonly thought of is an incoherent and self-contradictory idea. If by the word *spiritual* one means disembodied, a spiritual body would be a disembodied body, a body without a body. It would be like my saying that I am going to paint my house not-green green.[20]

Paul's idea of the spiritual *body* appears to be a physical, this-worldly body that is not under the power of this present evil age but is rather under the power of the Holy Spirit and the kingdom of God. In like manner, our actions, thoughts, habits and ways are spiritual or unspiritual as they are either obedient or disobedient to the will of God.[21]

Heaven

This world, then, is the scene of the consummation of the kingdom. This outlook in no way denigrates heaven, rightly understood. Heaven is important in the New Testament due to its association with Christ. Jesus is not only the mediator of the new covenant but the mediator between heaven and earth as well.

The coming of the Man from heaven opens heaven to the earth. When Jesus comes, he brings heaven and its powers with him. Catch the imagery in Jesus' statement to Nathanael, "You shall see heaven open, and the angels of God ascending and descending on the Son of Man" (John 1:51). It is as if a door has opened and the powers of heaven are coming to earth in Christ. The blessings of heaven are opened up and made accessible to those who live under the new covenant. The "ministering spirits sent out to serve those who will inherit salvation" (Heb. 1:14) are Christ's to command.

---

20. See Michael D. Williams, "Touch Me and Believe: Spiritual Resurrection Redefined," *Pro Rege* 24.3 (March 1996), 20–22 for a fuller discussion of the word *spiritual* and the nature of the resurrection body.

21. Our contention that Paul's distinction between the spiritual and the natural as being fundamentally moral and eschatological rather than ontological (constitutional makeup) holds for his distinction between the heavenly body and the earthly body as well. That which is heavenly is energized by heaven, attuned to heavenly wisdom, and oriented toward the moral righteousness of heaven.

Heaven has come to earth in Jesus. That was the case in the incarnation, and it will also be the case in the second coming (Mark 14:61–62). The future world is finally a matter of heaven coming to earth and endowing our earthly existence with the life of heaven. The New Jerusalem in the end comes to earth, wiping away all tears and utterly destroying the curse of Adam's sin (Rev. 21). Heaven and the kingdom of God, then, speak about the same thing: "the invasion of history by the God of heaven in the person of Jesus of Nazareth to bring history to its consummation in the age to come."[22]

But the sense of heaven present in the minds of many Christians does require a certain measure of relativization. Many think of heaven as the hope of the believer, but nowhere in Scripture is heaven presented in this way. Quite simply, there is no text that says, "Christians go to heaven when they die." Admittedly, this is a negative argument. But if heaven is our hope, our eternal abode, is it not reasonable to expect the Bible to say so somewhere? Some texts do indeed associate the believer with heaven (Matt. 5:12; 6:20; Col. 3:2; Phil. 3:20), but they do not say that heaven is either our rightful home or our fervent hope.

In reshaping our understanding of heaven, however, we need not dissociate it from the intermediate state. I see nothing wrong with the proposition that departed saints abide with God in heaven. Scripture says little about the intermediate state, except to affirm the presence of the redeemed dead with their Lord in heaven. And Scripture speaks its word about the intermediate state, as Hoekema points out, in hints, whispers, and murmurs. But the key to the intermediate state—however that reality is envisioned—is that it is intermediate. The heavenly existence of the dead is temporary, for it is one that awaits the resurrection of the body and the restoration of creation. When the intermediate state is seen as ultimate, however, the resurrection fails to exercise its intended function.

The resurrection of Christ (and our resurrection, which Paul aligns with it as its eschatological goal) targets unrelentingly, by the sovereign and restorative power of God, the flesh of the mortal body

22. Ladd, *The Pattern of New Testament Truth*, 45; see also 56–57.

and the creation in which it dwells. The hope of Scripture is an embodied hope, a hope that includes bodily resurrection and the renewal of creation, rather than souls flying off to heaven in release from earthly bonds and relationships. The Bible points us toward the future, but it is not a future of disembodied existence in an ethereal heaven. The future that the Bible looks toward is the resurrection of the body (Job 19:25ff.; 1 Cor. 15) and the renewal of our home, this earth (Matt. 19:28; Acts 3:21; Col. 1:20; James 1:18).

Living in Light of the Eschaton

As I have argued here, redemption does not scrap creation but rather advances to restore it. This restoration begins in the present life, called as we are to seek the kingdom of God already in the midst of this age (Matt. 6:33). Berkouwer declares, "The new earth is never a strange and futuristic fantasy, but a mystery that penetrates into this existence and will make itself manifest there, where steadfast love and faithfulness meet, where righteousness and peace kiss each other (Ps. 85:10)." To seek the kingdom of God is to bring our entire lives under the rule of the King who lays claim to every area of human life and endeavor. Abraham Kuyper expressed the Reformed understanding of the sovereignty of God when he said that "there is not an inch in the whole of the broad terrain of human life to which Christ does not lay claim."[23]

Thus, "life on this earth is not devalued, but called" into the service of God.[24] The kingdom of God calls the redeemed into faithful enlistment in the cause of Christ in the world, and for the world. Far from entailing a disdain for the creaturely realm, saying yes to Christ entails, not a rejection of creation but a rejection of sin and a deeply religious affirmation of the things of God. Our God-given calling includes reflecting God's self-sacrificial, redemptive concern for a sin-scarred world. The Bible's word about the *eschaton* offers us no excuse for an otherworldly retreat from this calling but rather sum-

23. Herman Ridderbos, "The Church and the Kingdom of God, *International Reformed Bulletin* (October 27, 1966), 9.
24. Berkouwer, *The Return of Christ*, 234.

mons the people of God to watchfulness and work. The biblical vision of the future does not negate our present existence but rather it enlightens and challenges our lives within God's creation.

We do feel the tension of the church in the present world. Nevertheless, we must not forget that it is this earth, the one in which we live, that is our rightful home. God created us here, not to live in some extraworldly realm. Christoph Blumhardt rightly observes that "it is to discard the whole meaning of the Bible if one argues, 'We have nothing to expect on earth; it must be abandoned as the home of man.' "[25]

The teaching of Scripture is that man has been turned out of his home by sin. A foreign power camps in the creational house and righteousness is exiled. This exile, however, is at odds with the will of God. In view of the blessed hope of Christ's promised return, we seek and claim that which is coming. And that which is to come is a restored and renewed cosmos. Blumhardt continues, "This is the homeland we seek. There is no other to be sought, because we do not have, and there cannot come to be, anything other than what God intended for us in the creation."[26]

The obvious danger of eschatology is that we may fall into all sorts of excesses and speculations that go far beyond what is affirmed by Scripture. Paul wrote that "no eye has seen, no ear has heard, no mind has conceived what God has prepared for those who love him" (1 Cor. 2:9). Thus we must exercise care when we attempt to describe the exact continuities between our world and the world to come. Nevertheless, the point remains that salvation is a holistic, earthly, concrete event that restores the created order, which God made and declared very good. This appears to be an essential element of the gospel proclamation.

"No Eye Has Seen . . ."

The age to come does not represent the destruction or replacement of God's material creation but its renewal. This eschatological

---

25. Christoph Blumhardt, *Thy Kingdom Come* (Grand Rapids: Baker, 1980), 4.
26. Ibid.

drama has already begun in this present age. Yet we cannot describe the ultimate character of the future life in the language of our present this-worldly experience. Paul's quotation of Isaiah 64:4, "no eye has seen," is no mere rhetorical flourish. While God's redemptive grace in Christ restores rather than destroys creation, the fact is that, along with the elements of continuity that we have noted, Scripture also sounds some haunting notes of discontinuity between this world and the age to come. Paul describes both continuity and discontinuity in this passage:

> What I mean, brothers, is that the time is short. From now on those who have wives should live as if they had none; those who mourn, as if they did not; those who are happy, as if they were not; those who buy something, as if it were not theirs to keep; those who use the things of the world, as if not engrossed in them. For this world in its present form is passing away. (1 Cor. 7:29–31)

The form of this world is passing away, not the world itself. And thus there is continuity. Yet we see the discontinuity in Paul's suggestion that marriage and the use of the things of the world are not eternally permanent.

Ladd stresses both the continuity and the discontinuity between our present world and the age to come when he writes,

> Both the divine visitation and the new order, while standing in continuity with the present order, will be so different from all human experience as to be truly ineffable. There are no terms of present experience that can accurately describe it; therefore, picturesque, symbolic language must be used. It is, however, not *merely* poetical . . . [W]hile the language is poetical, it designates real future events of cosmic proportions, indescribable though they be.[27]

It's about Jesus, Not Real Estate

We can better understand the nature of this discontinuity as we consider once again the relationship Yahweh intended Israel to main-

---

27. Ladd, *The Pattern of New Testament Truth*, 53.

tain with the land he gave it. Old Testament religion was grounded in Israel's vision of itself as the people of God, its relationship to God through his elective action, and its relationship to the land of promise. Accordingly, we may chart Old Testament religion as orienting toward three factors:

The three points of the triangle are not equally ultimate. God is the anchor of the covenant, not blood or soil. God promised a seed and the gift of the land, first to Abraham (Gen. 12:1–3), as blessings of Abraham's covenantal relationship to God, and also to aid Israel's calling to represent Yahweh among the nations. Secure space and familiar social relationships were spokes radiating out from the center of the covenant, Israel's relationship to God. The relative status of land was already prefigured in God's call to Abraham to leave the territory and tribe of his father, and later in God's expelling Israel from the land of promise under the Assyrian and Babylonian exiles. And in calling Abraham to give back his son Isaac, God powerfully signaled the relative status of the seed (Gen. 22).

In these terms, Israel's religion continually faced the temptation to absolutize the people and land points in the triangle. And repeatedly Israel succumbed, compromising its spiritual integrity by seeing its nation status and the land of Canaan as sharing the same ultimacy as its calling to stand in covenantal relationship to God. When Israel absolutized its status as a chosen people, it fell into a self-righteous condescension toward the pagan nations about it, and when Israel absolutized the promise of the land, it resorted to political compromise that led to spiritual apostasy.

Similarly, the eschatological perspective of Scripture relativizes both people and land. To think of the consummation of the kingdom as a mere return to a pre-fall creation, to hang our future hope upon simple restoration, on the gift rather than the giver, may be to reproduce Israel's sin of failing to appreciate the blessings of nationhood and the land as means for its worship and service of God.

A group of Sadducees asked Jesus about a woman with seven husbands (Luke 20:27–38): "At the resurrection whose wife will she be . . . ?" This question clearly concerns how the *eschaton* will alter God's present ordinances for human social relationships Jesus' reply is a most difficult one for a strictly restorational perspective: he says that in the age to come there will be no marriage.

It is easy to read too much into this text, but clearly Jesus promises that the institution of marriage will end.[28] God commanded marriage as a creational ordinance prior to the fall (Gen. 2:22–24). This ordinance served as the foundation for human social interaction. Thus marriage is pre-fall—it does not result from human sin. This suggests that, for human social bonding, the age to come does represent something different from the original creation. How different, we do not know, but it is different.

What of the land-creation point of the triangle? Here too Scripture offers provocative hints of discontinuity. This is especially so in Revelation 21. There will no longer be any sea (Rev. 21:1). There will be no need for the sun and moon as light bearers in the New Jerusalem, for the divine glory will shine throughout the new heaven and new earth (Rev. 21:23). Most commentators argue against an overly literalistic interpretation of these statements. Revelation often uses the sea to symbolize that which threatens harmony (e.g., Rev. 13:1; 17:5), so it may here as well. And the passage does not say that there will be no sun or moon but rather, metaphorically, that the light of the presence of God outshines them. Thus we should be careful

---

28. Hoekema makes the same point: "The similarity to angels, we may presume, applies only to the point being made, not to the absence of physical bodies. Jesus' teaching here does not necessarily imply that there will be no sex differences in the life to come. What we do learn, however, is that the institution of marriage will no longer be in existence." *The Bible and the Future*, 252.

not to push such statements too far. Yet they do suggest that we ought not to absolutize the present physical universe. As the *eschaton* relativizes social relationships, it also relativizes the structure of creation.

Indeed, aside from the broad affirmation that the body and the material creation are included within and transformed by the world to come, Scripture tells us precious little about the exact nature of that world. "It is interesting to observe that much of what the Bible says about the future existence is in terms of negations: absence of corruption, weakness, and dishonor; absence of death; absence of tears, mourning, crying or pain (1 Cor. 15:42–43; Rev. 21:4)."[29]

The anchor of the believer's existence is neither the people point nor the land point in the triangle. It is God. Christ is our anchor. Our hope is not so much in the restoration of creation but in Jesus Christ, the one who restores, the one who unites heaven and earth. The glory of the world to come is the glory of Christ. He is always the focus of faith.

The creation can become an idol when it, rather than Christ, becomes our comfort and our hope. Do not get too at home here. Do not find your stability or purpose here. In numerous ways biblically, it is clear that this world is included in the drama of the consummation of the kingdom. But that good news of God's victory over sin and death does not legitimate my building a little kingdom for myself here and now, in the hope that I can carry it with me into the *eschaton*.

Proper Heavenly Mindedness

This world will change, and change in ways beyond our imagining. That is why we are to live by the light of heaven. Heaven is the stable element of our current reality, not this earth. This is heaven's proper place in the discussion. At present, because Christ is ascended to the Father in heaven, heaven is the sphere of the present fulfillment of the promise of salvation. Andrew Lincoln appropriately writes, "Because Christ has been exalted to heaven, heaven rather than earth temporarily provides the chief focus for salvation and for

---

29. Ibid., 252; see also 285.

the believer's orientation until Christ's coming from heaven when salvation will then embrace heaven and earth."[30]

Because Christ is presently in heaven, the believer is united with him not only in his death and resurrection but also in his heavenly exaltation (Eph. 2:6). Thus the believer can be called heavenly (1 Cor. 15:48), for the heavenly dimension nourishes and directs the life of the people of God on earth (Gal. 4:26).

Paul calls the Christian to heavenly mindedness:

> Since, then, you have been raised with Christ, set your hearts on things above, where Christ is seated at the right hand of God. Set your minds on things above, not on earthly things. For you died, and your life is now hidden with Christ in God. When Christ, who is your life, appears, then you also will appear with him in glory. (Col. 3:1–4)

This text describes not merely a moral contrast between sin and holiness but also a redemptive-historical tension between the present age and the age to come. "Earthly things" refers not only to our sin but also to the age that is characterized by sin. Thus, to be heavenly minded is to live in light of the age to come. To maintain a heavenly orientation is not to withdraw from the earthly creation but rather to view the earthly in light of the heavenly. Believers embody the life of heaven within the present world as they look forward to the revealing of the glory of Christ.

The otherworldly Christian may cite Paul's claim that "our citizenship is in heaven" (Phil. 3:20). But this text does not claim "that heaven as such is the homeland of Christians to which they, as perpetual foreigners on earth, must strive to return, but rather that since their Lord is in heaven their life is to be governed by the heavenly commonwealth and that this realm is to be determinative for all aspects of their life."[31] We need only cite the rest of the same verse: "And we eagerly await a Savior from there, the Lord Jesus Christ."

---

30. Andrew T. Lincoln, *Paradise Now and Not Yet: Studies in the Role of the Heavenly Dimension in Paul's Thought with Special Reference to His Eschatology* (Grand Rapids: Baker, 1981), 193.
31. Ibid.

Yet we must not use the second statement as a denial of the first. This earth is not our home until Jesus comes, brings heaven with him, and makes all things new.

Until heaven is brought to earth and God brings our earthly bodies (and the earth itself) into conformity with the glory of Christ (Phil. 3:20–21), our hope is set on Christ above (Eph. 1:20; 6:9). Until the coming of the Lord we are strangers and pilgrims in this world (Heb. 11:13), living by the light of heaven. We long for "a better country— a heavenly one" (Heb. 11:16), a country where Jesus is Light and Lord. Heaven does qualify, even relativize, this life and this world. It leans in upon us reminding us that reality is more than merely what we can see and control or even comprehend. It reminds us that God— not man, even redeemed man—rules. And yes, until heaven comes to earth in the new Jerusalem, heaven's moral perfection indicts us in our sin and reminds us that the world in its present form will pass away.

Yet even in the *eschaton*, as always, it's about Jesus, not real estate. The *Who* question must exercise priority over the *Where* question. The glory of the age to come is not the glory of the earth but a heavenly glory, the glory of the Son of God. Christ will bring the glory of heaven to earth (1 Thess. 4:17; Col. 3:4) in the final coming together of the earthly and heavenly realms.

INDEX OF SCRIPTURE

303

307

308

INDEX OF
SUBJECTS AND NAMES

311

Michael D. Williams (M.T.S., Harvard Divinity School; M.Div., Grand Rapids Baptist Seminary; Ph.D., University of Toronto) is professor of systematic theology at Covenant Theological Seminary. He was professor of theology at Dordt College for six years before joining the Covenant faculty. Dr. Williams is author of *This World Is Not My Home* and co-author, with Robert A. Peterson, of *Why I Am Not an Arminian*. He is also highly regarded for his insightful articles on the nature of theology, theological method, history, and homosexuality.